Beyond What Is Written

Beyond What Is Written

The Performative Structure of 1 Corinthians

TIMOTHY MILINOVICH

☙PICKWICK *Publications* · Eugene, Oregon

BEYOND WHAT IS WRITTEN
The Performative Structure of 1 Corinthians

Copyright © 2013 Timothy Milinovich. All rights reserved. Except for brief quotations in critical publications or reviews, no part of this book may be reproduced in any manner without prior written permission from the publisher. Write: Permissions. Wipf and Stock Publishers, 199 W. 8th Ave., Suite 3, Eugene, OR 97401.

BWHEBB, BWHEBL, BWTRANSH [Hebrew]; BWGRKL, BWGRKN, and BWGRKI [Greek] Postscript® Type 1 and TrueTypeT fonts Copyright © 1994–2009 BibleWorks, LLC. All rights reserved. These Biblical Greek and Hebrew fonts are used with permission and are from BibleWorks, software for Biblical exegesis and research.

All translations in this book, unless otherwise stated, are from the author. The translations of the Greek New Testament are based on the Nestle-Aland *Novum Testamentum Graece*, 27th edition. Differences are marked with brackets and/or notes.

Pickwick Publications
An Imprint of Wipf and Stock Publishers
199 W. 8th Ave., Suite 3
Eugene, OR 97401

www.wipfandstock.com

ISBN 13: 978-1-60899-992-7

Cataloguing-in-Publication Data

Milinovich, Timothy

Beyond what is written : the performative strcuture of 1 Corinthians / Timothy Milinovich

xii + 248 p. ; 23 cm. Includes bibliographical references.

ISBN 13: 978-1-60899-992-7

1. Bible. Corinthians, 1st—Criticism, interpretation, etc. I.Title.

BS2675.52 M55 2013

Manufactured in the U.S.A.

*This book is dedicated to my parents,
Tom and Debbie Milinovich*

*Whose example showed me that the paradox of the cross
is truly God's power and wisdom.*

Contents

Acknowledgments / ix
List of Abbreviations / x

1. Listening to 1 Corinthians / 1
2. Events and Relationships behind 1 Corinthians / 18
3. Introduction to a Fractured Community, 1:1–17 / 26
4. Foolishness and Wisdom of the Cross, 1:18—3:3 / 39
5. Paul, Apollos, and the Community, 3:4—4:21 / 60
6. Sexual Immorality and Injustice, 5:1—6:20 / 82
7. Marriage, the Family, and the World, 7:1–40 / 99
8. Eating Disorder in Corinth, 8:1—11:1 / 117
9. Order in Worship and the Church, 11:2—14:40 / 143
10. Resurrection and Hope of the Community, 15:1–58 / 186
11. Closing and Preparations for the Next Visit, 16:1–24 / 211
12. Summary and Conclusions / 231

Bibliography / 241

Acknowledgments

I AM GRATEFUL FOR the many people in my life who aided the composition of this work in a variety of ways. Dr. Tanja Stampfl, Dr. Adrienne Ambrose, T.J. Rogers, and Prof. Samir Massouh offered necessary insights and comments in critical portions, and Fr. John Paul Heil remained a strong source of encouragement in beginning and continuing the research that picked up from my dissertation.

Special thanks are warranted for my wife, Leila, and my mother-in-law, Sylvia Williams. I also greatly appreciate the work of my editor, D. Christopher Spinks, and the editorial staff at Wipf & Stock in producing this text.

Lastly, two very special people need mention. My parents, Tom and Debbie, have been a part of this journey since I first told them that I was changing my major in college to Theology. They have never once missed an opportunity to encourage, strengthen, or embolden me throughout the difficult path since. And it is to them that this book is dedicated.

Abbreviations

AB	Anchor Bible
ACCS	Ancient Christian Commentary on Scripture
Adams and Horrell	Adams, Edward and David Horrell, eds., *Christianity at Corinth: The Quest for the Pauline Church.* Louisville: Westminster, 2004.
BBR	*Bulletin for Biblical Research*
BETL	Bibliotheca Ephemeridum Theologicarum Lovaniensium
Bib	*Biblica*
BibSac	*Bibliotheca Sacra*
BN	*Biblische Notizen*
BTB	*Biblical Theological Bulletin*
CBQ	*Catholic Biblical Quarterly*
CBQMS	Catholic Biblical Quarterly Monograph Series
CCor	R. Bieringer, ed., *The Corinthian Correspondence.* BETL 125. Louvain: Peeters, 1996.
CNTC	Cambridge New Testament Commentary
CTR	*Concordia Theological Review*
DNTB	*Dictionary of the New Testament Background*
DPL	*Dictionary of Paul and his Letters*
ESV	English Standard Version
ETL	*Ephemerides theologicae lovanienses*
ETS	tudies Evangelical Theological Society Studies

Abbreviations

EvQ	*Evangelical Quarterly*
ExpTim	*Expository Times*
GNS	Good News Series
Greg	*Gregorianum*
HNTC	Harper's New Testament Commentaries
ICC	International Critical Commentary
Int	*Interpretation*
JAAR	*Journal of the American Academy of Religion*
JBL	*Journal of Biblical Literature*
JFSR	*Journal for Feminist Studies in Religion*
JSNT	*Journal for the Study of the New Testament*
JSNTSup	JSNT, Supplement Series
JSOTSup	JSOT, Supplement Series
JTS	*Journal of Theological Studies*
LEC	Library of Early Christianity
LXX	Septuagint
NA27	Nestle-Aland 27th Edition
NAB	New American Bible
NCB	New Century Bible Commentary
NIBC	New International Bible Commentary
NICNT	New International Commentary on the New Testament
NIGTC	New International Greek Testament Commentary
NIV	New International Version
NovT	*Novum Testamentum*
NRSV	New Revised Standard Version
NT	New Testament
NTG	New Testament Guide
NTL	New Testament Library
NTS	*New Testament Studies*
NTT	New Testament Theology

Abbreviations

Od.	*Odyssey*, Homer
OTL	Old Testament Library
PCC	Paul in Critical Contexts
ResQ	*Restoration Quarterly*
RevExp	*Review and Expositor*
SBEC	Studies in the Bible and Early Christianity
SBL	Studies in Biblical Literature
SBLDiss	SBL, Dissertation Series
SBLSBS	SBL, Sources for Biblical Study
SNTSMS	Society for New Testament Studies Monograph Series
SP	Sacra pagina
TCGNT	B. M. Metzger, *A Textual Commentary on the Greek New Testament*
TDNT	G. Kittel and G. Friedrich (eds.), *Theological Dictionary of the New Testament*
TNTC	Tyndale New Testament Commentaries
TynBul	*Tyndale Bulletin*
VetT	*Vetus Testamentum*
WBC	Word Biblical Commentary
WUNT	Wissenschaftliche Untersuchungen zum Neuen Testament
ZNW	*Zeitschrift für die neutestamentliche Wissenschaft*

1

Listening to 1 Corinthians

INTRODUCTION

As AUDIENCES GO, WE modern readers of the New Testament are a beautiful accident. Paul (or any other NT author) did not imagine us reading these letters. A line of scribes and believers have made these available to us. Yet the distances in time, culture, and intention between modern text and ancient papyrus create overwhelming difficulties for interpretation. Perhaps the largest disconnect from the text's original context occurs within the very act of reading. These texts were meant to be communicated as a performance, not a written essay. Paul composed them aloud before his scribes and co-workers with the intention that they be performed to a largely illiterate audience. Imagine reading John F. Kennedy's moon speech merely in transcript form. A great deal would be lost in the media shift, including tonality, emphasis, rhythm, and many other important aspects of oratory.[1]

---

1. Paul Achtemeier raised the importance of the oral milieu of New Testament literature in his SBL presidential address (later published as "*Omne*" 3–27). He stressed that this literature was "oral to the core" due to its temporal and cultural location within late Western antiquity, and claims that the NT texts were composed and intended to be performed audibly, such that these texts should be studied with sensitivity to their oral nature. Sound patterns, such as repetition, inclusion, parallels, anaphora, and alliteration (among others) help to delimit borders, structures, and otherwise unheard meaning of the texts.

Beyond What Is Written

But what if the sound was not merely aesthetic? What if the patterns of the speech unfolded for the listening audience the structure and meaning of the author's argument like an oral blueprint? How then should we, as an accidental audience, seek a greater intimacy with Paul and his intended audience in Corinth, so as to understand that very precious, yet often elusive, original intention and meaning of 1 Corinthians? The answer, as this book argues, is not found in *reading like* the original audience. They did not *read* 1 Corinthians—it was performed to them.

So we must learn to engage and listen to the text of 1 Corinthians the way they would have, namely, within the oral culture of late Western antiquity. In doing so, we will be able to recognize the rhetorical structure that is inherent in the text to better understand the argument that unfolds for those who live within an oral culture. While other analyses treat the letter as a modern linear essay based on thematic content, this study engages the text of 1 Corinthians with a text-centered, grammatico-lexical method in order to demonstrate the rhetorical structure of the letter through objectively grounded criteria and analyze the concentric lexical correlations that are inherent within the text.[2] This structure, as this study will show, is a complex network of "ring" formations that is consonant with the oral milieu of late Western antiquity.

Reason for This Study

To this point, the problem remains that the structures proposed for 1 Corinthians in a linear format are unconvincing and multivalent, due in part to the implementation of subjective or thematic criteria in delimiting the text. That is, these analyses seem to fit a modern essay (in I, II, II . . . , A, B,C . . . , 1, 2, 3 . . . , i, ii, iii . . . , etc.) rather than ancient oratory. These structures are limited in that they treat the content of 1 Corinthians like wooden blocks that can be stacked upon another, only to build a single, unbalanced tower. But when one views the lexical repetitions of the letter, the text as an interconnected network of themes that anticipate, pivot, and reflect back on one another in a balanced rhetorical performance becomes evident. One reason for this discrepancy is the temporal and cultural divide between ancient author and modern reader. Today's audience engages the text with a linear

---

2. The grammatico-lexical method is utilized in a manner to engage a text's structure by Lambrecht ("Structure," 344–80) and Heil (*Ephesians*, 10), among others. Briefly put, the method demonstrates an outline for a text by underscoring objectively grounded textual evidence, such as repetitions in grammatical, terminological, and lexical forms. More will be said below regarding this method, its background, and its use in this book.

mindset and anachronistic expectations of how a letter and its argument should flow.

An example of this can be seen with modern scholars' discomfort with the rhetorical digression, when an author "interrupts" an argument to take on a second topic and then returns to complete the first in due time. This practice was common and encouraged in the highest schools of rhetoric in Greco-Roman antiquity, but many modern scholars wish to consider the secondary topic as foreign. By engaging the text with a grammatico-lexical focus that denotes the repetition of terms and sensitivity to the letter's cultural and literary milieu, this study presents a fresh analysis of the letter's structure that is fair to the original author and audience, as well as the modern reader. That is, it *communicates and shows to today's reader what the intended audience was anticipated to receive in performance*. This structure aids the interpretation of the letter by demonstrating the delimitations of larger arguments, particular units, and terms that parallel and correspond to one another. The textual elements themselves will be shown to determine the central points and developments of Paul's rhetorical arguments in the letter.

It is important to note that this book does not, per se, intend to "get into the heads" or hypothesize about how the particular historical audience heard this text. Rather, the goal here is to demonstrate what the text's structure itself intends the audience to receive through its repetitions. Since every author must imagine their audience and write so as to communicate effectively with them, it is understood that the structure within a text would then demonstrate a critical mass of information by which the audience can deduce and comprehend the author's message.[3]

Anticipated Contributions

This study contributes the following observations to the on-going conversation on this letter:

1/ The letter consists of three major ring sections: (A) 1:1—4:21; (B) 5:1—11:1; (A′) 11:2—16:24. Each major section itself consists of three ring sets. This means that the introduction (1:1–9) and conclusion (16:1–24) are not separate from the letter's body but in fact make up important parts of Paul's overall arguments. In total, there are nine ring sets and thirty-seven ring units in the letter.

2/ This study serves as the first monograph-length look at the oratorical, or performative, structure of the letter within its socio-historical location and oral milieu that was prevalent in late Western antiquity, and to

---

3. On this particular aspect of the text-centered approaches, see Heil, *Hebrews*, 3–7.

analyze ring formations within the letter using objectively grounded grammatical criteria that focus on concentric lexical correlations rather than synthetic, subjective, or thematic criteria.

3/ The first section (A), 1:1—4:21, consists of three ring sets: α, 1:1–17; β, 1:18—3:3; α´, 3:4—4:21. The central set regards wisdom and weakness in the cross (1:18—3:3), with the authority of Paul and Apollos and the division of the community (1:1–17; 3:4—4:21) acting as the primary concern.

4/ The central section (B), 5:1—11:1, consists of three complex ring sets: α, 5:1–6:20; β, 7:1–40; and α´, 8:1—11:1. This study demonstrates that the main issues regarding morality (5:1–13; 6:9–20) and relapsing to pagan syncretism (8:1–13; 10:1—11:1) are interrelated. In fact, the Corinthian slogan that Paul addresses, "Everything is lawful to me" (6:12; 10:22), denotes the bracket ring sets' connection. The discussion on marriage and peace with outsiders serves as the center of the section as a whole, while concern over lawsuits (6:1–8) and Paul's example of self-sacrifice (9:1–27) serve as central topics that develop the first and third ring sections, respectively.

5/ The third section (A´), 11:2—16:24, also consists of three ring sets: α, 11:2—14:40; β, 15:1–58; and α´, 16:1–24. The section pivots around the discussion on the resurrection. The α and α´ ring sets in this section prepare for Paul's return to the community's worship services by first instructing them on appropriate procedure, and then by discussing the collection and his imminent travel plans. The length of the α ring set, 11:2—14:40, bespeaks Paul's concern over the discrepancies in the community's worship services. The oration on the efficacy of love for spiritual maturity and communal transformation (12:31b—13:13) serves as the center of the longest and most complex ring set of the letter.

6/ This study demonstrates that the letter as a whole has a structure that is not linear but concentric. The central B Section (5:1—11:1) is focused on how this community presents itself to the outside world and how its members are to live as the elect of God and who are, at the same time, in Christ and in Corinth (see 1:1–2). Whereas the central section looks outward to the city, the bracket A and A´ sections (1:1—4:21; 11:2—16:24) look inward to the community itself. These sections concern the unity and worship of the community, and its relationship to Paul, the apostle who first brought them the gospel and the Spirit. For the community to capitalize on the grace they have received in Christ through the Spirit they must unite again under Paul by recognizing his authority as their apostolic father and acting more like God's sanctified elect. Hence, in both the A and A´ Sections, Paul brings up the Corinthians' association not just with the Spirit, but with the other sanctified church communities as well (1:1–2; 11:16; 11:34). It is in this larger group that the Corinthians are encouraged to invest with the collection and their changed behavior to show solidarity and peace with all of God's churches.

7/ The progression for each ring unit and ring set is not linear but concentric. The beginning points are developed through the central units and the final element/unit/set both informs, and is informed by, the initial parallel element/unit/set. In this way, the letter offers an intra-textual exegetical key to problematic sections, all the while presenting a balanced and aesthetically pleasing exhortation to the audiences, both ancient and modern.

8/ In every instance of ring formation there is objective grammatical and lexical evidence to support the proposed delimitations. In particular, these delimitations are based on the arrangement of repeated terms that form concentric/chiastic/ring-like formations in the text. This method of arrangement is consonant with the cultural literary milieu of Paul and the intended Corinthian audience.

9/ These structures also provide helpful data regarding existing exegetical debates throughout the letter. For instance, the analysis and explication of the ring sets in Section B helps to denote how the orations on sexual immorality, courts, marriage, and idol meat form a cohesive argument in 5:1—11:1 and are not randomly arranged. The structures also provide lexical and objectively grounded evidence for viewing the sections on women in 11:3b–16 and 14:34–35 as later "Paulinist" interpolations. Each of these, along with many other exegetical issues, will be explained at length in their respective chapters.

Analysis: The Performative Structure of 1 Corinthians

Section A, 1:1—4:24: Internal Issues: Reclaiming a Sanctified Identity amidst Divisions, Worldly Attachment, and Spiritual Immaturity

Ring Set α, 1:1–17: Divisions in the Church

Unit A, 1:1–3: Christ's Apostle Greets His Sanctified Church

Unit B, 1:4–9: Thanksgiving for the Elect's Spiritual Gifts Received in Christ

Unit A´, 1:10–17: Salvation Endangered by Divisions

Ring Set β, 1:18—3:3 "Foolishness" and Wisdom of the Cross

Unit A, 1:18—2:5: God's Plan in Christ Crucified Is an Assault on Worldly Conventional Wisdom, but Is Salvation for His Elect

Unit B, 2:6-13: God's Wisdom Is Hidden to Worldly Authorities and Ordinary Human Wisdom

Unit A′, 2:14—3:3: The Corinthians Remain Like Ordinary People because of Their Divisions, Spiritual Immaturity, and Attachment to the World's Standards

Ring Set α′, 3:4—4:24: Paul, Apollos, and God's Temple in Corinth

Unit A, 3:4-22: Paul and Apollos as Co-Workers, Constructing God's Temple

Unit B, 4:1-5: Do Not Yet Judge the Stewards of God's Mysteries

Unit A′, 4:6-24: A Father Exhorts His Children in Christ to Imitate Him

Section B, 5:1—11:1: External Issues: Living as the Sanctified in the Outside World

Ring Set α, 5:1—6:20: Sexual Immorality and Injustice

Unit A, 5:1-13: Leaven of Sexual Immorality and Arrogance in the Community

Unit B, 6:1-8: The Wrong People's Court and the Leaven of Imperial Injustice

Unit A′, 6:9-20: Sexually Immoral Persons cannot Be Connected to Christ's Body

Ring Set β, 7:1-40: Marriage and Outsiders

Unit A, 7:1-9: Concession to Marriage

Unit B, 7:10-16: Remain Married, Unless It Is Impossible

Unit B′, 7:17-24: Remain as God Called You

Unit A′, 7:25-40: Focus on the Lord as the World Fades Away

Ring Set α´, 8:1—11:1: Eating Disorder in Corinth

Unit A, 8:1–7a: God Is All in All

Unit B, 8:7b–13: The Weak Are Abused by the "Knowledge" and "Freedom" of the Strong

Unit C, 9:1–27: Paul's Life as Example of Self-Sacrifice for the Benefit of Others

Unit B´, 10:1–19: Israel in the Desert as an Example for Corinth

Unit A´, 10:20—11:1: Do Not What You Can, but Do What Is Right for All

Section A´, 11:2—16:4: Internal Issues: Identity in Peace, Order, and Love

Ring Set α, 11:2—14:40: Proper Order and Unity in Worship

Unit A, 11:2–3a, 16–34: Disunity and Disorder at the Lord's Supper

Unit B, 12:1–13: Many Gifts, but One Spirit

Unit C, 12:14–31a: Many Parts, but One Body

Unit D, 12:31b—13:13: Love as the Key to Unity and Transformation in Christ

Unit C´, 14:1–13: Prophecy Edifies Christ's Existing Body

Unit B´, 14:14–25: Prophecy Grows Christ's Body through Converts

Unit A´, 14:26–40: Order Is Required to Worship the God of Peace

Ring Set β, 15:1–58: The Resurrection of the Christ and the Elect

Unit A, 15:1–11: The Tradition of Christ's Resurrection as the Basis for Faith

Unit B, 15:12–34: The Second Adam's Climactic Campaign against the Cosmic Powers

Unit B´, 15:35–49: Christians Brought to Life by the Second, Spiritual Adam

Unit A´, 15:50-58: The Resurrection and Christ's Parousia as the Basis for Hope

Beyond What Is Written

Ring Set α´, 16:1-24: Preparations for Paul's Return to His Unified Church

Unit A, 16:1-4: The Collection and Paul's Arrival

Unit B, 16:5-12: Travel Plans for Paul, Timothy, and Apollos

Unit A´, 16:13-24: Christ's Apostle Offers His Grace to His Church in Closing

EXAMPLE OF THE PROBLEM

Structure

A brief overview of recent and multifarious delimitations of the text demonstrates the difficulty that scholars have in analyzing Paul's letter as a linear argument. Variants range from two to twelve sectional divisions. Bruce and Fee delimit the text into a dual system based on authorial intent: Paul's response to reports (1:10—6:20) and Paul's response to the Corinthian letter (7:1—15:58).[4] Barrett and Hays maintain the latter section but distinguish 1:10—4:21 and 5:1—6:20 based on content, making three total sections.[5] Gorman sees four sections determined by aspects of the major theme of chaos: unity (1:10—4:21), morality (5:1—7:40), liturgy (8:1—14:40), and theology (15:1-58).[6] Schnelle and Morris further divide the central sections as 7:1-40 (groups/marriage); 8:1—11:1 (eating meat); 11:2—14:40 (worship problems), for a total of six.[7]

But these delimitations are problematic since they separate the introduction (1:1-3[9]) and farewell (16:5-24) from the "body" of the text, thus inferring that these sections cannot interrelate with the theological content of the body of the text proper. Beyond this problem, the body of the letter is determined not by generic, but rather thematic and subjective criteria, which can skew the contextual perspective of each section. For instance, should 7:1-40 be separated strongly from the discussion on morality in 5:1—6:20? Should 8:1—11:1 be included within the context of liturgy if it concerns life outside the community? If one separates the discussion on the resurrection as a particular theological problem, why not also the discussion

---

4. Bruce, *1-2 Corinthians*, 25–27; Fee, *First Epistle*, 21–23.
5. Barrett, *First Epistle*, 28–29; Hays, *1 Corinthians*, xi–xiv.
6. Gorman, *Apostle*, 238.
7. Schnelle, *History and Theology*, 61; Morris, *1 Corinthians*, 31–33.

on weakness and the cross in 1:18—2:5? The problem remains, then, that the content of 1 Corinthians does not divide well in a linear model.

Recent rhetorical studies have been more successful in incorporating objective criteria for structure by the use of generic rhetorical forms, such as *narratio, probatio*, etc.; but, while these forms are useful, they are not definitive. Collins and Witherington, for example, differ on whether there are six or nine rhetorical demonstrations/arguments in the letter.[8] Both also exclude the introduction and farewell from the theological content of the body. Collins' delimitation of 11:2–34 diminishes the relationship of liturgical order with spiritual gifts and edification, and does not anticipate the return to problems of liturgy in 14:1–40.[9]

Witherington's numerous breaks have the benefit of equal treatment for each unit. He also, to his credit, addresses the use of digression as a rhetorical tool of antiquity in 12:31b—13:13.[10] But, although his model is closer to the socio-rhetorical setting of Paul and his audience, the analysis he provides still reads like that of an essay outline rather than a speech itinerary. And although he treats the digression, he does so as if it were just a strategic interruption rather than a pivot point around which two or more parts of a larger argument turn, develop, and reflect on one another.[11]

So the rhetorical studies are little less linear than their thematic-oriented and theological contemporaries, but all of these structures are limited in that they treat the content of 1 Corinthians like wooden blocks that can be stacked upon another, only to build a single, unbalanced tower. As we will see further below, the tools one can use to re-build and recreate Paul's rhetorical model are found in the oratorical aspect of late Western antiquity.

METHOD AND CRITERIA

The method used for this study is text-centered and grammatico-lexical-focused. It is text-centered in the sense that it bases its findings primarily on evidence found within the text and does not focus solely on authorial intent or over-utilize other Pauline literature that would be either irrelevant or anachronistic for understanding this particular correspondence as it exists within the relationship between Paul and the Corinthian community. The grammatico-lexical focus entails that I will address not themes or subjective evidence within the text but rather analyze lexical repetitions in how they

---

8. See also Margaret Mitchell, *Rhetoric*.
9. R. F. Collins, *First Corinthians*, 29.
10. Witherington, *Conflict*, 76.
11. Ibid., 77.

develop ring formations, and how these formations aid the interpretation of the letter's sections and its overall argument. Furthermore, these lexical connections are exclusive to their respective units or elements and do not overlap.

As a text-centered study, this work presumes that the letter is the product of an author who wrote to communicate with a particular audience in a manner that both parties would understand and so would be greatly influenced by the author's cultural and historical situation. For this reason, we will next turn to the oral milieu of late Western antiquity and its impact on the interpretation of the letter.

Ring Formations within the Oral Milieu of Late Western Antiquity

What It Is and Where It Is Found

Common formulae within an oral culture's literature included parallelism (the pairing of synonymous or antithetical terms or themes) and the chiasm, or ring formation.[12] In its most general structure, a ring formation consists of "inverted parallelism—a passage in which the second part is inverted and balanced against the first."[13] This may also be referred to as a "concentric pattern," or a "chiasm." For practical purposes, we will prefer the term "ring formation," although there is no generic difference between the three terms.

The prevalence of the ring formation in non-literary and literary cultures is vast, and its importance for interpretation was realized by ancient scholars and commentators. Some rabbinic commentaries interpret texts using their chiastic or ring formation.[14] The Homeric commentator Aristarchus also utilizes the inverted structure of the discussion between Odysseus and his mother in his literary analysis (*Od.* 11:170–74).[15] These inverted patterns in Homer, sometimes referred to as *hysteron proteron*, were also noted by Crates and the Stoics of Pergamum as essential to the analysis of the text.[16] Other examples may be found in Isocrates, Demosthenes, Aristotle, Cicero, Dio-Chrysostom, and the Cynics.[17] As a

---

12. Achtemeier, "*Omne*," 18. See also Milinovich, *Now*, 9–11.

13. Stock, "Chiastic Awareness"; see also Bailey and Vander Broek, *Literary Forms*, 49–50.

14. Klaus (*Pivot Patterns*, 15) notes such comments used to interpret Lev 6:16; Josh 24:4; Ruth 1:5. See also Fishbane, *Interpretation*, 472.

15. Welch, "Greek and Latin," 254.

16. Ibid., 256.

17. Harvey, *Listening*, 71–82; Douglas, *Thinking*, 110–18.

testimony to their ubiquity, ring formations are even found in public and private letters of antiquity.[18]

Ring-like literary structures were likely perpetuated in Greco-Roman literature by the culture's method of education. Adolescents in school began to memorize the alphabet in concentric rather than linear repetitions.[19] In later rhetorical training the students were taught to begin and end a speech with similar material.[20] They were also often encouraged to arrange the content of their argument in three or five-part groups of concentric patterns in order to emphasize a central point.[21]

How It Works

The ring formation works by presenting a set of terms within an argument, reaching a central or pivot point, and then repeating previous terms in a concentric pattern. This system adds form and balance to the author's argument or story, but also presents opportunities for interrelation of the unit's elements. That is, the structure is as much a part of the argument as is the content. An example can be seen in Amos 5:4–5:

a: *Seek* me and you shall *live*:

b: But do not seek *Beth el*

c: Nor enter into *Gilgal*

d: And do not pass to Beer-sheba;

c′: For *Gilgal* shall surely go into exile

b′: And *Beth-El* shall come to nought:

a′: *Seek* the Lord, and *live*.[22]

Observe how the initial ideas of the *b, c,* and *d* elements are completed in their later parallels. Why should one not seek Beth el? Because, the parallel *b′* element explains, it will come to nothing. Why should one not enter Gilgal? Because, the parallel *c′* element explains, it will surely go into exile. The text is not clear on what will happen to the central city Beer-sheba (*d*), but based on what happens to the others, one can presume that it is just as

---

18. Heil, "Philemon," 179–206; Stowers, *Letter Writing,* 73.
19. Stock, "Awareness," 24.
20. Ibid., 25.
21. Wuellner, "Arrangement," 78–79.
22. The translation and structure are from Klaus, *Pivot,* 15. However, the insertion of elements is my own for emphasis.

precarious. Notice also how the final line (*a′*) does not merely repeat the first (*a*), but develops it. Seeking the Lord assures one life in the future but, in the final element, one receives life as a present state that is as certain as the destruction that Gilgal will receive.

An example of this concentric lexical correlation can be found even in everyday correspondence in late Western antiquity. In a letter to his wife who is expecting their child, a husband who is traveling writes:

a: *Do not worry* if they all come back except for me . . . *I urge you* . . .

b: Be concerned about the *child* . . .

c: And if I should receive my wages soon . . .

b′: And if you should bear a *child* . . .

a′: How can I forget you? So *I urge you not to worry.*[23]

The lexical repetition aids the reading of the letter. Who is this child whom the wife should worry over? The *b′* element explains that this is the child the wife presently carries in her womb. The pivotal element concerns the most important matter of the writing, namely, that the wages the man is earning will be sent shortly to aid his pregnant wife. The repeated exhortation in the bracket elements is supported by the central portion. His wife should not worry about her husband because he will be sending his wages soon to care for the child, even if he himself does not return. The existence of such a pattern within correspondence of Twitter-like length shows its pervasiveness in the life and thought of late Western antiquity.

Why They Used It

Any popular cultural trait naturally leads outsiders to ask why it is so pervasively used. The ring formation, or concentric lexical correspondence, has several benefits that aided its perpetuation in ancient societies from Sumeria to Rome.

- First, since ancient texts lacked paragraphs, line breaks, word spaces, or punctuation, a ring formation offered structure and delimited the beginning and ending of a particular section. The verbal repetitions informed the audience when one section ended and another began.
- Second, the corresponding elements within the structure acted as an initial interpretive key to the author's message.

---

23. Translation comes from Borg and Crossan, *First Paul*, 29; however, the structure is my own.

- Third, the structure offers an aesthetic as well as interpretive quality to the text: "the mid-turn is written so that it makes correspondences with the prologue and with the . . . ending [and] the result is a well-integrated composition" with "symmetry and balance."[24]

Why We Should Care

Since ring formations frame particular sections of an author's argument and distinguish the central point, literary scholars have for centuries used ring structures for effective textual analysis. Still, the strongest and most basic benefits from the study of chiasms and rings are the ability to deduce the structure and main point of the author's argument and perceive the development of that argument as it progresses through the concentric structure. In Pauline studies, in particular, the concentric structure demonstrates a rhetorical strategy that is otherwise unapparent to the modern reader, and the comparison of parallel elements aids the exegesis of any given textual unit.[25] This is made all the more important when a letter's structure is presumed to be unclear. Beyond setting the borders, a chiasm or ring also denotes the center point, or pivot, of a unit. This pivot may operate in one of two ways: as "the interpretive focal point of the passage," or as "an important transition in the movement of thought" of the unit.[26] Overall, the utilization of ring patterns is as useful and imperative to interpretation as form criticism.

Why Now?

An additional question the reader might ask at this point is why attention was given to this genre by ancient pagan interpreters and post-modern biblical scholars, but not by more ancient Christian commentators on Scripture, such as Augustine, Chrysostom, or Origen. This is a good question, and it hinges on the fact that these early Christian pastors sought at length to argue that Scripture's rhetorical effect was entirely from spiritual—rather than human—origin. That is, the effect of the text, in their view, should be attributed only to God's design and not to any human rhetorical convention.

Nils Lund extrapolates this issue in his powerful monograph on the topic of chiasmus in Scripture, and his comments are beneficial to note at this point. From an early stage of interpretation, Tertullian had demanded

---

24. Douglas, *Thinking*, 35–37.
25. Baily and Vander Broek, *Literary Forms*, 51.
26. Ibid., 53.

a separation between Church and academy, such that secular literary methods were not to be used on the sacred: "What concord is there between the academy and the Church? . . . Away with all attempts to produce a mottled Christianity of Stoic, Platonic, and dialectic composition."[27] In a similar era of the Church's history, Origen agreed, "it was not any power of speaking, or any orderly arrangement of their message, according to the arts of the dialectics or rhetoric" which was the effective cause of the gospel message.[28] These comments and their particular points seem to presume that others had in fact seen "orderly arrangement" and "arts of the dialectic or rhetoric" in Scriptural texts. The commentators of the day themselves, however, refused to acquiesce to these observations.

The complicit blindness to literary formulation in scripture continued into later Christian antiquity. Augustine agreed that Paul's rhetoric was exceptional, but that it could not be learned in schools like Stoicism or Sophism. According to Lund, Gregory the Great expressed the opinion, "It is an indignity that the words of the oracle of heaven should be restrained by the rule of Donatus."[29] To use rhetorical methods of interpretation on scripture seemed to be simply inappropriate. To be fair, early interpreters did note the use of oratorical forms such as *probatio* and *narratio* within some of Paul's letters, but this was never to insinuate that Paul's secular education in anyway affected his ability to proclaim; it merely showed that Paul could proclaim the gospel well within a letter. The early Christian commentators appeared to draw a distinct line between the form of the text and its means of persuasiveness. The former could be human, sure enough; but the latter could only come from heaven above.

This aversion to literary analysis in the early Fathers should all the more compel us to seek out the possible (if not presumed) existence of ring formations in New Testament texts and all Scripture. In the centuries that separate us from Tertullian there was considerable shift in the theory of methodology and interpretation. Pope Pius XII's encyclical *Divino Afflante Spiritu* made clear to the deposit of Catholic tradition that denoting a text's genre was an imperative first step to interpretation.[30] Within the Protestant tradition there has always been a similar interest: from Luther, to R. C. Sproul, and to Bishop Spong. So, while we should aspire to be like the earliest commentators in many ways (particularly as orators, a gift which our culture has too long dismissed), their aversion to literary analysis of

---

27. *Against Heretics* 7, cited by Lund, *Chiasmus*, 5.
28. *Against Celsus* 1.42, cited by Lund, *Chiasmus*, 6.
29. Ibid.
30. Milinovich, *Revelation*, 80–84.

Scripture must be reconsidered. In this particular area, the Catholic liberal arts intellectual tradition has developed in a consistent manner to correct their concern, and Protestant methodology, open to inspiration, can rest easy in its trajectory.

In short, we have a lot of time to make up for.

Criteria

Lambrecht and Concentric Patterns

For an example of how we can study ring formulations and objective structures in ancient texts we turn first to the work of Jan Lambrecht.[31] Lambrecht discerns and utilizes a complex, tiered concentric structure in 2 Cor 2:14—4:6.[32] The A section (2:14—3:6) has three parts: the first and last (a, 2:14–17; a´, 3:4–6) focus on ministry while the central part (b, 3:1–3) addresses the Corinthians directly. The B section (3:7–18) has two separate concentric units within it. In the first (3:7–11), lesser to greater arguments (3:7–9, 11) flank the central point that the glory of the Law is limited when compared to the new covenant in Christ (3:10). In the second (3:12–18), emphases on first person plural pronouns (3:12–13a, 18) flank third person plural pronouns (3:13b–17), along with other terminological distinctions. The final A´ section has a similar set-up ("we" in 4:1–2, 5–6; "they" in 4:3–4).

Lambrecht denotes over fourteen lexical connections between the A (2:14—3:6) and A´ (4:1–6) sections. For instance, Paul's "ministry" in 4:1 relates to the "ministry of life" in 3:6. The meaning of 4:1–6 is enhanced by denoting this interrelation along with the development of the argument found in his discussion of "glory" of the old and new covenants in the central 3:7–18 portion. Paul's ministry that reveals the knowledge of God's "glory" (4:1, 6) also gives life (3:6), despite Paul's weakness (2:14–17); and it can do this because the "glory" of the new covenant is so great that it outshines the old (3:7–11) and gloriously transforms those who perceive the new covenant on the face of the risen Christ (3:12–18).[33]

The additional lexical connections bolster this correlation and bind together 2:14—4:6 as a cohesive argument; but, as Lambrecht's deft analysis

---

31. For several scholars, the utilization of chiasms has become associated so much with subjective criteria that the term "chiasm" has become taboo. An example of this is found in Lambrecht, who uses objective lexical and grammatical criteria to determine and analyze so-called "concentric patterns." He then utilizes this analyzed structure to aid his interpretation of the text.

32. Lambrecht, "Structure," 340–47.

33. Ibid.

shows, the terms denote a structure that enhances exegetical insight for the text. A anticipates A´. A´ builds on, points back to, and reflects on A. And B offers support for the thesis in A and the concluding statement in A´. Structure informs the content's meaning. As seen in the examples above, lexical connections objectively denote and interpret that structure.

Additional Criteria: Blomberg, Douglas, and Heil

Lambrecht's exemplary work will serve as a preliminary model for what this study hopes to find in 1 Corinthians. However, his method was more by practice than by design, and so further definitions may be presented at this point from equally notable scholars. Craig Blomberg presents a set of seven criteria for finding chiastic/ring patterns in ancient texts that offers more fine rules than did Lambrecht. The rules are as follows:

- There must be a problem in perceiving the structure of the text in question, which more conventional outlines fail to resolve.
- There must be clear examples of parallelism between the two 'halves' of the hypothesized chiasm, to which commentators call attention even when they propose quite different outlines for the text overall.
- Linguistic (or grammatical) parallelism, as well as conceptual (or structural) parallelism, should characterize most, if not all, of the corresponding pairs of subdivisions.
- The linguistic parallelism should involve central or dominant imagery or terminology important to the rhetorical strategy of the text.
- Both linguistic and conceptual parallelism should involve words and ideas not regularly found elsewhere within the proposed chiasm.
- Multiple sets of correspondences between passages opposite each other in the chiasm, as well as multiple members of the chiasm itself, are desirable.
- The outline should divide the text at natural breaks which would be agreed upon even by those proposing very different structures to account for the whole.
- The central or pivotal, as well as the final or climactic, elements normally play key roles in the rhetorical strategy of the chiasm.
- Ruptures in the outline should be avoided if at all possible.[34]

---

34. Blomberg, "Structure," 4–8. This criteria is also used in Milinovich, *Now*.

Douglas, Harvey, and Heil all utilize and perpetuate Blomberg in their analysis of other texts. Douglas' work finds ring patterns in texts ranging from the Odyssey to the book of Numbers, and her work is helpful in explaining all of the benefits that authors and audiences received from using this genre.[35] Heil has found chiastic patterns of various complexities in Ephesians, Colossians, Philippians, Philemon, and, most recently, in the letter to the Hebrews. Heil slightly modifies Blomberg's criteria within his work by denoting some additional rules:

- Ring/chiastic patterns appear in varying complexities and sizes. Heil distinguishes between chiastic units (a passage of 4 to 14 verses with a concentric pattern), macrochiasms (a chain of chiastic units that may span an entire letter, as in Ephesians), and microchiasms (a concentric pattern within a unit's element). Heil also finds that macrochiasms can group together into sections that also form overall concentric patterns in a larger letter, such as in Hebrews. A similar pattern may be seen in 2 Corinthians.[36]
- Prepositions and conjunctions are as important as nouns or verbs and may denote parallel elements within a unit.
- Terms may be found in more than one element, so long as those elements do not touch one another.
- Chiastic/ring units contain "linking terms" that connect the units together into a cohesive, united argument.

This set of criteria, both practiced and defined, serves as the genesis for the analysis of 1 Corinthians presented in this study. Following the next chapter's brief overview of the circumstances behind 1 Corinthians, the remaining chapters of the book will analyze the concentric lexical correlations and demonstrate how the performative structure contributes to understanding the letter's rhetorical arguments within its original oral milieu.

---

35. Douglas, *Thinking*, 11; see also Harvey, *Listening*, 108.
36. Heil, *Hebrews*, 10–13.

2

Events and Relationships behind 1 Corinthians

SETTING THE STAGE FOR A MAJOR PERFORMANCE

Introduction

THIS PARTICULAR LETTER (LIKELY the second of four that he sent them) exists within an ongoing conversation and complex relationship that Paul and the Corinthian community shared. Every relationship, in itself, is a story. And this letter is one particular event within that unfolding drama. This chapter offers a context for engaging the letter and subsequent chapters by giving a brief overview of Paul's overall ministry, his relationship with the Corinthians (i.e., the events that led up to the writing of the letter), particular reasons for writing, and profiles of the factions in the community.[1]

---

1. We take at face value that Paul the apostle, who is said to found a community in Corinth in Acts 18, is the presumed author of the letter and that this letter exists within the temporal context of his career and within the narrative of his relationship with the community.

Events and Relationships behind 1 Corinthians

The Context of Paul's Life and Ministry

A citizen by birth and tent-maker by trade, Paul enjoyed a status, opportunity for education, and stable lifestyle that was shared by few in the Empire at that time. His professional renown for knowledge of the Jewish Scriptures and Pharisaic traditions, as well as his ability to zealously lead Jewish communities, is well attested in the Acts of the Apostles. His influence stretched from Jerusalem (where he oversaw Stephen's execution, Acts 7:40–51) to Damascus (where he attempted to present warrants to authorities to arrest Christians, Acts 9:1–5). This profile serves to underscore the character and zeal of the man behind the message of 1 Corinthians.

Damascus Event and Early Ministry

If we take as a guide the account of Paul's career that is preserved in Acts, then we can see from the start several important trajectories. Along with Barnabas, Paul was considered one of five prophets and teachers in the Antiochian community. From there, he and Barnabas initiated a mission through the regions of Phrygia, Galatia, and Iconium (Acts 14:1–20). They were successful in building communities, but nearly at the expense of their own lives. In time, Paul came to consider this danger as necessary in the proclamation of God's Kingdom (14:8–23).

Ministry in Greece

Paul began his mission into Europe after a vision in which a man asked him to help them in Macedonia (15:34–38). He and Silas were arrested and nearly killed in Philippi because of the seditious nature of their teachings (16:19–40). The mission had more treacherous moments, including a clandestine escape from Thessalonica to evade local leaders who were seeking to kill him for his message of a new Lord and new Kingdom (17:2–8). Such a proclamation naturally implied that he was also calling for the absolution of the authority and power of the Roman Empire as a whole (17:6). They even chased him into Beroea. He then received a mixed, if not patronizing, review in Athens (17:16–33).

It is no wonder, then, that he arrived to Corinth "in much fear and trembling" (1 Cor 2:3). The persecution his community in Thessalonica still suffered (1 Thes 2:1–13) likely made Paul hesitant to start a community in Corinth with the same bravado he had in other cities. Over several months, he developed a core of followers (possibly thirty to forty in number) who ranged broadly in status and situation in life: married, widowed, single, engaged; slave, free, freed; Jew, God-fearer, pagan; respected community leaders and former prostitutes.

While in Corinth, Paul's ministry would take a considerable turn. He would write 1 (and possibly 2) Thessalonians while there to faithful but anxious and struggling Christians in Thessalonica. This letter may be a point in which he crystalized his teachings on Christ's return and sexual ethics, both of which would be shared with the Corinthians at that time, and would remain pertinent in 1 Corinthians. He was also likely influenced during the visit when he and fellow-member Sosthenes were tried for sedition before Gallio, proconsul of Achaia (Acts 18:10–18). Paul escaped unharmed, but he watched as Sosthenes was beaten by activists outside the court (18:17). This event no doubt reminded Paul of the toxicity that his gospel represented for his converts in a pro-Roman environment. He was the proclaimer of a new Lord and a new Kingdom, but the subjects of the present emperor and status quo were not willing to give up so easily.

After leaving Corinth, Paul returned to Ephesus, where he stayed for three years (and may at this time have written his letter to the Galatians). He is still in Ephesus as he awaits Timothy's return with a report when Chloe's people bring news of factions and immorality (1 Cor 5:1). Given the anxiety Paul already demonstrated in fear of losing the Thessalonians to violent mobs, or the Philippians and Galatians to opponents, when Timothy arrives with his own report (and possibly also a letter of rebuke from the Corinthians), Paul realizes that his ministry has yet again come to a defining moment. A poor response now could cost him a community that is also in one of the most important cities in the empire.

Paul's Relationship with the Community in Corinth

We know relatively little of Paul's initial time in Corinth. At best, we can discern from Acts that he was there for roughly eighteen months (18:11), and that this visit was during the proconsul of Gallio. Whether we take an earlier or later approximate date for Gallio's administration of the city, it is clear that Paul was already an experienced and accomplished missionary (for fifteen to twenty years) and spent an adequate amount of time teaching and getting to know the members of the community. This can explain why many of the members remain devoted to Paul in the drama that unfolds in 1 Corinthians.

While there, he partnered professionally with Prisca and Aquila, Jewish-Christian refugees from Rome (Acts 18:2), and began preaching in the synagogues (18:4). His speeches were successful in gaining as members the God-fearer Justus (18:7), and two synagogue officials Crispis (with his whole household), and Sosthenes (18:8, 10). Overall, Luke tells us that "many" were baptized in the city (18:10).

After Paul Left

APOLLOS

At least a few things are clear about the relationship between Paul and the Corinthians after he left. First, Apollos arrived in Corinth while Paul was traveling to Ephesus (Acts 19:1; 1 Cor 3:3—4:21; 16:20–22). Apollos is briefly described as "eloquent" and "expert in the Scriptures" (Acts 18:24). His knowledge of the faith, however, was somewhat limited. He spoke passionately about "the Way" but did not know about the baptism in the name of Christ and the Holy Spirit (18:26). Prisca and Aquila took it upon themselves to train him and joined others in writing letters of recommendation for Apollos to take with him to Corinth and Achaia (18:27). His ministry there is deemed a rich success by both Luke (18:28) and also Paul (1 Cor 3:4–10).

(LOST) LETTER A FROM PAUL TO CORINTH

It is equally clear that Paul wrote another letter (Letter A) to the Corinthians regarding sexual morality and associating with non-believers (1 Cor 5:9). Based on his recalculated comments in 1 Corinthians regarding this lost letter, Paul seems to have instructed the church to refrain from associating with any immoral persons. However this message was worded, it appears that some members (likely the libertine faction) ridiculed Paul for what they viewed as an impossible request. In order to leave immoral people, they argued, they would need to leave the planet altogether. It is unclear whether Apollos' arrival to Corinth had any relation to the need for Paul's letter or the Corinthians' subsequent response to it. What is clear, however, is that some members began to have negative feelings toward Paul and to rebuke his leadership as unfounded.

Beyond What Is Written

Theological Differences

As in most religious communities, differences of opinion in Corinth did not grow out of a vacuum, but rather from problems in everyday life. Setting aside for now the issue of the involvement of Apollos or other apostles, we can deduce from 1 Corinthians several practical issues over which the Corinthians were arguing:

- Sexual immorality (5:1–13; 6:9–20)
- Marriage and sexual relationships (7:1–40)
- Eating meals at temples and idolatry (8:1–13; 10:1—11:1)
- Abuses of the Lord's Supper (11:2–3, 17–34)
- Treating the Spirit like a status symbol (14:1–25)
- Disorder in worship proceedings (11:2—14:40)
- Members suing one another in pagan courts (6:1–8)
- Timothy's upcoming visit (4:17)
- Discomfort with the "weakness" of the cross (1:18—3:3)
- Denial of the resurrection of the dead (15:1–58)
- Paul's collection (16:1–5)
- Paul's relationship or news about Apollos (16:20)

All of these problems stem from four basic issues in the community:

- Misunderstanding of the Spirit that led to arrogance and over-emphasis on empowerment
- Many members were too connected to the Roman imperial view of power and status
- This status-oriented focus cyclically reinforced a perception of the Spirit as a material commodity
- A sense that the main aspects of the eschaton had already taken place (realized eschatology)[2]

Problems of this sort distinguish Corinth as a Christian community on the verge of collapse.

---

2. See Thiselton, "Realized," 109–11.

Events and Relationships behind 1 Corinthians

THE CORINTHIANS' LETTER TO PAUL AND CHLOE'S PEOPLE

Perhaps due to disagreements, at least one faction in the church wrote a letter to Paul with regard to several pertinent issues in the church. Since Paul begins some of his orations in 1 Corinthians with "now concerning" (περὶ δέ), it is likely that the Corinthians asked Paul about sexual immorality in general (perhaps in response to Letter A); whether a Christian can or should remain married; food at temples; the resurrection of the dead; and the collection. In addition to this letter, "Chloe's people" brought Paul a negative report of the church (1:10–12). It is likely that the major topics found in 1 Corinthians that are not introduced with "now concerning" (e.g., 1:10–17; 5:1–9) were contained in this group's report. This means that there were some things the Corinthians wanted Paul to know about their community, and some things that they did not want him to know. Paul, however, wants to make clear that he can always find out the truth about their state of holiness and practice of his gospel.

FACTIONS

Following Apollos' departure, factions began to develop in the Corinthian church. The particular number and substance of the parties existing in the Corinthian church is one of the more fascinating and murky exegetical issues in the letter. The variety of theories underscores the ambiguity of the text, the complexity of the historical situation to which Paul responded, and the extent of academic imagination within doctrinal and scholarly developments.

The arguments pertaining to this debate can be separated themselves into four major positions. The first, following the work of Baur, sees four groups within the four slogans of 1 Cor 1:10–12: Hellenists associate with Apollos; Judaizers associate with Peter (Cephas); spiritual enthusiasts associate with Christ; and Paul's loyalists respond by affirming their association with him.[3] A variant of this theory sees the Christ slogan as a rhetorical mockery of the first three groups. The Cephas party is allegedly apparent in the food issue later in the letter (8:1—11:1).[4]

A third position sees only two factions in the community that associate with either Paul or Apollos. The Peter and Christ slogans are added for rhetorical weight. This position is bolstered by the sparse mention of

---

3. Baur, "Parties," 55–57. See also Barrett, *First Epistle*, 44; Thiselton, *First Epistle*, 133–39.

4. Fitzmyer, *First Corinthians*, 137–39.

Peter in the remainder of the letter, the rhetorical turn to say that all in the community should associate with Christ (1:12; 3:22), and the emphasis on the equal-yet-separate relationship between Paul and Apollos as leaders and teachers of the community (3:5–7; 4:6; 16:10). The simplicity and clarity of this theory makes it the more widely held position among commentators today.[5] A minority view sees the slogans as pointing not to distinct parties, *per se*, but rather to a rampant factionalism and discord within the community and, as a result, a move against Paul's overall authority.[6]

A fusion of the last two theories is possible to outline the following scenario: after Paul and Apollos arrived, taught, and departed (respectively), different opinions developed regarding theological issues, such as spirituality, worship, and life outside the church. Groups with differing opinions began to fester, not so much around Paul and Apollos, but rather around what they embodied for the members: innate apostolic authority of the gospel in Paul and sophistic talent and persuasiveness in Apollos. I differ from other scholars in that I view the factions' development around the preachers as a product of the factions rather than their source. Based on the textual evidence, it is likely that theological questions (e.g., if one can eat idol meat, or how one should deal with a non-believing spouse) caused groups to form around preferred responses and party lines. The distinct styles and perspectives of Paul and Apollos merely aided this division, but were no less a part of the farce.

When combined with the problems enveloping the community above, the factions and their particular stances can be deduced as the following:

Pauline Faction:

- "Weak"
- "Foolish"
- Ascetic
- Open to divorce
- Views consumption of idol meat as scandalous
- Preferred Paul
- Accepted resurrection of the dead
- Future-oriented

---

5. See, e.g., Fee, *First Epistle*, 59; Keener, *1–2 Corinthians*, 24–25; Horsley, *1 Corinthians*, 43; Witherington, *Conflict*, 83–87.

6. R. F. Collins, *First Corinthians*, 73.

- Emphasis on Jewish Apocalypticism and more future-oriented view of spiritual gifts
- Counter-cultural

Apollos Faction:

- "Strong"
- "Wise"
- Libertine
- Anti-divorce
- Embarrassed of the cross
- Comfortable with eating idol meat
- Overemphasized the Spirit as a status commodity
- Preferred Apollos or themselves to Paul
- Questioned resurrection of the dead as foolish
- Present-oriented
- Emphasized Hellenism and realized aspects of spiritual gifts
- More willing to acquiesce to imperial and pagan cultural status quo

Overall, the polar positions stem from the two factions' perceptions of the Spirit. The Pauline faction viewed the Spirit as a sanctifying force that prepared their bodies for the future eschaton, and their asceticism and apocalyptic outlook led the libertine group to define them as "weak" and "foolish." The Apollos faction viewed the Spiritual gifts of liberty and spiritual knowledge more in the present. For this reason, they could see themselves as empowered to overcome customary views of sexuality and eating meat as a non-issue.

Paul and Apollos, who appeared to maintain cordial communication with each other, may well have been stunned by this communal spiral in their names.[7] Paul writes now to reestablish his authority in the midst of these factions.[8]

---

7. Keener, *1–2 Corinthians*, 27; Horsley, *1 Corinthians*, 45.
8. Fitzmyer, *First Corinthians*, 137.

3

Introduction to a Fractured Community, 1:1–17

Section A, Ring Set α

ANALYSIS OF UNITS

Unit A, 1:1–3: Greeting

a: 1/ Paul, called to be an apostle of Christ Jesus by the will of God (θεοῦ), and Sosthenes our brother, 2/ to the Church of God (θεοῦ)

b: that is in Corinth, those who are sanctified (ἡγιασμένοις) in (ἐν) Christ Jesus,

b′: called to be sanctified (ἁγίοις), with all those in (ἐν) every place who call on the name of our Lord Jesus Christ—theirs and ours.

a′: 3/ Grace to you and peace from God (θεοῦ) our father and the Lord Jesus Christ.

Paul, Called to Be an Apostle (a), 1:1

The introductory section of the letter serves to lay the foundation for Paul's overall rhetorical appeal to the audience. In this unit, Paul stresses his call

Introduction to a Fractured Community, 1:1–17

as an apostle of Christ by the will of God to preach to the elected members of the community. The unit pivots around the adjective "holy/sanctified" and the repetition of the preposition "in" (Corinth/Christ). The borders are defined by the repetition of "God," who is the organizer of activity for both apostle and audience in the unit.

In the first element, Paul states that he is called to be an apostle from, and on behalf of, Christ Jesus. An *intitulatio* defines "the modality" of the author's presence that is conveyed in the letter.[1] In this case, the portrait he wishes them to envision is the ambassador who speaks for God's Son, Christ the risen Lord. He substantiates his authority as Christ's emissary by saying that he remains as their pastor by God's own will. The dense, verbless clause denotes Paul's credentials. He is called by the will of God to be an ambassador for Christ Jesus. His title "apostle" identifies him as a witness of Christ's resurrection,[2] which both supports his claim as ambassador and empowers him to proclaim faith in, and salvation from, the risen Christ. The term "Christ" refers to the promised Messiah of Israel, who is king of God's peculiar people and of the whole world (Isa 11:10; 1 Cor 15:25–28).[3] As such, Paul presents himself as affiliated with the fulfillment of God's promises through the Law and the prophets, namely, that he would raise up an heir of David to renew his people's obedience to his will and, in so doing, recreate the cosmos with order (see Ezek 34:1–6; Jer 31:1–4; Isa 24:1–18).

The Sanctified in Corinth (b), 1:2a

The second element presents a paradox existent in every Christian community. The audience are addressed both as those who are "in Corinth" and "in Christ Jesus." Being in Corinth and in Christ Jesus are antithetical statuses. The former defines the Corinthians in terms of the present, fading age, while the latter explains who the Corinthian community truly are now that they have received the gospel from Paul and God's invitation to take part in his salvific act toward humanity and creation through Christ. They have been brought into Christ Jesus by Paul's apostolic ministry, and so also by God's will. This element affirms the church's identity as God's own (1:1a) in that they are sanctified by God[4] for himself in Christ Jesus. This phenomenal benefit of sanctification was offered by invitation, and they accepted

---

1. R. F. Collins, *First Corinthians*, 43.
2. Garland, *1 Corinthians*, 25.
3. Garland, *1 Corinthians*, 29, citing N. T. Wright, *Climax of the Covenant: Christ and the Law in Pauline Theology*, 41–49.
4. Barrett, *First Epistle*, 32.

that invitation when they received by faith Paul's gospel about Christ and were baptized.

All of the Elect Are Called to Be Sanctified in Christ Jesus (b′), 1:2b

The *b′* element confirms the special benefits that the audience in Corinth receive but also expands the view of God's plan. Christ Jesus of the *a* and *b* elements is now described as "the Lord Jesus Christ." The transposition of the names emphasizes the pivotal shift in the unit's structure. Jesus is further defined as "Lord," heightening both Jesus and his ambassador. Furthermore, those who are "sanctified" in the *b* element are now "called to be sanctified in the Lord Jesus Christ" in the *b′* element. The audience is "called" to be sanctified to God in Christ just as Paul is "called" to be an apostle for Christ, to preach to them, and bring them the opportunity for sanctification.[5]

The repetition of the term "sanctified" in the *b′* element (1:2c) demonstrates this term to be of central import to the unit. Paul addresses the Corinthians as those "sanctified" in Christ in the *b* element (1:2b) because they were "called to be sanctified" with all those in every place. This special status for the elect, who are in this world and in Christ, is affirmed by their declaration of loyalty in calling on the Lord's name. These pivotal elements serve to demonstrate to the Corinthians that they and all believers, regardless of their physical location in the Empire, find their true identity and home as those who, through Christ, are set apart for God. In addition, the elect find Jesus Christ to be their shared heavenly Lord, by whose name they are sanctified to God (i.e., set apart for God).

The Corinthians are not alone in being called and sanctified—rather, in their baptism they join those who are sanctified by God in Christ "in every place." The Spirit is not confined to Corinth alone, as some of their factions have contended (see 11:1—14:36).[6] Rather, partnership in Christ Jesus comes through acceptance of God's election that is announced by the ministry of divinely appointed apostles (3:1–9; 9:1–9; 12:9–13), and may be received by all of the elect who call upon Christ's name (1:2b) and are baptized in his name (see 1:14-17 below). It is their baptism in Christ's name by which God sanctifies them as his own church in Corinth—as he

---

5. Inasmuch as "sanctified in Christ" implies the concept of Christ's agency of salvation on the cross, it also encapsulates in sum the whole of Paul's gospel of God sanctifying his elect in (through, by means of) his Son, Jesus Christ in history (on the cross) and in baptism (for identity and in practice). Here ἐν has more to do with agency and instrument (like διά) than the spatial or mystical concept of being within the sphere of Christ (see Conzelmann, *1 Corinthians*, 21).

6. Garland, *1 Corinthians*, 28.

Introduction to a Fractured Community, 1:1–17

does with the elect everywhere—"in Christ." So the audience's blessings are neither unique nor of their own doing. Rather, they come from God in Christ by way of the ministry of an evangelical apostle. However, while they are not unique, they do have an implied responsibility since they have been called and sanctified into their newfound relationship with God, and did not make amends on their own. An ambassador was required to broker their salvation.

The Apostle Sends Greetings from Those Who Sent Him (a´), 1:3

The final *a´* element ties together the unit as a whole by developing the themes of the central elements and connecting with the initial *a* element (1:1–2a). If the pivotal *b* and *b´* elements focus on sanctification, the bracket elements focus on God as the main actor in the lives of Paul and his audience. Just as "God's will" calls Paul to preach to Corinth and establish them as his ("God's") church—whom he calls and sanctifies—now, in the *a´* element, God affirms the election of his sanctified ones by sending his ("God's") grace and peace, as a loving Father, through his emissary Paul.

This community, that belongs to God and is called to be sanctified in Jesus Christ by his will, is also able to call God their Father. They receive this benefit from the ministry of Paul, as do other churches. Their partnership grants them divinely instituted removal from the local authorities and places them under the auspices of a new heavenly Lord. From God and Christ the apostle brings to the audience both grace and peace. The mention of both greetings may serve to address both Jews and Gentiles in the community in their regular greeting pattern.[7]

Unit B, 1:4–9: Paul's Thanksgiving for God's Faithfulness

a: 4/ I give thanks to my God (θεῷ) always concerning you since God's (θεοῦ) grace has been given to you in Christ Jesus, 5/ so that in every way you have been filled in him—in every word and all knowledge—

b: 6/ just as the testimony of Christ was established (ἐβεβαιώθη) among you,

c: 7/ such that you are not lacking in any spiritual gift as you eagerly await the revelation of our Lord Jesus Christ,

---

7. Barrett, *First Epistle*, 34; Keener, *1–2 Corinthians*, 21.

b′: 8/ who will establish (βεβαιώσει) you as blameless until the day of our Lord Jesus.[8]

a′: 9/ Faithful is God (θεός), by whom you were called into fellowship with his Son, our Lord Jesus Christ.

Established in Christ by God's Grace (a, b), 1:4–6

The central unit of the α ring set (1:1–17) concerns Paul's thanks to God for the spiritual benefits that the Corinthians have gained in Christ. As in the first unit, God is the active party and brackets the unit as a whole. Christ is the focal figure of the unit (mentioned six times in six verses), but his primary function is that of agent. God, whose faithfulness guarantees all the benefits the audience has and will receive, is the ultimate source and most active party in the overall transaction.

In the *a* element (1:4–5), Paul gives thanks to God concerning the audience because the grace that is given to the Corinthians in Christ Jesus ultimately comes from God himself. This gift in Christ is defined as the eschatological gifts of all wisdom and all knowledge, which regards the receipt of the gospel that makes known to the Corinthians their election and by which they accept their sanctification. This knowledge regarding the gospel is affirmed in the *b* element (1:6) that speaks of the testimony (i.e., Paul's initial proclamation of the gospel at the founding of the community) as the root of contact between the community, their saving God, and his ambassador, Paul.

Awaiting the Revelation of Jesus Christ (c), 1:7

The unit—which has an eschatological focus throughout—centers organically around the eager expectation of the Lord Jesus Christ, whom all believers expect to receive (1:2). The complete fullness of their spiritual benefits (1:4–6), is affirmed as "not lacking in any way." This statement is somewhat paradoxical since the community is presently divided (1:10). Paul knows it, and they know it. But Paul's point is not entirely contradicted. The power of the gospel is wholly effective in that its initial proclamation of salvation is complete. So that part is valid. However, as will be shown in 1:10–17 and later, the problem is not the message but the audience's execution of this message in their lives, both within and outside the community, which may

---

8. I omit "Christ" on account of P[46] and B. Its inclusion in numerous witnesses may be due to assimilation to 1:8. Cf. NA[27].

bear weight on their eschatological status. The central point of this unit is that the product of salvation was delivered to them intact to prepare them for the Lord Jesus' return.

God will Establish the Elect as Blameless (b´), 1:8

The structure begins to fold back to its initial topic with the repetition of the *b* term "establish." Just as the gospel about Christ "established" God's spiritual gifts of knowledge for the community in Christ, so too will Christ, whom the audience eagerly awaits, "establish" them as blameless until the day of this revelation (1:7). This revelation is a public event in the future in which God completes the spiritual gifts of prophecy and knowledge that the community holds partially through Christ.[9] The term "establish" denotes a sense of permanent or significant effectiveness in God's saving action in Christ, and the repetition of the term further emphasizes the sense of "impression" that the gospel is to have made on the audience. This "impression," which develops their sanctification above (1:2–3), qualifies the audience as "blameless," a status which has significant meaning given the judging faculties of Christ expected at his return (cf. 2 Cor 5:1–10). The gospel Paul has brought them "establishes" in them the eschatological knowledge for salvation (1:6), and Christ will "establish" them as blameless until his return (1:8).

God Is Faithful to Give Fellowship with His Son (a´), 1:9

The final *a´* element ties together and develops the unit as a whole by returning to the initial main actor. "God," to whom Paul gives thanks because he is the ultimate source of the Corinthians' eschatological knowledge (1:4), and who sanctifies the church in Christ (1:2), is further defined as "faithful" and as "the one who has called" the audience into fellowship with Christ his Son (1:9). This fellowship is not only a personal relationship, but also a "share in the [glory] of the exalted, eschatological Lord."[10] This fellowship with the Son is the entire basis for the life of the community, to whom Paul now writes.[11]

The clarification of Christ as God's Son redefines the new relationship that the community receives with God in him. Reception of the gospel does

---

9. Horsley, *1 Corinthians*, 41; Thiselton, *First Epistle*, 100.
10. Barrett, *First Epistle*, 40.
11. Keener, *1–2 Corinthians*, 23.

not simply remove them from their present earthly rulers to be under the auspices of a heavenly Lord, but also invests them into one who is God's Son. This redefines their relationship to be more than possession and subjection to become one that is familial and has the sense of promise for inheritance. The "son" was the legal heir who was culturally guaranteed a massive (if not total in the case of a single child) apportionment of the patriarch's wealth and assets. If the Corinthians are in fellowship with God's Son, then they and all the saints have a special relationship with the Father that supersedes the rest of creation and further affirms the delivery of the spiritual gifts they have, and will continue to receive, in Christ.

The unit's theme of assurance is punctuated by the lexical emphasis on God's identity and his faithfulness. That God can complete that which he has sought to do in calling, sanctifying, and establishing the community for blamelessness in Christ for their salvation is to be taken as a foregone conclusion—denarii in the bank. The status of the "calling" of the community is developed from its initial mention in 1:1–3. They are called not just to be God's gathering—his new Israel—but are also called to have fellowship with his Son, with whom they share a filial relationship with God the Father, to receive his spiritual blessings.

Unit A′, 1:10–17: Salvation Endangered by Divisions

a: 10/ I exhort you, brothers and sisters, by the name of our Lord Jesus Christ, that (ἵνα) you all speak (λέγητε) in harmony and have no divisions among you, in order that (ἵνα) you are properly ordered in (ἐν) the same mind and in (ἐν) the same purpose.

b: 11/ For it has been made clear to me regarding you (περὶ ὑμῶν), my brothers and sisters, by Chloe's people, that there are fractures among you. 12/ And it is said of you (ὑμῶν) that some of you say, "I am with Paul (Παύλου)" and another, "I am with Apollos," and another, "I am with Cephas,"

c: yet even another, "I am with Christ (Χριστοῦ)!"

c′: 13/ Is Christ (Χριστός) divided?

b′: Or was Paul (Παυλός) crucified for you (ὑπὲρ ὑμῶν), or were you baptized into Paul's (Παύλου) name? 14/ I give thanks to God[12] that I baptized none of you (ὑμῶν)—except for Crispus and Gaius—

---

12. The words "to God" are omitted in key witnesses (a* B), but they fit with Paul's style and do not hinder or change the meaning of the text.

Introduction to a Fractured Community, 1:1-17

a′: 15/ so that (ἵνα) no one might say (εἴπῃ) that he was baptized in my name.—16/ And I baptized the household of Stephanas, but I don't remember the rest that I baptized. 17/ For Christ sent me not to baptize but to proclaim the gospel, not in (ἐν) a word of wisdom, so that (ἵνα) the meaning of Christ's cross might not be wiped away.

An Exhortation to Unity (a), 1:10

The A′ unit (1:10–17) of the α ring set (1:1–17) develops the eschatological intensity of the B unit (1:4–9), and also returns to the issue of Paul's identity as Christ's apostle, called within God's will, to proclaim to the audience that they are called to be sanctified for the purpose of their future salvation at Christ's return. The divisions in the community addressed in this unit are shown to stifle this gift of salvation intended for them. Such a shift following a thanksgiving is not uncommon in ancient rhetoric, and can be considered a reasonable deliberative strategy.[13]

Paul addresses the community as brothers and sisters and exhorts them in the name of the Lord whom they await. The two causal clauses denote that both are equally important and intended to precipitate from his pastoral call. The primary placement of the factions issue in the body proper of the letter demonstrates its importance. His contention that the audience be (1) united, and (2) not divided, covers the matter both positively and negatively and explains exactly in what state Paul demands for the community to be in order to reflect the full spiritual blessings, blamelessness, and sanctification they received from God (1:2, 4, 7, 9).

The repeated use of the preposition "in," with regard to the locale and state of the community, echoes the greeting and puts forward that the community are to be "in harmony," "in one word," and "in one mind," just as they are the church of God "in Corinth" who are sanctified "in Christ." Paul's point is that the Corinthians did not receive the Spirit to be empowered as individuals, but instead are called to be united in one mind as one church that is bound together in fellowship with God's Son, the Lord Jesus Christ.

Divisions in the Community (b), 1:11–12a

In the next element Paul explains that the report of factions in the community he received from Chloe's people necessitates a harsh pastoral response. We are not certain whether Chloe or her people were church members, but

---

13. Keener, *1–2 Corinthians*, 23.

their mention serves to validate his admonishment of the community.[14] The use of the phrase "each of you" may be hyperbolic, but it denotes a rampant and viral divisiveness throughout the group. As such, this section admonishes everyone as a group—perhaps the only thing they have done together in months.

Dividing Christ (c, c'), 1:12b–c

In the pivotal elements of the unit, Paul addresses and mocks the audience's factions concentrically. The divisions are presented in the *b* and *c* elements (1:12a, b) as groups that show allegiance to Paul, Apollos, Cephas, and Christ. This order is reversed to Christ, then Paul, in the *c'* and *b'* (1:12c, 13) elements. Paul's initial rebuke asks whether Christ the Lord Jesus—in whom God has filled the community with all spiritual blessings and knowledge, in whom they were called and sanctified, and who will return to judge them—can be divided. The obvious answer, if their faith in him is anything worth its salt, is "no." The mention of Paul with the cross and baptism serves to subordinate the apostle to Christ who sent him. These next questions point the audience back to Jesus Christ, whom they all share as Lord (1:3), in whom they are called to be God's elect (1:2), and with whom they share a filial relationship with God (1:9). Paul was merely the messenger (1:1, 3).

The order of names within the progression of the structure sheds some light on the nature of factions occurring at the time. The centrality of Christ is likely rhetorical. Since it does not appear again, the supposed "Christ group" was likely a convention of the pattern by which Paul subordinates himself to Christ and calms tensions in the community by first admonishing those who are perpetuating the feud by remaining overly loyal to him and his apostleship.[15] Rhetorically this move also serves to disarm and pacify those who had broken from Paul and his authority to side with Apollos. As we'll see further below, the nature of Apollos' authority and relationships with the members in Corinth are likely key issues behind the factions and Paul's concern therein.[16] Since Cephas does not appear substantively again in the discussion on divisions and authority in the church (1:10–17; 3:3—4:24), it is likely that this "group," like the supposed "Christ party," is also a rhetorical

---

14. Thiselton, *First Epistle*, 121; cf. Witherington, *Conflict*, 99.

15. Paul does not thank this group because the resulting discord within the community was a distortion and contradiction of his gospel. See Barrett, *First Epistle*, 43; Fee, *First Epistle*, 56.

16. Witherington, *Conflict*, 83: "According to Acts 18:24–26, Apollos was from Alexandria and was . . . eloquent, possibly implying that he used Greco-Roman rhetoric in the presentation of the gospel."

creation. This apostle of considerable weight was likely placed third after Apollos to dilute the tension that had grown regarding the authority of Paul and Apollos in the community.[17]

So how many groups are there in Corinth? It is more likely that there are two parties rather than four (or three).[18] Paul's language (here, and elsewhere in the letter) presumes factions in the community that have attached themselves to either Paul or Apollos, identified spiritual characteristics with each (evangelical and apostolic authority with Paul, wisdom and rhetorical talent with Apollos), and subsequently associate themselves and develop their own spiritual identities, goals, and subsumed status in the community (and thus also the new eschatological age) based on these criteria of association.[19] Paul is disappointed in both groups since such arrogant factionalism flies in the face of his gospel that proclaims God's grace in saving the elect through Christ's action and the Spirit's sanctifying presence. The factions began with theological differences within the community, but were perpetuated by cultural systems. It was common for rival traveling Sophists to develop equally rival groups of disciples.[20] In this case, the groups who lionize one Christian preacher over another feel their wisdom or sanctification put them on a higher spiritual status than the others.[21]

Paul Sent to Proclaim the Gospel (b´, a´), 1:13–17

In the b´ element (1:13b–14) Paul again demurs from any overemphasis on his importance to the Corinthians' new status with God. Paul hoped to proclaim the gospel of Christ equally to the elect in Corinth so that they all might be as one in Christ. In fact, his decision to baptize only a few was intended to prevent divisions.

The passage focuses on Paul's pastoral decisions that were meant to support the church's unity. In the *a* element (1:10), Paul exhorts the community for two reasons: "in order that" they be united in word and mind and that they have no divisions. In the *a´* element (1:15–17) his pastoral directives are for the same purposes: he restates that he baptized only a few in Corinth "in order that" divisions might not occur, just as Christ sent him to

---

17. See Chapter 2 above on the problems and factions in the community.
18. According to Smit, "Coherence," 248, Paul intentionally uses four slogans rather than two "as a form of *insinuatio*" to avoid direct confrontation with the two existing sides.
19. Fee, *First Epistle*, 57.
20. Fitzmyer, *First Corinthians*, 139.
21. Horsley, *1 Corinthians*, 45.

proclaim the gospel "so that" the cross might not be emptied of its power—that is, so that the gospel might be effective for the community's salvation.

So everything that Paul seeks to do as pastor is meant to make the saving gospel effective in the life of the community and maintain that powerful state by administering his apostolic duties to prevent divisions and build harmony among God's elect. Since Christ cannot be divided, they are to be of one word and one mind, just as they are in one Lord Jesus Christ. Those who wish to divide him are in danger of losing the spiritual benefits of election, sanctification, and fellowship with his Son (1:4–9). They were not baptized in Paul's name, nor was Paul crucified for them. Christ is the agent of their salvation by God's will, and he should be their focus—not Paul or Apollos. The overemphasis on Paul's agency, either by dismissal or loyalty, diminishes Christ's sacrifice on the cross. And the overemphasis on Apollos' persuasive speech and wisdom does the same.[22] If salvation could come by the work of Paul, Apollos, or any other apostle, then what is the meaning of the crucifixion and resurrection?

INTERRELATION OF UNITS

Outline

Christ's Apostle Greets those who Call on the Lord's Name (A, 1:1–3)

Paul addresses his relationship with the community through God and Christ, namely that he was "sent" (ἀπόστολος) from God to proclaim the gospel to those who call on Christ's "name" (ὄνομα).

Thanksgiving for the Church's Blessings (B, 1:4–9)

The community in Corinth has received blessings from God through Christ and the gospel, and God binds them together in Christ in order to preserve them for salvation.

---

22. Horsley, *1 Corinthians*, 46–47. See also Thiselton, *First Epistle*, 145.

Introduction to a Fractured Community, 1:1–17

God Sent Paul for the Church to Receive Spiritual Gifts in Christ's Name (A´, 1:10–17)

Paul addresses the divisions in the community and a proper understanding of his authority: God "sent" (ἀπέστειλεν) Paul to them so that they adhere to one gospel, and they received spiritual gifts in Christ's "name" (ὄνομα), not Paul's, so that they might be united in Christ.

Conclusion

At the center of this ring set Paul positively addresses the spiritual blessings the community has received in Christ within an imminent eschatological context (1:7). The community has been called by God into fellowship with his Son to confirm their election and sanctification in order to make them blameless for salvation on the day of Christ's revelation. The unit is grounded in determinism, a common aspect of Jewish Apocalypticism. God's faithfulness guarantees the effectiveness of the gospel and Paul's apostolic authority to sanctify and confirm the Corinthians as an elect church in Christ (1:9). The guarantee, however, is on God's end; the Corinthians must still maintain their state of grace. The unit also bolsters Paul's authority. The Corinthians received the spiritual blessings of eschatological knowledge and fellowship through his proclamation and ministry. Paul's claim to be an apostle sent by Christ is affirmed by the community themselves since his message has been at least relatively effective in bringing them the gift of the Spirit (1:4–5).

The introduction of the letter serves to present Paul's pastoral credentials and give a cast of characters that will remain prominent throughout the rest of the letter and their interrelationships: Christ, God, the Spirit, Paul, Apollos, the Church in Corinth, and the elect everywhere. Paul is Christ's apostle and serves at God's behest to proclaim salvation to all those who are called to sanctification. This includes the audience in Corinth, who are God's own Church, set apart for himself in the spiritual realm of Christ. Paul represents Christ, who works as an agent in accordance with God to bring salvation to his elect everywhere who are baptized and call upon his name for sanctification and affiliation in his spiritual realm (1:2–3). For now, though, the particular focus will be those called who are in Corinth.

The A´ unit (1:10–17) of this ring set makes use of the A (1:1–3) and B (1:4–9) units by mocking the community for misusing and misunderstanding the gospel that they had received from Paul that was to be their sanctification and unification in Christ (1:9). The key issue in this unit is that the community is divided, and the text implies that at least some Corinthians feel Paul has played some part in this division (1:10–12). Paul's response is threefold: (1) Christ is the center of their identity as God's Church and their salvation, not Paul; (2) Christ sent Paul to proclaim a message, not to baptize them; and (3) the community cannot be divided and still be in Christ. Hence their divisions may cause them to lose benefits received from the gospel.

The lexical connections between the units draw out these main points of Paul's exhortation to the community (1:10). "Paul" was called by God's will to be an "apostle," an ambassador, for Christ (1:1), but he was "sent" by Christ (1:16–17) not to baptize but to proclaim the gospel for the community's salvation. The community finds confirmation of their identity in Christ through baptism when they call on Christ's "name" (1:2, 15–17). One cannot be baptized in a minister's (e.g., "Paul's") "name" because the minister does not bring salvation—only the message of its possibility.

The Corinthians had misunderstood the minister's role in their baptism and, as a result, the role of baptism in their Christian identity. The baptism that sanctifies them (1:2) also binds them together in Christ to receive salvation as one church with all the elect (1:7). If they are using it to boast over one another then they have entirely misunderstood their fellowship in Christ and may altogether endanger their salvation.

4

The Foolishness and Wisdom of the Cross, 1:18—3:3

Section A, Ring Set β

ANALYSIS OF UNITS

HAVING ADDRESSED THE DISUNITY of the Corinthian church, Paul now engages their relationship with him and his message. At least one contingent thinks that the apostle's abilities are not satisfactory for an ambassador of the glorious heavenly Lord and his powerful Spirit. They prefer the more grandiose style of Apollos and develop a theology of spiritual power, wisdom, and personal freedom therein.[1] At the same time, the idea of a crucified messiah is antithetical to their cultural view of power and authority. They appear to base this judgment on their own spiritual knowledge. Paul's rebuke is that their conclusions are wrong because their reasoning is not spiritual at all. Instead, their judgment of him and his message shows that they are still too trapped in the earthly conventional wisdom of Greco-Roman culture and are fracturing the community. Paul's ministry, in its weakness and lack of beauty, embodies the cross of Christ, God's most powerful and brilliant plan to justify and redeem humanity. This pivotal β ring set serves to underscore his exhortation in 1:10–17 by countering the Apollos group's

---

1. Bruce, *Circle*, 53; Fitzmyer, *First Corinthians*, 143.

concept of the Spirit and wisdom and impugning that the community is spiritually immature.[2]

Unit A, 1:18–25: God's Plan in Christ Crucified Is an Assault on Worldly Conventional Wisdom but Is Salvation for His Elect

a: 18/ For the message of the cross (σταυροῦ) is foolishness to those who are perishing, but to we who are being saved it is the power of God (δύναμις θεοῦ). 19/ For it is written, "I will destroy the wisdom of the wise ones and I will abolish the brilliance of the brilliant." 20/ Where is the wise person? Where are the scribes? Where are the seekers of this age? Has not God made foolish the wisdom of the world? 21/ For since in God's wisdom the world does not think by God's wisdom, God saw fit to save by "foolish" proclamations (κηρύγματος) those who believe (πιστευόντας). 22/ Jews demand signs and Greeks seek wisdom, 23/ but we ourselves proclaim (κηρύσσομεν) Christ crucified (ἐσταυρωμένον)—a stumbling block to the Jews and foolishness to Gentiles. 24/ But to those who are called—Jews and Greeks alike—is Christ, the power of God (θεοῦ δύναμιν) and the wisdom of God. 25/ For the foolishness of God is wiser than any human, and the weakness of God is stronger than any human.

b: 26/ Consider your own calling, brothers and sisters: not many of you were wise by standards of the flesh (σάρκα), not many of you were powerful, not many of you were well-born.

c: 27/ But God chose (ἐξελέξατο) the foolish things of the world in order that he might destroy (ἵνα καταισχύνῃ) the "wise" things,

c′: 28/ and God chose (ἐξελέξατο) the lowborn and hated of the world, those who are nothing, in order that he might destroy (ἵνα καταισχύνῃ) those who are something.

b′: 29/ As such, no flesh (σάρξ) may boast before the Lord. 30/ And it is because of him that you are in Christ Jesus, who became for us God's wisdom, righteousness, holiness, and redemption. 31/ For it is written, "The one who boasts must boast in the Lord!"

---

2. In the previous chapter, I outlined the performative structure accordingly: sections of the overall letter (A, B, A′), ring sets within each section (α, β, α′); ring units within each set (A, B, A′); and elements (a, b, a′) within units. In this section I will also discuss some elements that are micro-rings in themselves. I will refer to the parts of these micro-rings as "lines" (x, y, x′) in order to distinguish them from the elements. In the interest of space, I have not included the Greek with the micro-rings. However, all translations demonstrate lexical correspondence in the original Greek.

a´: 2:1/ When I came to you, brothers and sisters, I came not with a powerful message or wisdom, but announcing to you the mystery[3] of God. 2/ For I decided to know nothing among you except Jesus Christ and this one who was crucified (ἐσταυρωμένον). And I—in much weakness, fear, and trembling—arrived to you, 4/ and my message and my proclamation (κήρυγμα) were not in persuasive words or sound-bites, but in the manifestation of the Spirit and power, 5/ in order that your faith (πίστις) might not be based on human wisdom but in the power of God (δυνάμει θεοῦ).

God's Assault on the World's Wisdom (a), 1:18–24

The theologically rich text of the *a* element contains a micro-ring structure.[4] The pivotal question in the *z* line (1:20b) presumes that God has, in fact, rendered foolish the wisdom of "the world," such that he has made it irrelevant for entering the new age. The *z´* (1:21) line explains why: since "the world" did not know or act by God's merciful wisdom, God saw fit to save those who believe through a gospel that appeared to be foolish by worldly standards. Faith is required to believe that a message of weakness can be powerful in any way.

Next, the wise person, scribe, and "seeker" of this age who are nullified by God's wisdom in the *y* line (1:20a) are paralleled in the *y´* line (1:22) by Jews, who demand signs, and Greeks, who *seek* wisdom. These groups are set in contrast with those who find the power of God's salvation in a foolish and weak proclamation because of their faith. The rhetorical questions that make up these lines act together.[5] Why are those who base their wisdom

---

3. Some other witnesses read "testimony" (μαρτυριον). I follow NA[27] to read "mystery" (μυστεριον), which has early witnesses (a* A 88 Hippolytus Ambrose).

4. a: (*x*) 18/ For the message of the *cross* is foolishness to those who are perishing, but to we who are being saved it is the *power of God*. For it is written, "I will destroy the wisdom of the wise ones, and I will abolish the brilliance of the brilliant."
(*y*) 20/ Where is the wise person? Where are the scribes? Where are the *seekers* of this age?
(*z*) Has not God made foolish the wisdom of *the world*?
(*z´*) 21/ For since in God's wisdom *the world* does not think by God's wisdom, God saw fit to save by "foolish" proclamations those who believe.
(*y´*) 22/ Jews demand signs and Greeks *seek* wisdom,
(*x´*) 23/ but we ourselves proclaim Christ *crucified*—a stumbling block to the Jews and foolishness to Gentiles. 24/ But to those who are called—Jews and Greeks alike—is Christ, the *power of God* and the wisdom of God. 25/ For the foolishness of God is wiser than any human, and the weakness of God is stronger than any human.

5. The response to the last of these is presumed based on the responses to the initial three. Paul here appears to borrow from the *rib* trial scene imagery in Isaiah (40–55). Like the idols in Second Isaiah, the lack of response serves to denote their

on power rendered powerless? Because, Paul's last question presumes, God has made foolish the "wisdom of this world" through the saving action of the gift of the cross. The wisdom of God's plan is contrary to the world's. The wisdom of "this world" likely encapsulates two different but not entirely exclusive categories. The first is that this wisdom concerns some Hellenistic philosophy that honored knowledge but demeaned the material aspect of the human condition.[6]

A second option is that this wisdom would refer to materialistic and power-based status concerns of the Roman Empire's conflict society.[7] Paul likely has both aspects in view, and so, in contrast to the "wisdom of this world" that relies on a show of strength, God's wisdom grants salvation through the allegedly "weak" gift of the cross. The world, the corrupt system of humanity's social structures, is based on something entirely antithetical to God's wisdom. Because of this, those who are connected to the world cannot think of the gospel as anything but foolishness.

Since the corrupt system worked antithetically to God's plan of salvation by grace, God saw fit to save his elect who would believe and recognize his powerful gift in the gospel. By doing so, those who believe choose God's wisdom over the corrupt systems of greed and power of the world. Their loyalty to God and denunciation of the world logically saves them from his wrath when God completes his abolition of the worldly wisdom at the parousia (1:4–9, 19).

So, how can a crucified messiah manifest God's power? The bracket lines (1:18–19, 22–24) present Paul's thesis that those who are perishing reject the message of the cross as foolishness, but "we who are being saved" recognize that this message truly manifests the power of God. Paul finds support for this paradox in Scripture that speaks of God destroying the wisdom of the wise and the understanding of scholars (x, 1:18–19). The x' line develops this thesis by asserting that, despite the world's continued interest in seeking salvation by their own standards of human power (i.e., signs and wisdom), Paul and all Christians proclaim Christ crucified to be the power of God (1:23–24).

Humanity is made up of two groups: Jews and Gentiles (here, literally "Greeks"), as is the community at Corinth. Both are caught up in the world's standards of wisdom in their own way: Jews seek God's hand in signs and Greeks seek reason in wisdom. So the cross was preached in foolishness in order that those Jews and Greeks who are called might believe the

---

powerlessness—in this case, in the face of the gospel.

6. Collins, *First Corinthians*, 97.
7. Witherington, *Conflict*, 114.

foolishness of the cross despite its apparent lack of miraculous power or wisdom. This is a slight against the pneumatic Apollos faction in the audience. They have been called, yet they do not recognize God's wisdom that was intended specifically for them to understand.

The weak elect's salvation by faith ("*we* who are being saved") and their election ("*we* who are called") demonstrate to the world that God's power to save humanity is truly present in the merciful gift of the cross. Their ability to recognize God's wisdom in the foolishness and weakness of the cross, despite human conventions to seek power elsewhere, is what separates the elect who are being saved from those who are passing away (1:18). Christ and the cross are the power of God (1:18, 23–24), not despite human expectations, but because of them. Since humans expected this power to be shown in signs and wisdom, God saves the elect through a message that is, by all appearances, complete foolishness.

Christ crucified is God's power and God's wisdom for those who are called to believe (1:18, 21, 24–25).[8] Christ's power as God's wisdom is counterintuitive to humans precisely because it lacks signs and worldly wisdom and, further, because God's wisdom and power are far beyond the comprehension or abilities of humanity. What humans consider to be common sense is incapable of recognizing the power and wisdom of God. By the cross, then, God has shown human wisdom to be irrelevant (1:18–20).

Those who are perishing do not receive the gospel because they are caught up in the conventional wisdom of the world and reject a crucified Messiah as pure foolishness. Citing Scripture (Isa 29:14), Paul claims that God will abolish the wisdom of the so-called "wise" (1:19). Wisdom refers here not to rhetoric only but also philosophical and conventional assumptions of Roman culture.[9] Those who perish do so because they cling to human wisdom and reject as foolishness God's power and plan for salvation through grace that is manifest in the cross because it does not conform to their present values of power and material gain. Their decision to view God's action through the lens of their own standards (rather than vice versa) betrays their loyalty.[10]

---

8. Here Christ is treated as the personified Wisdom seen in Jewish sapiential literature (Prov 8:24; Wisd 7–9). See Witherington, *Conflict*, 117.

9. Keener, *1–2 Corinthians*, 28.

10. According to Keener, *1–2 Corinthians*, 28–29, there is a precedent in Jewish Apocalypticism for salvation being dependent on one's response to God's wisdom (*1 Enoch* 5:8; 98:3; 99:10; *2 Bar* 51:7). For Paul, the same results now apply to one's response to the gospel, the manifestation of God's wisdom.

Beyond What Is Written

Not Powerful According to Human Standards (b), 1:26

Having addressed in the *a* element that God has seen fit to save the elect through a foolish gospel, Paul now uses the audience themselves as an example of how God's powerful salvation is hidden in foolishness and weakness. The point of departure is whether one can judge the truth of God's wisdom according to human standards. The elect who are in Corinth are not rulers of this age, generally of high status, or conquerors, yet they have been invited to take part in the new age and the glory of the risen Lord Jesus Christ. This is indeed a foolish plan!

God Selects the Foolish to Conquer the Wise (c), 1:27a

Drawing from the imagery and message he set forward in the *a* element (1:18–26), Paul now states that God completes his assault on human wisdom that was foretold in Scripture (1:19) by selecting the foolish things of the world as his instrument. God's wisdom is so superior to human wisdom (1:25) that he can conquer human standards of wisdom by seemingly foolish things. Since the world rejected God in favor of its own sense of order (1:21), God sought to save those who believe through a message that the world would find to be "foolish" according to its own wisdom.

God Selects Weak Things to Conquer the World's Power (c'), 1:27b-28

The pivot of the A unit (1:18—2:5) is denoted by the repetition of the terms "elected" and "nullify" in the *c* and *c'* elements. These central elements complete the example of the community that began in the *b* element (1:26). Just as God in the *c* element "elects" the foolish things of the world to "nullify" human wisdom (1:27a), he likewise in the *c'* element "elects" the weak and hated things of the world to "nullify" those things that humans consider powerful (1:27b-28). The result is that those things that are considered nothing and negligible now replace the existing powers. There is not only a complete inversion of standards and status, but also a complete inversion of existence and relevance.

Paul develops his argument of divine design in the gospel's appearance by presenting the Corinthians themselves as an example. Paul's description of the elect here denotes the community not only as poor.[11] More to the point, "not many" in this group exemplify the powerful conquering

---

11. On "calling" referring to socioeconomic status, see Witherington, *Conflict*, 113–14.

ideal figure or the system of corruption manifest in the Roman Empire at that time (1:26). Instead, they are the lowly, conquered, occupied, and colonialized who have been elected by God, not despite their lowliness, but because of it (1:21), and as such become a demonstration of God's wisdom to the rest of the world.[12] Like Christ's cross, their election is scandalous and denounces the existing power structure as corrupt and temporary. God's eternal plan will soon replace it. The community's election, confirmed externally by the Spirit (1:4–9), denotes the inevitability of God's victory for the elect. Through a crucified Lord, God conquers the conqueror on behalf of the conquered.

Paul's wording in 1:26–28 echoes Jer 9:22–23 and presents a christocentric interpretation of the prophetic text.[13] The aspects (wisdom, power, and wealth) that Jeremiah claimed separated the sixth century audience from the Deuteronomic covenant are now what Paul views as a threat to God's new covenant people in Corinth. Paul's allusion to boasting before the Lord denounces any mixing of worldly status and spiritual context. One's spiritual gifts come from God, *not* the world; and one should abide in God's church by the standards of the Spirit, *not* the world. Paul's use of Jeremiah is apt for the Corinthians' crisis. The false standards of the sixth century BCE Judeans that violated the covenant are the same that cause the Corinthians to misunderstand the gospel, misuse their Spirit-given abilities from baptism, and create worldly status-oriented conflict and division in their own community.[14]

The elect in Corinth were lowly and not of influence by the world's wisdom but are now filled with eschatological knowledge and all spiritual gifts, sealed in the Spirit, and bound in fellowship with God through Christ. They must recognize their renewed status is not due to anything based on human standards, but rather comes from the gift/grace of God's wisdom (i.e., his plan for their salvation). God has called them to play a game in which he has drastically changed the rules but also informed his elect so that they might believe and be saved.[15] God is now, as demonstrated by the cross and by the presence of the Spirit among the community, "engaged in overthrowing the world's false standards."[16] The gospel and the election of the worthless by the Spirit both show how God's wisdom abrogates and ren-

---

12. For an excellent discussion on colonization in the context of Paul's letters to his communities, see Lopez, *Conquered*.

13. See O'Day's illuminating article, "Intertextuality," 259–67, on the intertextual relationship between 1 Cor 1:26–28 and Jer 9:22–24.

14. Ibid.

15. Garland, *1 Corinthians*, 79.

16. Barrett, *First Epistle*, 57.

ders foolish the wisdom of this world.[17] The wisdom of God's plan receives its support from the Corinthians themselves.

No Human May Boast before God (b'), 1:29–31

Following God's nullification of human wisdom and power through the election of foolish and weak things (such as the audience), in the next element Paul asserts in a micro-ring structure that no person may boast before God.[18] The central *y* line (1:30) puts forward that God's election of the foolish and weak community in Corinth has placed them in Christ, who has become "for us" the wisdom, righteousness, sanctification, and redemption that are from God.

The surrounding *x* and *x*´ lines (1:29, 31) explain that, because the foolish things are not great in themselves but only by God's election, they have no right to boast before God. It is in Christ that their boast rests, not in themselves. This idea completes the development from the *b* element, which stated that the elect are not wise or powerful according to "human" standards (1:26). Since these standards have been made irrelevant by the election of foolish and weak things, the elect fulfill Scripture in that they and all "humanity" can no longer boast in their own standards of power for salvation; instead, they must now boast only in the weakness and foolishness of the cross and Christ, through whom they receive salvation and righteousness.

The qualities that Christ becomes for "us" who are called to believe—righteousness, sanctification, and redemption—compound the extent to which God has nullified the conventional wisdom of the world. Those great gifts were not achieved by signs, wisdom, wealth, influence, or nobility, but rather by Christ crucified. Christ has achieved these renewed states for the elect who are in him. He is righteousness in the sense that they are brought into right relationship with him. He is sanctification for them in that in him they are set apart as God's own church. And he is redemption for them in that he is the price by which God bought them from the present age and the wisdom of the world so that they might belong to God, have fellowship in Christ with him, and have the gift of all eschatological knowledge (1:18).

Through Christ, they become something even more powerful than the standards which had judged them as worthless. For if God's foolishness is

---

17. Conzelmann, *1 Corinthians*, 50.

18. b´: (*x*) 29/ As such, no flesh may *boast* before the *Lord*.

(*y*) 30/ And it is because of him that you are in Christ Jesus, who became for us God's wisdom, righteousness, holiness, and redemption.

(*x*´) 31/ For it is written, "The one who *boasts* must boast in the *Lord*!"

wiser than human wisdom, and they have become God's wisdom, then they are that much wiser and more powerful than even the mightiest human rulers.

Paul Preaches the Mystery of God: That Christ Crucified Is God's Power (a´), 2:1–5

This element presents Paul's preaching as an example of God's wisdom and points back to the *intitulatio*, in which Paul self-identifies as Christ's ambassador to the community (2:1–5).[19] In the central line of the element's micro-ring structure, Paul declares that while he was among the Corinthian community he discerned to know nothing except Jesus Christ, "this one who is crucified" (2:2).[20] In contrast to the wisdom that the Corinthians are using to compete with one another, Paul states that for him the sum of the gospel is manifest most fully when one understands the power that is present in Christ on the cross. The element thus hinges on the weak, fearful, and trembling manner in which he first arrived with the gospel of salvation (*y*, 2:3).

The bracket lines present Paul's arrival and teaching with the audience as support for this central claim, and the close of the ring develops the initial thesis. That he arrived in Corinth ("to you") in great fear and trembling (2:3) underscores that he did not proclaim his message with lofty words of wisdom (also "to you," 2:1). Rhetorical demonstration was not necessary because, as the *x´* line (2:3–5) explains, Paul's message and preaching were validated by the Spirit and power of charismatic activity in the community (2:4). That Paul wishes for their faith to be founded in the power "of God" and not human wisdom (*x´*, 2:5) clarifies that the mystery "of God" (*x*, 2:1) that Paul proclaims is mysterious because its content—salvation and glory in Christ crucified—is contrary to human wisdom. God's election of the Corinthians, which is manifest in the charismatic gifts and powers they experienced after they received the gospel with faith, is made possible through fellowship with Christ. However, the spiritual riches the Corinthians receive

---

19. Collins, *First Corinthians*, 115.

20. a´: (*x*) 1/ When I came to you, brothers and sisters, I came not with a *powerful* message or *wisdom*, but announcing to you the mystery *of God*.

(*y*) 2/ For I decided to know nothing among you except Jesus Christ and this one who was crucified.

(*x´*) 3/ And I—in much weakness, fear, and trembling—arrived to you, 4/ and my message and my proclamation were not in persuasive words or sound-bites, but in the manifestation of the Spirit and *power*, 5/ in order that your faith might not be based on human *wisdom* but in the *power of God*.

are due to Christ's sacrifice on the cross. It is this paradoxical image that Paul claims to portray in his fearful and trembling ministry before them.

The initial line explains that Paul did not preach God's testimony eloquently or showing superior "wisdom" because he endeavored to know the mysterious salvation found in Jesus Christ who was crucified (x, 2:1–2). The final line (x', 2:4–5) completes the ring by restating that he did not preach with "wise" words in Sophistic style, but rather in the demonstration of the Spirit's power, in order that the Corinthians would know that the true source of their salvation is found in Christ crucified, who is God's "wisdom" (1:31), and not in human "wisdom" (2:5).[21] Paul preached about Christ by God's wisdom in the manifestation of the Spirit, which is God's power. This image serves to sum up the paradoxical nature that he and the gospel take on when the audience receive him by human standards and not with spiritual understanding.[22]

This final element reconnects to the initial a element and brings the A Unit (1:18—2:5) as a whole to a close. That Paul wished to know nothing while among the Corinthians except this one "crucified," so that through his "proclamation" their "faith" might be in "God's power" and mystery rather than human standards (a', 2:1–5), recalls the message of the "cross" that separates the elect who "believe" in Paul's foolish "proclamation" from those who rely on signs and human wisdom. And the elect are saved by their faith precisely because they are able to recognize "God's power" in Christ "crucified," whom Paul "proclaims" (a, 1:18–24).

In the lead up to the letter, some in the Corinthian community had rejected the cross and crucified Lord as foolishness but wished to keep the powerful Spirit as a pawn in their worldly status competition. But the reciprocal structure of the unit in the parallel a and a' elements refutes their position as illogical. The powerful Spirit of God and the cross are inseparable. Christ crucified is the content of the gospel that Paul proclaims, and it is only by receipt of this "foolish" message that the power of the Spirit can be demonstrated or experienced (2:4–5). God's mystery (2:1) to the world

---

21. Despite Paul's comment, he demonstrates considerable rhetorical skill in this argument (Collins, *First Corinthians*, 91). Underselling one's own skills was a common and accepted strategy that was used by talented orators such as Isocrates, Cicero, Seneca, and Quintilian; see Keener, *1–2 Corinthians*, 34.

22. Paul's defensive tone implies that something had been said to challenge him and his preaching abilities. So what exactly was the problem? Many different ideas have been proposed. One explanation points out that it was common practice for Sophists to preach and develop groups of devotees. Paul may have had an accent or blasé delivery that caused some elite members embarrassment when they compared Paul to their friends' respective speakers who have been more influenced by Sophistic showmanship. On this theory, see Keener, *1–2 Corinthians*, 34–35.

The Foolishness and Wisdom of the Cross, 1:18—3:3

is that he offers the power of his Spirit to the low-status elect through a message of foolishness and weakness (1:18–28). True wisdom—God's wisdom—can only be comprehended when this presumably ridiculous equation is recognized as the perfect, logical truth that brings salvation.

Unit B, 2:6–13: God's Wisdom Is Hidden to Worldly Authorities and Regular Human Intuition

a: 6/ Now we can speak wisdom (σοφίαν λαλοῦμεν) to adults, but it is a wisdom not of this age, nor of the rulers of this age who are being destroyed. 7/ But we speak the wisdom (ἀλλά λαλοῦμεν σοφίαν) of God that is a mystery and hidden (ἀποκεκρυμμένην),

b: which (ἥν) God set forward before this age for our glory (δόξαν),

b′: 8/ which (ἥν) none of the rulers of this age know. For if they knew, they would not have crucified the Lord of Glory (δόξης).

a′: 9/ But (ἀλλά) just as it is written, "Eye has not seen, and ear has not heard, and a person's heart has not understood, such things that God has prepared for those who love him." 10/ Now to us God has revealed (ἀπεκάλυψεν) this through the Spirit; for the Spirit searches everything, even the depths of God. 11/ For what person can comprehend a person except that person's spirit within? And who can know the depths of God except the Spirit of God? 12/ We did not receive the spirit of the world but (ἀλλά) the Spirit that is from God, in order that we might comprehend the depths that have been given to us from God. 13/ We do speak (λαλοῦμεν) of such things—not in words taught by human wisdom (σόφιαν)—but (ἀλλά) as taught by the Spirit, explaining spiritual things to spiritual people.

We Speak to the Mature a Wisdom Not of This Age (a), 2:6–7a

The opening element of this central unit in the ring set initiates a veiled rebuke of the Corinthians' accusations that Paul does not speak well and that his gospel is foolish. He does in fact speak wisdom, but only to "adults." This element contains a micro-ring structure.[23] The central lines purport that the wisdom Paul preaches is "not of this age" (y, 2:6b) and "not of" the rulers of "this age" (y′, 2:6c). The closing line (2:7a) clarifies

---

23. a: (x) 6/ *Now we can speak wisdom* to adults,
(y) but it is a wisdom *not of this age*,
(y′) *nor of the rulers of this age* who are being destroyed.
(x′) 7/ But *we speak the wisdom* of God that is a mystery and hidden.

that the "wisdom" spoken to adults in the *x* line (2:6a) is in fact God's "wisdom" that Paul speaks mysteriously to those whom it has been revealed. Adults, then, would include those who are transformed into spiritually mature believers who recognize the mystery apparent in the gospel. Given the arguments in 1:18—2:5 seen above, this word-choice is a harsh indictment of the Corinthians' spiritual development and comprehension. Their rejection of the cross and their divisiveness demonstrate their spiritual shortcomings and immaturity.

The stagnation of their development centers around their refusal let go of the worldly standards of this age. This stunt in growth is represented well in the Apollos faction who have intertwined the gifts of the gospel (tongues, wisdom, interpretation, etc.) with aspects of human status and conflict.[24] But Paul's loyalists are held accountable for boasting in him. They do not see themselves as the unified body of Christ, but rather as competing leaders of a dawning empire. Their present actions demonstrate that they misunderstand the core of the gospel and will not be spiritually mature until they let go of the worldly misuse of the Spirit in competition against one another.[25]

This element initiates a new direction from the previous unit with the caveat that Paul's gospel is in fact wisdom to "mature" (i.e., complete) persons. The combination of the words "wisdom" and "mature" echoes Wisd 9:17; Sir 1:6-9; 3:31-52, which emphasize that no human can be complete or mature without God's revealed knowledge.[26] This wisdom, however, is contrary to the wisdom of this age, and the rulers of this age, who are fading away. These rulers would include both heavenly and earthly authorities who will be subsumed under Christ's lordship on the day he returns (1 Cor 15:21–25). The liberal use of "wisdom" in this section likely presumes it as a major topic or catch-word among the community in Corinth.[27]

God's Wisdom and the Ignorance of the Rulers of this Age (b, b'), 2:7b-8

Paul does not speak this wisdom in a way that is apparent to this age but, rather, he preaches mysteriously the wisdom and power of God that are truly present in the cross.[28] This spiritual power is not apparent to those who judge speech or other matters by the standards of this age, but only by the

24. Fee, *First Epistle*, 96.
25. Barrett, *First Epistle*, 68.
26. Keener, *1-2 Corinthians*, 38.
27. Conzelmann, *1 Corinthians*, 57.
28. Barrett, *First Epistle*, 70-71.

elect who are spiritually mature enough to recognize the world's systems as corrupt and judge through the aid of God's Spirit and wisdom (1:7).

That the rulers of this age crucified the Lord of glory, who will rule over them, demonstrates the hidden nature of God's plan for salvation. For their part in his death, the rulers will see the eclipse of their authority and temporal reign by the new age of the Spirit that is demonstrated in the reception of the gospel by the low-status elect (2:4). Since these worldly powers did not recognize Christ's mission while on earth, they are also unable to evaluate the gospel that the apostles now proclaim.[29] As spiritual infants, the Corinthians remain aligned with the leaders of this age because they are still obsessed with worldly standards of power and status and blind to the true power of God in the gospel.[30]

Human Wisdom cannot Intuit the Depths of God's Gifts for the Elect (a´), 2:9–13

The *a´* element, like its parallel complement, contains a concentric micro-ring pattern.[31] The central *y* and *y´* lines (2:10–12) are denoted by the repetition of the phrase "the depths of God." The *y* line (2:10) explains that the Spirit is a successful communicant of God's wisdom to the elect because the Spirit has searched "all things," even "the depths of God." The *y´* line (2:11) continues that, just as only a person's spirit can know his/her internal plans and motives, so too can only the Spirit of God explore "the depths of God" to know and make known his most hidden plans (2:7, 10). Paul and the elect did not receive the spirit of the world, which is blind to God's plans (2:6–9); rather, they received the Spirit of God in order that they can know "the depths of God" and the wisdom that has been given to them.

The elemental micro-structure is bracketed by the *x* and *x´* lines, which are denoted by the repetition of the term "things." In particular, the

---

29. Keener, *1–2 Corinthians*, 39.
30. Ibid., 38.
31. a´: (*x*) 9/ Now just as it is written, "Eye has not seen, and ear has not heard, and a person's heart has not understood, *such things* that God has prepared for those who love him."
(*y*) 10/ But to us God has revealed this through the Spirit; for the Spirit searches everything, even *the depths of God*.
(*y´*) 11/ For what person can comprehend a person except that person's spirit within? And who can know *the depths of God* except the Spirit of God? 12/ We did not receive the spirit of the world but the Spirit that is from God, in order that we might comprehend *the depths* that have been given to us from God.
(*x´*) 13/ We speak of *such things*—not in words taught by human wisdom—but as taught by the Spirit, explaining spiritual things to spiritual people.

"things" that God has prepared for the elect who love him, but that cannot be intuited by human senses or wisdom, in the *x* line (2:9), are the "things" that in the *x′* line Paul proclaims in his gospel not in human words but by the Spirit that discerns God and can interpret the depths of his wisdom to his elect (2:13). Paul cites Scripture (Isa 64:3) to support his thesis: no human sense has perceived, or can intuit, that which the gospel has made clear. God has prepared salvation in Christ crucified for those who love him, are in right relationship with him, and are obedient to his will. The "us" is emphatic. God alone saves, but the full impact is determined by "how each person understands him/herself as the receiver of the gift."[32]

Paul then explains how the audience is not able to understand the gospel by their own human faculties. In fact, God revealed his plan to his elect, those whom he has destined for glory (2:7) and fellowship with him in his Son (1:9), by his Spirit and its powerful demonstration in the worship and faith of the community. God has revealed his plan through the Spirit and not by human intuition so that the elect might understand God's gift in Christ crucified as something wholly contrary to the present, corrupt system of the world. Human intuition cannot understand this by worldly faculties; only the Spirit who delves into the mind of God can illuminate the human mind to see the truth. And so this spiritual reality, as foolish as it may sound, must be the content of Paul's gospel, because if he began to express it in human terms or rhetoric, it would be robbed of its power and truth.

The *a′* element reconnects to the *a* element (2:6–7a) through the repetition of key terms and brings closure to the central B unit (2:6–13). That Paul does mysteriously "speak" God's wisdom, not the world's, to adults in the *a* element (2:6–7a) is developed in the *a′* element in that Paul "speaks" of the incredible things that God has prepared for his elect that are hidden in his depths but are revealed by the Spirit to spiritual people who recognize Paul's gospel as God's wisdom apart from human conventional wisdom (2:9–13).

Throughout this unit Paul builds on the tradition of Jewish Apocalypticism that views spiritual wisdom as the disclosure of God's plan for the end times that is equally and completely outside the grasp of ordinary people. Only those who understand the particular texts, be they *1 Enoch*, Daniel, or (in this case) Paul's preaching, can consider themselves sufficiently informed by the Spirit for the imminent onslaught of God's plan.[33]

---

32. Conzelmann, *1 Corinthians*, 64–65.
33. See Brown, *Cross*, 45–60.

Unit A´, 2:14—3:3: The Corinthians Remain Like Ordinary People because of Their Spiritual Immaturity and Divisions

a: 14/ An ordinary person (ψυχικὸς ἄνθρωπος) cannot receive the Spirit of God, for it is foolishness to him, and he is not able (δύναται) to judge spiritually. 15/ But the spiritual person can judge all things, and he is judged by no one.

b: 16/ For who has known the mind (νοῦν) of the Lord, and who has searched him?

b´: But we do have the mind (νοῦν) of Christ![34]

a´: 3:1/ But, brothers and sisters, I was not able (ἠδυνήθην) to speak to you as spiritual people but only as fleshy people, and as undeveloped children in Christ. 2/ I fed you milk, because you could not handle (ἐδύνασθε) bread. And you still cannot handle it! 3/ For you are still fleshy. For when contention and strife are among you, are you not fleshy and acting just like ordinary people (σαρκικοί ἄνθρωπον)?

Between Ordinary and Spiritual Humanity (a), 2:14-15

The A´ unit of the β ring set (1:18—3:3) produces the logical conclusion of the argument to this point. Since God's wisdom can be known only by the Spirit, a person without the Spirit cannot understand the gospel. God reveals his wisdom to his elect through the single conduit of the Spirit. Only upon the successful receipt of this wisdom can they begin to be transformed from "ordinary" people to "mature" and "spiritual" people.[35] But this conclusion has an added twist: although the Corinthians are in Christ, and have the Spirit and the mind of Christ to understand God, they are still immature in their faith and so are unable to fully understand God's wisdom as would a spiritually mature person. This immaturity and resistance to the gospel seems to arise from the members' attachment to the world's corrupt views of power.

Their spirituality is in fact so childish that it nearly renders them ordinary (i.e., like the unsanctified who are perishing, 1:18-20). This has two consequences: 1) Paul cannot preach the full gospel to them because they could not receive it in its purest form, and 2) their worldliness ("fleshiness")

---

34. There is some textual evidence for κυρίου (B D* F G 81) instead of Χριστοῦ. The majority of scholars and translations, however, prefer the text above. See Metzger, *TCGNT*, 482.

35. Fitzmyer, *First Corinthians*, 170.

creates a vicious cycle of misunderstanding the gospel and creating factions in the community—leading them to live just like "those who are perishing," rather than "those who are being saved" (1:18).[36] All believers have some wisdom, but a spiritual and mature believer has faith to accept the Spirit and the painful truth of the gospel that this world's standards have been eclipsed by God's truth and power that are manifest in the cross.[37] The divisions and contention over spiritual gifts demonstrate that a number of the audience members have fallen short.[38]

The initial element picks up from the last unit and explains that an ordinary, unspiritual person who is not predestined for glory (and so has not received the Spirit in order to understand the gospel) is incapable of receiving the gifts of the Spirit (namely the eschatological knowledge, fellowship in Christ, and faith in the cross that brings righteousness, sanctification, and redemption) because all of these things are foolishness to him/her, or rather, he/she considers them foolish and cannot accept that these gifts can come as a gift from the cross.[39]

Who has Known the Mind of the Lord? (b), 2:16a

The *b* element continues that they are not only unable to accept the results of the Spirit, but are also unable to understand them, or rather, are unable to reconcile the spiritual gifts with their counterintuitive origin in the cross. They are unable to do these things because these gifts must be understood spiritually apart from the world's presumed standards of power. The spiritual person can judge all things with full eschatological knowledge and God's wisdom, but, because of his/her place in Christ, is immune to judgment by human standards. The question here echoes Isa 40:13. The answer for the original context was "no one," but Paul does presume an answer here—the Spirit. For Paul, the "mind" of the Lord "is equivalent to the spirit coming from God."[40]

Paul implicitly echoes OT (Wis 9:13; Isa 40:13) with the rhetorical question, "Who has known the mind of the Lord?" Not only do the elect spiritual persons have the knowledge of the Spirit, they also have the mind of Christ, God's Son, who has become for them the wisdom of God (1:31).

36. See Conzelmann, *1 Corinthians*, 71.
37. Fitzmyer, *First Corinthians*, 170.
38. Francis, "Babes," views the Corinthians' baptism and receipt of the Spirit, but refusal of the gospel, as a paradox that Paul refuses to accept.
39. On ψυχικῶς, see the excursus in Conzelmann, *1 Corinthians*, 67–68.
40. Fitzmyer, *First Corinthians*, 185; see also Conzelmann, *1 Corinthians*, 69.

As in many other uses of OT scripture where God the Father is the original implied referent for "Lord," Paul has transferred the title to refer to Christ. So, the passage asks, who has known the mind of Christ? The answer, as has been provided in the letter so far, is that the elect who have received the Spirit from the gospel, and are incorporated into Christ to receive knowledge and all other spiritual blessings from God, also receive the mind of Christ. This point explains why the spiritual person cannot be judged by worldly standards.

Only God's Spirit can reveal his plan because only the Spirit has searched the Lord to find and communicate that wisdom. Being in receipt of the Spirit and God's wisdom, the believer is transformed into a spiritual, mature being in Christ (1:7, 17) and thus through him also into a blameless, sanctified, and redeemed state (1:30–31) that is immune to the accusations of unspiritual people (1:31; 2:14). That is, of course, unless these sanctified people disqualify themselves by remaining overly connected to the world in divisions and arrogance.

The Elect have the Mind of Christ (b´), 2:16b

The b´ element continues the concentric folding of the argument as the structure progresses. The b element (2:16a) already explained to the audience that the spiritual person judges all things but cannot be judged in return. However, the b´ element explains further that the Corinthian audience does not yet fit in this category.[41] They cannot yet judge everything, nor receive immunity from the judgment of others, because Paul impugns that they are not, in fact, spiritual people. They are still worldly ("fleshy"). And he had to address them in such a manner because, even though they are God's elect who have an inclination to receive the gospel and faith to gain a portion of the Spirit and spiritual blessings, they are still spiritually immature from their dependence on worldly standards of power. The spiritual person is able to do much with his/her spiritual blessings (b, 2:15); the audience in Corinth, however, cannot. The b´ element explains that their infantile nature in Christ is such that they were not even able to receive the gospel that conveys the cross as God's wisdom to them. Instead, Paul presented a simplified version of the gospel with the demonstrable power of the Spirit that was to be more digestible for them, like milk instead of solid

---

41. The "we" here likely refers to Paul, the co-authors, and all other Christians who have received the Spirit and become mature, spiritual people through faith and understanding the true power of the gospel (cf. Conzelmann, *1 Corinthians*, 69, who feels the "we" phrase mocks a slogan from the pneumatics).

food, to aid their meager faith. But even that mild form was hard for them to stomach, so connected were they to the worldly standards to which they were accustomed.[42]

Only the mature, spiritual, and faithful elect can claim to know the wisdom of God because he has imparted his Spirit, the sole communicant of this wisdom (2:9–13), to them. Here the mind of Christ is equivalent to the mind of the Lord (the Father) because of the Spirit, and this ambiguity furthers the paradox of the cross. The Spirit teaches the elect that the crucified Lord is the emphatic nexus of God's wisdom. These sanctified who possess the mind of Christ should then also reject the standards of the world and believe in the truth of God's gracious saving power.

Corinthians' Spiritual Immaturity Restricts their Understanding (a'), 3:1–3a

The final a' element completes the unit and further imparts the accusation of the Corinthians' worldliness. Not only would they not successfully receive the gospel that Paul presented, but their factions further demonstrate their spiritual immaturity.[43] Connecting back to the initial a element (2:14–15), the a' element reiterates that the audience are merely human in their divisiveness, and so are no different from ordinary unspiritual person who cannot accept the gifts of the Spirit.

The word choice is deliberate and unfolds the progression of Paul's argument. The Corinthians are not just ordinary people (2:14); they are worldly and consumed by the desires of the world (3:2). They are not perfect, as they presume, but rather are fleshy and contrary to the Spirit.[44] The accusation is followed with insult. The Corinthians are still immature with regard to Christ, far from the mature and spiritually knowledgeable persons they imagined themselves to be.

If the Corinthians cannot recognize the spiritual gifts found in the cross because of their attachments to worldly standards of power, and if they are quarrelling and forming divisions, what is the difference between them and the ordinary, unspiritual person who is perishing with the age that is passing away (1:18–25; 2:14–16)? The painful truth of Paul's message in this unit is that *there is no difference*. Although they have received the gospel,

---

42. Francis, "Babes," 41–43, views the immaturity not in the terms of stunted spiritual formation but rather in their childish attachment to worldly standards. We view the two problems as being co-existent and equal.

43. Fitzmyer, *First Corinthians*, 150.

44. Collins, *First Corintihans*, 140; Barrett, *First Epistle*, 80.

faith in Christ, and the Spirit, the Corinthians are still acting as though they had not received any spiritual gifts—and their actions confirm their lack of understanding and reception of the truth found in the gospel.[45]

INTERRELATION OF UNITS

The second major ring set in the letter's first large section (A, 1:1—4:24) argues as a whole that the cross is not "foolishness" to the elect who understand that God's wisdom and power are truly demonstrated in the spiritual blessings that come from Christ's sacrificial act. Rather, the worldly standards of conventional human wisdom are shown to be foolishness because they are not able to recognize God's power and wisdom. Only the Spirit can distinguish the pseudo-foolishness of the gospel from the true foolishness of human intuition and conventional wisdom's pursuit for material power.

Outline

God's Plan in Christ Crucified Is an Assault on Worldly Conventional Wisdom, but Is Salvation for His Elect (A, 1:18—2:5)

Paul preaches that the audience are "in Christ" (ἐν Χριστῷ, 1:29) because they have received the Spirit from a "foolish" (μωρία, passim) gospel. The audience were selected because they are not special by human (σάρκα, 1:26) standards. And God did so in order that no flesh (σάρξ, 1:29) may boast before him.

God's Wisdom Is Hidden to Worldly Authorities and Regular Human Intuition (B, 2:6–13)

The spiritually mature recognize Paul's gospel to demonstrate the power and wisdom that are inherent in the grace of the cross. However, the rulers of the world, those who symbolize the status-obsessed emphasis on worldly power and knowledge, are blind to the true power and wisdom found in the cross.

---

45. Witherington, *Conflict*, 126.

Beyond What Is Written

The Corinthians Remain Like Regular People because of Their Spiritual Immaturity and Divisions (A´, 2:14—3:3)

Paul has treated the Corinthians as children because they are still underdeveloped "in Christ" (ἐν Χριστῷ, 3:2). That is, they are not able (or refuse) to accept the truth of the gospel's message of power through weakness. Their dysfunction is demonstrated both by their rejection of the cross as "foolishness" (μωρία, 2:14) and by the divisions among them. As such, the audience remain "fleshy" (σάρκινοι, 3:3), worldly, like ordinary people who have not received the Spirit.

Conclusion

The pivotal B Unit holds that the gospel's apparent "foolishness" is part of God's plan to save those who are called while hiding it from rulers of this age and ordinary humanity (2:6–13). This desire for material power is reflected most fully in the central B unit's imputation that the rulers of this age act contrary to God's wisdom. Their attachment to the ways of their culture led them to crucify God's Son while he was on earth. Their blindness continues in the new age in that they cannot recognize that their reign is already passing away, nor that they will soon be subordinated to the glorious crucified Lord when he returns. Only God's elect are able to recognize the subtle truth of the cross in the gospel, which is perceived by the Spirit, who manifests God's power, and by whom God reveals his plan for them in Christ crucified.

The Corinthians' attachment to worldly power has constricted their reception of the gospel, such that they misunderstand the cross as "foolish" and "weak" when they should recognize by the Spirit that it is their salvation, wisdom, power, and hope for future glory. This lack of spiritual knowledge betrays their truly "fleshy" or worldly state—far from the mature, spiritual people that God has called to edify.

The bracket A and A´ Units argue that the foolishness of the gospel is contrary and therefore indecipherable to worldly wisdom, and the Corinthians are too close to the latter to recognize the former (1:18—2:5; 2:14—3:3). The A unit explains that, since the world rejected God's wisdom, he was pleased to save those who believe through the "foolishness" of the gospel. This message of Christ crucified was unacceptable to most because it did not meet the standards inherent in human conventional wisdom that focus on demonstrable power and material gain. But, although he may appear foolish to others, Christ crucified should be apparent to the elect as the power of

God and the wisdom of God. This truth is beyond human wisdom and can be understood only by faith. Since God's foolishness is greater than human wisdom, much more is Christ crucified, who is God's wisdom made apparent by the Spirit to those who are called and empowered to believe. Christ's act on the cross, which supersedes human understanding and circumvents human conventional wisdom by bringing righteousness, sanctification, and redemption to his elect by grace, is the means by which God abolishes worldly wisdom.

The A′ unit develops the A unit. The audience are in Christ (A, 1:29) but they are immature in Christ (A′, 3:3). Rather than being Christians who live in Rome, they are acting like Romans who attend a Christian assembly. They cling too strongly to the Roman Empire's (i.e., the "world's") ideals of power and wisdom that can be measured by human conventional wisdom and material or status-oriented gain. Their attachment to the ways of the world that is fading away is like squeezing a deflating life-preserver while stranded in the ocean, and this rejection of God's wisdom in the cross is damaging their opportunity for salvation.

First, it demonstrates their lack of understanding the gospel and failure to be illuminated properly by the Spirit. Second, their desire for power causes arrogance and divisions among them, such that they tear apart that which God has bound together in the Spirit. Consequently, while they are still entrapped in human (fleshy) standards (A, 1:26) and, though fleshy, attempt to boast before the Lord as if their talents were their own (A, 1:29), they prove themselves to be fleshy persons still who act just like the ordinary, fleshy people who have not received the gospel or God's Spirit (A′, 3:3). Paul's clear message to the audience within the eschatologically-laced ring set is that they need to change their outlook on the cross and fix their present divisions—or else face the imminent consequences.

5

Paul, Apollos, and the Community, 3:4—4:21

Section A, Ring Set α´

ANALYSIS OF UNITS

The modern Christian tends to focus on the questions of wisdom in 1:18—3:3 and immorality in 5:1—6:20 and, as a result, we often miss that 3:4—4:21 is Paul's main point and the climax of his argument in the first major section of the letter. The section on wisdom in 1:18—3:3 is placed rhetorically at the center to support Paul's overall thesis in Section A: despite what they think, the Corinthians cannot judge who or what is spiritual because they are not yet mature in Christ. They say they have spiritual knowledge, and that this empowers them to judge between apostles. Having pointed out that their idea of "wisdom/foolishness" is backwards, Paul will now set out to explain that their presumptions about the faculties of an apostle, and how he and Apollos relate to their salvation, are also misconstrued.

Unit A, 3:4–22: Paul and Apollos as Co-Workers, Constructing God's Temple

a: 4/ For when someone says, "I am with Paul (Παύλου)," and another says, "I am with Apollos (Ἀπολλῶ)," are you (ἐστε) not like ordinary people? So

Paul, Apollos, and the Community, 3:4—4:21

what is Apollos (Ἀπολλῶς), and what is Paul (Παῦλος)?—Stewards through whom you came to believe—to each as the Lord (κύριος) gave. 6/ I planted, Apollos (Ἀπολλῶς) watered, but God did the growing. 7/ So it is not the one who plants who is anything of account,[1] nor the one who grows, but God who does the growing. 8/ The one who plants and the one who waters act as one, and each will receive his own wage according to his own work, 9/ for we are co-workers of God. And you are (ἐστε) God's field and God's building.

b: 10/ According to the grace of God which is given to me, as a wise architect I set a foundation, but another built (ἐποικοδομεῖ) upon it. But each must watch how he builds (ἐποικοδομεῖ). 11/ For no one is able to set a foundation other than what is already set, which is Jesus Christ.

b′: 12/ And if one builds (ἐποικοδομεῖ) on a golden foundation with silver, then valuable stone, wood, hay, and stubble, 13/ the work of each person will become visible. For the day will reveal, as it manifests in fire, and the fire will show the work of each. 14/ If the work of the one who builds (ἐποικοδόμησεν) remains, then he will receive his wages; 15/ if his work is consumed in fire, his wages will be lost, but he [himself] will be saved—but only as if through fire.[2]

a′: 16/ Do you not know that you are (εστε) the temple of God, and the Spirit of God dwells in you? 17/ If anyone should destroy God's temple, God will destroy him; for God's temple is holy, just as you are (εστε) holy. 18/ Do not let yourselves be deceived: if anyone among you wishes to be wise according to this age, he must first become foolish, so that he can become wise. 19/ For the wisdom of this world is foolishness to God. 20/ For it is written, "The wise ones are caught up in their own craftiness." And again, "The Lord (κύριος) knows the schemes of the wise, and that they are worthless." 21/ So let none of you boast in ordinary people; for that is what you really are (εστε)— 22/ whether under Paul (Παυλος), or Apollos (Απολλως), or Cephas, or the world, or life, or death, or presence, or absence—all things belong to you! 23/ But you are Christ's, and Christ is God's.

---

1. The phrase "that is anything of account" translates the pronoun τι that is placed in a difficult manner.

2. The phrase "his wages" is added to the translation to clarify the referent. Following the NA[27], I place "himself" in brackets to denote that some witnesses omit it.

Beyond What Is Written

Paul and Apollos as Co-workers of God (a), 3:4–9

The *a* element of the initial unit (3:4-22) contains a concentric pattern.[3] Building on the most recent accusations in the last unit (2:14—3:3) of the previous ring set (1:18—3:3) that indict the Corinthians for being spiritually immature, the *x* line asks rhetorically whether the audience are acting in a worldly manner when they divide in factions under Paul and/or Apollos. Their arrogance bespeaks that the Corinthians have forgotten their dependence on God and instead judge by their own wisdom and desires.[4]

In the central *z* line (3:6) Paul metes out each actor with their role: Paul "planted" as the church's founder; Apollos watered with his pastoral teaching; but the one who "grows" is God. This point is affirmed in the *z'* line: God does the "growing," not the ones who "plant" or water (3:7). The secondary layer addresses what God has given to pastors and believers. In response to his own rhetorical questions, Paul claims that he and Apollos are to be considered as God's stewards, through whom members in the audience came to believe. The grammar implies that several members came to the community through Apollos' evangelization style (which may, in turn, have contributed to the factions).[5] Just as, in the *y* line, "each" person—whether pastor or believer—receives their faith from God and not of their own accord (3:4b), so too, in the *y'* line, "each" worker will receive wages as evaluation for their work in building the community (3:8). A community of united believers who are sanctified to God and illuminated by his Spirit to understand his gospel (1:4–9) gives evidence of apostolic success (1:9, 31).

The bracket lines contrast the community's present state with what they should be as God's church, particularly with regard to Paul and Apollos. While Paul impugns in the *x* line that "you [the audience] are" like ordinary people who cause divisions by boasting in individual teachers (3:3b–4), the closing *x'* line demands that they see the reality that "you are" God's building, united together (3:9). God owns the field (3:9) and is the ultimate

---

3. a: (*x*) 4/ For when someone says, "I am with Paul," and another one says, "I am with Apollos," *are you* not like ordinary people?

(*y*) So what is Apollos, and what is Paul?—Stewards through whom you came to believe—to *each* as the Lord gave.

(*z*) 6/ I planted, Apollos watered, but *God did the growing.*

(*z'*) 7/ So it is not the one who plants who is anything of account, nor the one who grows, but *God who does the growing.*

(*y'*) 8/ The one who plants and the one who waters act as one, and *each* will receive his own wage according to his own work,

(*x'*) 9/ for we are co-workers of God. And *you are* God's field and God's building.

4. Barrett, *First Corinthians*, 81; R. F. Collins, *First Corinthians*, 141.

5. Barrett, *First Epistle*, 84. See Chapter 2.

source of its growth; Paul and Apollos are merely his servants, and their work is in coordination, not competition. Their diversity of talents actually benefits the community.[6]

The underlying message of the element is that the successful edification of the community comes from God, not the community members or the pastors. The community's insistence that their spiritual power comes from themselves or their pastors rejects God's merciful wisdom and betrays their spiritual immaturity. True wisdom would recognize that God is the ultimate author of their spiritual life.

Christ Is the Only Foundation (b), 3:10–11

Emphasizing again that all apostolic activity comes by God's grace (3:4–5), the micro-ring *b* element now presents Paul and Apollos as wise[7] architect and builder, respectively, who work on the same building.[8] While Paul is the founder, it is necessary that another "build" on Paul's work (*y*, 3:10b), but each must be careful how he (or she) "builds" on the preliminary foundation because their work is not their own doing, but from (and for) the glory of God's grace (*y´*, 3:10c).[9] "Building on" here refers to preaching and forming the community in continued meetings and worship, and thus has in mind that each preacher must be conscious of what he or she teaches the growing body of new believers.[10]

The bracket lines remind the audience that Paul was the one who "placed the foundation" (*x*, 3:10a), but the "foundation" that was "placed" is Jesus Christ, not Paul or Apollos (*x´*, 3:11).[11] This image recalls the centralization of Christ who died for them and in whose name they were baptized,

---

6. Fee, *First Epistle*, 130–32.

7. According to Garland (*1 Corinthians*, 114), Paul's self-description as "wise" architect is intended to engage the rhetoric and assessments of the opposition group in the community.

8. b: (*x*) 10/ According to the grace of God which is given to me, as a wise architect I *set* a *foundation*,

(*y*) but another *built* upon it.

(*y´*) But each must see how he *builds*.

(*x´*) 11/ For no one is able to set a *foundation* other than what is already *set*, which is Jesus Christ.

9. This micro-ring in 3:10–11 is presented as an isolated chiasm in Fee, *First Epistle*, 137.

10. Garland, *1 Corinthians*, 115.

11. According to R. F. Collins, *First Corinthians*, 150, the singularity of the foundation "underscores the uniqueness of the edifice being built," namely, the gathering of his new elect, whom he invested with his Spirit and fellowship with his Son.

in Paul's initial address of factions and exhortation to unity (see 1:10–17, esp. 1:12–14). Reconfigured by the Spirit in baptism as God's people in Christ, the community is obligated to remain intact upon its singular foundation.[12]

The Day of the Lord Will Reveal Each Apostle's Work (b ′), 3:12–14

Having explained the roles of Apollos and himself as God's workers for the community, the *b ′* element continues this comparison by using traditional motifs of Jewish Apocalypticism.[13] The pivotal *b ′* element contains a micro-ring structure.[14] The *y* line (3:13a) states that the fiery event of the day of the Lord will manifest the work of each apostle. The parallel pivotal line explains that the work of "each" apostle will be manifest by the fire of the Lord's day (*y ′*, 3:13b).

The bracket lines argue that, regardless of the apostles' style or trappings (analogized in the materials of varying value, *x*, 3:12) that he uses to "build" the community, it is only the remnant of what he "built" and survives the fire that truly evaluates the apostle's work (*x ′*, 3:14). In other words, the external trappings of the apostle do not determine his worth so much as the spiritual substance of his community on the Day of judgment. Parallel language in the *Testament of Abraham* depicts a judgment scene in which a person whose work is burned up by fire is placed with sinners while a person whose work withstands fire is set with the righteous. Other differences are considerable, but the example offers insight into Paul's concern for where the apostles fit in the unfolding apocalyptic narrative of the new era.[15]

---

12. Garland, *1 Corinthians*, 114, notes that the images of Israel as God's field and building are also found together in Jer 1:10; 18:9; 24:6; Sir 49:7.

13. R. F. Collins, *First Corinthians*, 151.

14. b′: (*x*) 12/ And if one *builds* on a golden foundation with silver, then valuable stone, wood, hay, and stubble,

(*y*) 13/ the work of *each* person will become visible.

(*y ′*) For the day will reveal, as it manifests in fire, and the fire will show the work of each.

(*x ′*) 14/ If the work of the *one who builds* remains, then he will receive his wages; 15/ if his work is consumed in fire, his wages will be lost, but he [himself] will be saved—but only as if through fire.

15. Hollander, "Testing," 96–99, discerns that Paul and the author of the *Testament of Abraham* are both familiar with the same Jewish Apocalyptic tradition of testing people by fire; however, he argues, Paul has developed the tradition to include a recompense for the builder and a distinction between those who are merely flawed builders (and are saved, but as though through fire) and those who destroy the church (and who will then be destroyed by God).

The *b´* element returns to the concentric image of "one who builds" from the *b* element (3:10–12). In the earlier parallel, "the one who builds" refers to Apollos and his pastoral work that built upon Paul's foundation of the gospel. The *b´* element then explains that if what "the one who builds" survives, then "the one who builds" will receive his paycheck accordingly. But if the building fails the test and is consumed by fire—presumably due to a lack of understanding and poor execution of the gospel's moral imperatives—the worker's payment (recompense, not reward) will be forfeit. He will be saved, but only like a person who escapes a burning house, and loses everything inside. The work of neither Paul nor Apollos can be judged at this time, but rather all evaluation must be reserved for Christ at his return.

God's Temple and True Wisdom (*a´*), 3:16–23

In a shift from the general examples in the *b* and *b´* elements, the *a´* element noticeably returns to directly address the audience.[16] Like its complement above, the *a´* element contains a concentric structure.[17] In the *x* line (3:16) Paul reminds the community that they, as a church, are God's temple and God's Spirit dwells within them. Furthermore, God will destroy anyone who destroys his temple. The central lines (3:18–19) presume a situation in the church where members consider themselves wise enough to know how the apostles should be paid and the source and quality of their work. The *y* line asks these individuals who think themselves wise by standards of this age to first become "fools." This paradox recalls how the cross overturns and re-orders the world in God's wisdom rather than humanity's.[18] The community must leave behind human standards of power so that they may become truly wise and judge everything with spiritual knowledge (2:14–15).

---

16. Garland, *1 Corinthians*, 119.

17. *a´*: (*x*) 16/ Do you not know that *you are* the temple of God, and the Spirit of God dwells in you? 17/ If anyone should destroy God's temple, God will destroy him; for God's temple is holy, just as *you are* holy.
(*y*) 18/ Do not let yourselves be deceived: if anyone among you wishes to be *wise* according to this age, he must first become foolish, so that he can become *wise*.
(*y´*) 19/ For the wisdom of this world is foolishness to God. 20/ For it is written, "The *wise* ones are caught up in their own craftiness." And again, "The Lord knows the schemes of the *wise*, and that they are worthless."
(*x´*) 21/ So let none of you boast over ordinary people; for that is what *you really are*—22/ whether under Paul, or Apollos, or Cephas, or the world, or life, or death, or presence, or absence—all things belong to you! 23/ But *you are* Christ's, and Christ is God's.

18. Witherington, *Conflict*, 135; R. F. Collins, *First Corinthians*, 163.

The y' line confirms this argument by claiming that the wisdom of the world is foolishness in God's sight, and cites two supporting examples from Scripture. The first citation (from Job 5:13) claims that God will catch the Corinthians who wrongly presume themselves to be "wise" in their misunderstanding and (from LXX Ps 93:11) that the "wisdom" of these alleged "wise" persons are known by God to be useless because, as described above, they reject God's wisdom and rely entirely on human intuition (2:1-13). The x' line (3:22-23) then concludes this element and the unit as a whole with the summary exhortation to boast no more in people, such as the apostolic workers Paul and/or Apollos. Since the audience are members of Christ, the Lord of all, all things belong to them as well. One cannot simply claim hold of one of the apostles (Paul, Apollos, Cephas) or reality (the world, life, death, present, future)—all things belong to all of them because, as a group, they are bound together and incorporated in Christ to receive the fullness of God's spiritual blessings. Since Christ belongs to God, the members also are God's temple who house God's Spirit.

For the A unit (3:3-23) as a whole, the correlation of the a (3:3-6) and a' (3:16-23) elements reminds the Corinthians of their true identity in Christ. Their divisions had led them to act like unspiritual people ("you are fleshy," 3:3b) who boast in one apostle over another. But Paul reminds them "you are God's building"—not because of either apostle, but because God has caused them to grow on the foundation of his Son Jesus Christ. This image is developed in the a' element when Paul states that, as God's sanctified people, they are more than a building—"you are God's holy temple," in whom dwells God's wisdom-giving Spirit (2:9-13).

The spiritually immature members who are causing factions because of their so-called "wisdom" need to reject human wisdom as foolishness and accept God's wisdom that is taught by the Spirit, who dwells in God, and reveals his plan to the spiritual elect through the gospel of the cross. So no group should boast in Paul or Apollos (2:9-13; 3:5). God has elected, given faith to, and appointed respective apostles for the community to be united as one holy temple, founded on Christ, to house God's Spirit. No mere apostle could be responsible for such gifts. More than just an apostle or an ideology, the community should embrace their identity in Christ, throw aside the conventional wisdom and pride that is causing them to divide the community over allegiance to apostles, and embrace the spiritual wisdom of the cross.

In sum, the A unit (3:4-23) reprises the issue of divisions that were first addressed in 1:10-17. Throughout the unit, Paul's goal is to address the parties involved in the salvific, symbiotic relationship of God, Christ, the Spirit, apostles, and the elect community. Christ assigns and sends the apostles their duties in building the community. Paul and Apollos are equals as coworkers with God, tending his field and building his temple, and each will be paid according to his work by the Lord upon his return. Those in the community who think they can judge the quality of the workers by human standards are foolish and should instead judge by the alleged "foolishness" of God's wisdom, so as to understand the true relationship of the apostles to the community. Comprehension of this fact will show them why they should not boast in the men so as to divide God's temple, but rather unite in Christ to be a proper building to house God's Spirit.

Unit B, 4:1–5: Stewards of God's Mysteries

a: 1/ So this is how men must think of us: as servants of Christ, and stewards of the mysteries of God (θεοῦ). 2/ Furthermore, the rest must search the stewards in order that they be found trustworthy.

b: 3/ So it is of little concern to me if I am judged by you, or by a human court; for I do not (ἀλλ' οὐδέ) even judge myself (ἐμαυτόν).

b': 4/ For I know of no issue against myself (ἐμαυτῷ), not that (ἀλλ' οὐκ) I am justified in any way, but the Lord himself is my judge.

a': 5/ Even so, do not judge before the time that the Lord returns—he who brings to light the things that are in darkness, and manifests the secrets of the heart. That is when approval comes to each from God (θεοῦ).

Stewards of God's Mysteries (a), 4:1–2

The strategic digression in this ring set again focuses on eschatological themes. Paul and Apollos are stewards of God's hidden mysteries, and must be proven faithful by their work. But they are to be evaluated by the Lord when he returns—not, presumably, by themselves, each other, or the community. Every person will receive due praise from God, but only at the appropriate time. The unit is a self-defense and affirmation of his working relationship with Apollos as God's stewards. The overtly forensic language possibly has his opposition in mind,[19] although all who cause tension are probable targets.

In the *a* element (4:1–2), Paul stresses that people (perhaps alluding again to the "ordinary" status of the community's spiritual immaturity) should regard him and Apollos as two categories: (1) as servants of Christ,

---

19. R. F. Collins, *First Corinthians*, 169.

and (2) as those entrusted with the secrets of God. The latter recalls that God's plan is secret (1:18) and hidden from the authorities of this age, but revealed to his elect through the Spirit and the gospel. Paul admits that individuals who are entrusted with such duties must be evaluated and proven faithful for the task, but his laborious explanation in 4:1–2 betrays how he regards the audience as immature children in the faith.[20]

Paul Does Not Judge Himself (b), 4:3

The central *b* and *b'* elements (4:3–4, 5) describe how these evaluations may and may not take place. First, Paul considers it useless to be judged by the audience or by any human authority. He does not judge himself (positively or negatively) because the Lord will judge him. The Corinthians likely felt a right to judge Paul (and Apollos), as it was customary to do with philosophers and rhetoricians.[21] They did, after all, often contribute money and allegiance to these traveling preachers. Here, again, Paul implicitly indicts the Corinthians for being too attached to their previous life and human wisdom. They should recognize that God's stewards act within God's paradoxical wisdom that is contrary to the world's ideas of power and success. If the Corinthians truly understood the spiritual wisdom of the gospel that Paul preached they would realize how contradictory it is to criticize the manner in which it was preached to them (4:1–2).

The Lord Alone Judges Paul (b'), 4:4

The *b'* element's caveat that Paul does not judge himself because he knows that the Lord will judge him upon his return (see also 3:12–15) clarifies why the audience are not to judge him (or Apollos) now. First, the verb "judge" recalls that the unspiritual person cannot judge anything because he/she cannot understand God's wisdom or Paul's part as his apostle to the elect (2:14–15). Second, the evaluations of the Corinthians would be worthless compared to that of Christ, who sent both Paul and Apollos and has the proper faculties for judgment (3:1–3).

---

20. Witherington, *Conflict*, 137.
21. Ibid.; Keener, *1–2 Corinthians*, 42.

He Who Brings to Light the Secrets of the Heart (a´), 4:5b

The *a´* element (4:5) concludes the unit and reconnects with the *a* element (3:1–3). Just as "God's" secret wisdom has been entrusted to Paul and Apollos in the gospel (*a*, 4:1–2), so too will Christ's revelation of things hidden in darkness and men's hearts precipitate in "God's" just evaluation of each apostle (*a´*, 4:5b). So Christ sends and evaluates but, since God entrusts his apostles with his wisdom and plan that are hidden, he is also the ultimate source of their payment. Comments from the audience are unsolicited and void of influence in the theological schema. They should instead turn their attention to their own misunderstanding of the Spirit and recognize that they too will be judged based on their work in, and reception of, the gospel.[22]

Unit A´, 4:6–21: A Father Addresses His Children in Christ

a: 6/ Into such as these, brothers and sisters, Apollos and I have been transformed for your benefit, in order that you might learn from us not to go beyond what is written, so that you might not be puffed up (φυσιοῦσθε), one against another. For what makes you different from others? And what do you have that you did not receive? 7/ If you received it, why do you boast as if it were your own? 8/ Already you are rich! Already you have been filled and become kings (ἐβασιλεύσατε) without us! And I wish that you were kings (ἐβασιλεύσατε) already so that we might also be kings (συμβασιλεύσωμεν) along with you!

b: 9/ For it seems that God has displayed us apostles as least of all, as those paraded around. We have become a spectacle to the world, and angels, and humanity. 10/ We are fools because of Christ (διὰ Χριστόν), but you are wise in Christ (ἐν Χριστῷ); we are weak, but you are mighty; you are glorified, but we are shamed. 11/ For to this very moment we hunger, and thirst, and go naked, beaten, and homeless; 12/ and we toil, working with our own hands. When cursed, we bless; when persecuted, we endure; 13/ when slandered, we exhort; we have become the grime of the world, the lowest of dirt, to this very moment!

b´: 14/ I do not write these things to shame you, but rather I admonish you as my beloved children. 15/ For you may have many babysitters in Christ (ἐν Χριστῷ) but not many fathers; for in Christ (ἐν Χριστῷ) Jesus I arrived to you with the gospel. 16/ So I exhort you, be imitators of me! 17/ For this reason I sent you Timothy, who is my beloved child and faithful in the Lord,

---

22. R. F. Collins, *First Corinthians*, 170.

whom you will remember from my travels in Christ (ἐν Χριστῷ) [Jesus],[23] just as I teach in all the churches everywhere.

a′: 18/ And there are some of you who are puffed up (ἐφυσιώθησαν) as if I were not returning to you. 19/ But I will be departing soon to you—if the Lord wills it—and I will teach you something not in puffed up (πεφυσιωμένων) words but with power. 20/ For the kingdom (βασιλεία) of God is not in word but in power. 21/ What do you want—for me to show up with a rod or a loving and caring spirit?

Do Not Overstep Your Present Arrogance (a), 4:6–8

The *a* element contains a concentric pattern.[24] The central lines ask a set of harsh rhetorical questions that presume arrogance within the community. The first asks what makes them different from anyone else, since everyone's gifts are ultimately from God, not from either of the pastors.[25] As such, the Corinthians have no reason to think associating with one apostle over another is worthwhile. The referents for "what you have" may well include the whole sum of the spiritual benefits they received in the gospel (1:7–11).

The *y′* line (4:7) develops the questions in the *y* line (4:6b): the Corinthians do not have anything that they did not "receive" (4:6b), and so they should not be arrogant as if they attained their gifts by their own merit (4:7). The expected answer within the progression of these pivotal lines is that they have nothing in the new age that they did not "receive" from God, in Christ, by the Spirit, and so they have no reason to boast as if they themselves had attained this salvation. To be sure, God's act in Christ was an assault on human arrogance (1:18–25) and, through him, rendered conventional human wisdom and corrupt worldly systems irrelevant.

The *x′* line (4:8) shifts the tone from accusatory to sarcastic and develops the argument from the *x* line (4:6a). That Paul tells the audience that

---

23. Early witnesses differ on the inclusion of "Jesus" in 4:17. P[46] a 33 include while A B omit. The brackets follow NA[27] to denote this problem. See Metzger, *TCGNT*, 484.

24. a: (*x*) 6/ Into such as these, brothers and sisters, Apollos and I have been transformed for your benefit, *in order that* you might learn from us not to go beyond what is written, *so that* you might not be puffed up, one against another.

(*y*) For what makes you different from others? And *what* do you have that you did not *receive*?

(*y′*) 7/ If you *received* it, *why* do you boast as if it were your own?

(*x′*) 8/ Already you are rich! Already you have been filled and have become kings without us! And I wish that you were kings already *so that* we might also be kings along with you!

25. Fee, *First Epistle*, 170.

he and Apollos have been made examples for their "benefit" in order that they not go beyond what is written, so that they might not boast in one over another, now is inverted sarcastically in the x' line when Paul states that he wishes the Corinthians, who presume to dominate the cosmos by their own power, had actually succeeded in order that he and Apollos might "benefit" by having a portion of their superiority.[26]

The enigmatic line "beyond what is written" (4:6) likely refers to the Scripture passages in the complement A unit, 3:3–23, within the α' ring set (3:3—4:21). The passages from Job 51:13 and LXX Ps 93:11 in 1 Cor 3:20–21 support Paul's paradoxical exhortation to become foolish in the new age so that the audience understand their communal identity and unity with true spiritual knowledge rather than causing divisions with their human conventional wisdom. These Scripture passages warn that those who try to be wise by human standards will be "caught up in their own craftiness," and that they cannot outwit God or undo his re-ordering of the world with new spiritual wisdom by dividing his church over worthless concerns. Such people will be dealt with by God himself (3:19).

Within this context, then, the meaning of 4:6 could be that, despite Paul and Apollos' different styles, they are co-workers with God and are made to be examples of unity for the community's benefit. In light of this fact, the Corinthians should not go beyond that which they were warned in the written Scriptures in 3:19–21, lest they be caught up in their craftiness and destroyed by God for dividing his church.[27] The mockery of the term

---

26. Fee, *First Epistle*, 172, and Thiselton, "Realized," 110–12, view the Corinthians' "over-realized eschatology" as the background for Paul's sarcasm; but this does not preclude spiritual arrogance as a concern to his argument.

27. Several good explanations for this difficult phrase "do not go beyond what is written" have been offered. See Fitzmyer, *First Corinthians*, 214–17; Fee, *First Epistle*, 166–70, for excellent overviews of the issue. According to Tyler, "Pedagogy," 101–103, Paul is using an elliptical Hellenistic pedagogy to encourage the audience to follow the example set by him and Apollos. Hanges, "By-laws," posits a sort of pre-existing written code that the Corinthian church had developed like contemporary pagan cults, while Wagner, "Call," sees the referent as the command to boast in no one but the Lord (1 Cor 1:31; 3:21).

The opinion that "what is written" refers to the several citations of Scripture that Paul has given in the letter to this point is well-founded, and I would be inclined to agree with it. However, within the present context, it appears to me that the performative structure dictates for the audience to understand the particular Scripture references in the most immediate parallel unit (A, 3:4–23) as the proper point of referent. There is no question that the numerous Scripture citations with "what is written" are useful, and many concern the same issue of wisdom/foolishness as found in 1:29–31. However, the performative structure appears to hold 3:20–21 as the primary referent for "that which is written" for the Corinthians to beware in 4:6. It is notable also that even scholars who stop short of defining a meaning for 4:6 (e.g., R. F. Collins, *First Corinthians*, 178; Fee,

"benefit" within the concentric elemental structure further underscores that the church's disunity is at the center of this obscure statement.

Here Paul jabs that the Corinthians (whom he already accused of spiritual immaturity and being like "ordinary people" who are perishing) already have been filled, have become rich, and have become kings—all without Paul and Apollos. The last jab is perhaps the sharpest. Paul takes the Christian eschatological hope that all the elect will share in Christ's reign (1 Cor 6:1; 15:1–34) and mockingly turns it to say that his eschatological "hope" is to reign with the Corinthians, who have allegedly already conquered the cosmos.

A Powerful Church and Their Weak Pastors (b), 4:9–10

Following the satire from the previous element, in the *b* element Paul describes the situation with mockery and hyperbole. The Corinthians who are spiritually immature feel they should rule the cosmos, yet those through whom they received the gospel are set on display like prisoners in a parade on their way to the coliseum or execution. The whole universe, the realm that some in the audience feel they should (or already) rule, is an audience to the apostles' suffering.

The contrast between Paul and the audience intensifies the rhetoric of the micro-ring's central lines.[28] In the *y* line (4:10a), "we" are foolish for Christ with his gospel, but "you" are wise enough in Christ to evaluate his apostles. Likewise, "we" are weak, but "you" are mighty enough to seek to rule the world. These are summed in the *y'* line (4:10b), "you" are honored as recipients of the gospel, but "we," its bearers, are shamed.

The bracket *x* and *x'* lines (4:9, 11) describe the extent of the spectacle that God has made Paul and the apostles to become, but also shows how the apostles engage these obstacles with God's grace (1:4–5; 3:10–12): they bless when cursed; they endure when persecuted; and they answer when slandered. They respond with humility, not arrogance. The stewards of

First Epistle, 171) agree that it is intended to discourage factionalism and bring unity to the church and pastors.

28. b: (*x*) 9/ For it seems that God has displayed us apostles least of all, as those paraded around. *We have become* a spectacle to *the world*, and angels, and humanity.

(*y*) 10/ We are fools because of Christ, *but you* are wise in Christ; *we are weak but you* are mighty;

(*y'*) *you* are glorified *but we* are shamed.

(*x'*) 11/ For to this very moment we hunger and thirst, and go naked, beaten, and homeless; 12/ and we toil, working with our own hands. When cursed, we bless; when persecuted, we endure; 13/ when slandered, we exhort; *we have become* the grime of *the world*, the lowest of dirt, to this very moment!

God's hidden wisdom not only proclaim it, but live it out in their apostolic ministry. Having stated in the *x* line (4:9) how God displays the apostles as a defeated spectacle, such that "we have become a spectacle before the whole world," in hunger, thirst, beatings, and homelessness, in the *x´* line (4:11) Paul punctuates these images by declaring that "we have become the refuse of the world" and the scum of the earth.

This element serves to accentuate the contrast between how the apostles and Corinthians demonstrate their spiritual knowledge in their lives. While the apostles dangerously proclaim the goodness of the risen Lord, the Corinthians seek to be lords themselves. The hyperbole is intended to demonstrate that true discipleship reflects the paradoxical shift in power that is inherently found in the cross. Paul shows the Corinthians' view of lordship to be severely outdated, and their self-assessment to be a sham.

A Father Exhorts His Children to Imitate His Foolish Example (b´), 4:14–17

Having addressed the conflicting states of the "glorified" audience and the "shamed" apostles, in the *b´* element Paul shifts his tone to pastorally admonish rather than mock his audience. The *y´* line's exhortation that the audience become imitators of Paul stands out as the pivotal thesis statement of this concentric micro-structure (4:16).[29] In the *x* line (4:14–15) Paul reminds the Corinthians that they may have many babysitters "in Christ," but they have only one father—him. This underscores his unique function in their existence as a community of God's elect and heightens their need for them to be reconciled to their founding apostle. The *x´* line (4:16) develops this point in that even if these alleged leaders of the community are "in Christ," Paul is ever more important because he initiated the gospel among them "in Christ." They should therefore imitate him, just as children are expected to adhere to their fathers' example and instruction in an agrarian society. The rhetorical connection is further supported in that Paul offers to support their imitation by sending "my beloved child" Timothy, who

---

29. b´: (*x*) 14/ I do not write these things to shame you, but rather I admonish you as *my beloved children*. 15/ For you may have many babysitters *in Christ*, but not many fathers; for *in Christ* Jesus I arrived to you with the gospel.
(*y*) 16/ So I exhort you, be imitators of me!
(*x´*) 17/ For this reason I sent you Timothy, who is *my beloved child* and faithful in the Lord, whom you will remember from my travels *in Christ* [Jesus], just as I teach in all the churches everywhere.

is faithful enough to teach the audience, "his beloved children," to imitate their father.[30]

As a whole, the *b′* element reconnects the structure of the argument by developing the *b* element (4:14–17) through the repetition of the phrase "in Christ." Both Paul and his community gained spiritual blessings "in Christ" through the gospel, but some in the community had viewed Paul's portion as foolishness while their own was brilliance and might. In the *b′* element the benefits of the gospel are developed in that what they receive "in Christ" is the symbiotic relationship with each other that establishes them as God's elect, fills them with God's wisdom and eschatological knowledge, and brings them into familial fellowship with God "in Christ" Jesus his Son. Hence, just as they receive spiritual blessings in Christ (*b′*, 4:15), so too does the audience receive each other to aid their spiritual growth and complete their present duty as God's eschatological family who imitate the paradoxical example of their spiritual father who suffers towards victory "in Christ" (*b*, 4:9–13).

A Father Threatens to Return to Deal with Arrogant Children (*a′*), 4:18–21

The *a′* element concludes the unit, the ring set, and the section as a whole, and as such contains powerful statements for the audience via a concentric micro-structure regarding Paul's upcoming visit.[31] The *y′* line develops the *y*: that God's kingdom is not about words but "power" (4:20) recalls and doubles down on Paul's earlier sarcastic line that he will arrive to find the true nature of the arrogant groups' disunity is not so much about "power" as it is petty gossip (4:19b).

Having stated in the *x* line (4:18–19a) that some arrogant members of the church are acting as though Paul will not return (even though he is trying to return, and will do so if God wills it), in the *x′* line (4:21) Paul asks the audience whether they want him to return with a rod or with a caring and gentle spirit.[32] Both of these aspects emphasize his fatherly authority over those he claims as his beloved children in Christ.

30. Fee, *First Epistle*, 189.

31. a′: (*x*) 18/ And there are some of you who are puffed up as if I were not *returning* to you. 19/ But I will be *returning* soon to you—if the Lord wills it—
(*y*) and I will teach you something not in puffed up words but with *power*.
(*y′*) 20/ For the kingdom of God is not in word but in *power*.
(*x′*) 21/ What do you want—for me to *return* with a rod or a loving and caring spirit?

32. Fee, *First Epistle*, 191, considers that Paul's absence led some arrogant leaders at Corinth to think that he would not return and began to disdain him as an absent father

This *a´* element (4:18–21) concludes the A´ unit by repetition of the terms "arrogant" and "king." In the *a* element (4:6–9) Paul indicts the people who are "arrogant," presume to boast in one apostle over another, and wish to "become kings" (instead of Paul or Christ); now, in the *a´* element, Paul warns that he will engage these "arrogant" people and their words when he returns and show them, by rod or gentleness, that true power is found not in their words but in God's authoritative "kingdom."

The A´ unit (4:6–21) as a whole seeks to persuade the community to reconcile with Paul through familial imagery. In particular, Paul tries to remind them of his paternal and apostolic authority over them. He is the founder of the community—an image that doubly serves to separate his work in the church from that of Apollos and any other teachers. The Corinthians are reminded that they were made into a family with Paul and Apollos. This family relationship comes with a burden, however. The father is calling on his children to imitate aspects that they find to be foolish and weak. But, once they understand and successfully imitate Paul's example of the gospel, they will exit their downward spiral and enter a new trajectory that will help them to gain true spiritual knowledge and maturity in Christ. But they must first understand the gospel, so that they can believe and act correctly. Proper faith can only come when one properly understands the object of faith.

INTERRELATION OF UNITS

Outline

Paul and Apollos as Co-Workers, Constructing God's Temple (A, 3:4–23)

1) While the Corinthians are boasting, "I am with Paul," and others, "I am with 'Apollos'" (Ἀπολλώς, 3:4), they are called to recognize that they are the unified body of Christ whom God has benefited with the work of Paul and "Apollos" (Ἀπολλώς, 3:6), co-workers and stewards of God's mysteries who both contributed to God's growing of the community. 2) When the Corinthians divide themselves between pastors they are (ἐστε, 3:3, 21) acting like ordinary people. They should instead recognize that they are (ἐστε, 3:9, 17) God's holy building (ἐστε, 3:9, 17), united in Christ under these diverse preachers. 3) If they wish to become "wise" (σοφός), as they

---

or itinerant philosopher. As such, Paul concludes this section of *imitatio patri* with a soberly toned threat of return.

believe they are already, then they must first become "fools" (μωρός), since the world's standard of "wisdom" (σοφία) is still "foolishness" (μωρία) to God (3:18–19). 4) Afterall, "it is written" (γέγραπται, 3:19) in Scripture that these so-called "wise" ones are caught up in their own craftiness, and their schemes are worthless. 5) For this reason, the Corinthians should not "boast" (καυχάσθω) in either Paul or Apollos (3:21). Such boasting in human agents betrays their spiritual immaturity (3:3, 21) and ignorance of Paul's and Apollos' true mission among them.

The Stewards of God's Mysteries Will Be Judged by God Alone (B, 4:1–5)

Both of these apostles are to be regarded by the Corinthians as servants of Christ and stewards of God's mysteries, and whose approval comes directly from God (4:5). As such, the Corinthians should not judge for or against either one, since they do not even judge themselves. They await the Lord to judge their work in the churches on the day when all things are revealed (4:3–5).

A Father Calls His Children to Imitate Him in Christ (A´, 4:6–21)

1) Paul and "Apollos" (Απολλως, 4:6) have been transformed by God to benefit the Corinthians' edification into the unified body of Christ. 2) Their arrogant delusion of supremacy is mocked when Paul says that already they are (εστε) rich, filled, and have become kings without their pastoral leaders (4:7). 3) Afterall, Paul chides, the apostles (God's trusted emissaries) are "fools" (μωροί, 4:10), weak, and shamed while the Corinthians are "wise," powerful, and honored. 4) So Paul cites "what is written" (γέγραπται, 4:6) in Scripture to warn the Corinthians not to be puffed up against one another. 5) They "boast" (καυχᾶσαι, 4:7) in their apostles and their spirituality as if they somehow attained these things on their own and now stand as conquerors of the universe.

Conclusion

The B unit (2:6–13) serves as the pivot between the arguments about this community's divisions over apostles. Paul never mentions Apollos by name in this unit. Instead, he points to their shared commission and future evaluation from God. They have been entrusted to reveal God's mysteries, and this approval must be considered before any criticisms are laid before them. Secondly, the one who chose them for this job is the one who will judge all at the end of the age (4:5). This passage builds on the earlier unit's view that Paul and Apollos are co-workers whose judgment will come only from the Lord at the appropriate time, and anticipates Paul's accusation that the audience is acting arrogantly by taking on a task that is neither timely nor in their power to discern.

The A and A´ units (3:4–23; 4:6–21) aim both to affirm the positive relationship that Paul and Apollos have as co-workers, who were equally called by God to serve this community of the sanctified in Corinth in different ways, and to impugn the Corinthians for their arrogant appraisal and division over these apostles. Their so-called "wisdom" has shown them to be truly foolish in terms of the gospel.

The repeated terms tie together the large ring set as a whole and underscore the major points of Paul's argument against the Corinthians.

1/ When the Corinthians boast that one is for "Paul," and another that he or she is for "Apollos," they miss the fact that both "Paul and Apollos" were called by God to serve the community with their own God-given gifts (A, 3:3, 21), be stewards of his mysteries who would reveal them to his elect at this climactic time of the age (B, 4:1), and who have been transformed by God to demonstrate humility to the community and build them into the unified body of Christ that God intended (A´, 4:6).

2/ Second, the Corinthians are plagued by an identity crisis and delusions of grandeur. They think themselves to already be rich (A´, 4:17), kings, and fulfilled; but they betray themselves to be like ordinary people who act as though they have never known the Spirit (A, 3:18–20). They should instead recognize that "they are" God's holy temple and the unified body of Christ. Only then will they be able to outgrow their present spiritually immature state.

3/ In their deluded state they consider the apostles to be "fools" and themselves "wise" enough to judge and appraise these ambassadors of the Spirit (A´, 4:10). But if they truly wished to be "wise" and understand the fullest extent of the apostles' mission and worth, they would first need to become "foolish" in terms of the gospel, since in Christ God has already subverted the worldly wisdom that they hold so dear (A, 3:19–21; see also 1:18—2:5).

4/ What "is written" in Scripture testifies to God's unfolding demolition of human wisdom and is demonstrated in the preaching of the apostles (A, 1:19–20), whose example warns the elect not to go beyond "what is written" in their arrogant disputes (A´, 4:6), lest their pride cause them to be swallowed up with the rest of arrogant human wisdom that is fading away.

5/ As it stands, they betray their misunderstanding of the Spirit when they improperly "boast" in one apostle over another (A, 3:21; A´, 4:7) as if they had attained these spiritual talents on their own merits. In truth, though, they have misused the Spirit to be puffed up against one another rather than be edified together into one coherent body. Their plans to conquer the world endanger their own salvation and place among God's elect.

INTERRELATION OF RING SETS

The initial section serves many technical, but also imperative, purposes in this letter to a community that is in the process of implosion. On the technical side, this section conveys the usual greeting and thanksgivings common in every letter, and introduces the addressees to the most pertinent items and reasons for writing. But even within these pro forma genres Paul strategically puts forward an argument that serves to disarm the Corinthians of their arrogance, explain their true identity as corporate and in Christ, and remind them that their spiritual talents are gifts. Paul then moves on to disabuse them of the misunderstandings of the gospel that have led to their divisions. The cross is more powerful and wise than human wisdom and power, and he and Apollos serve together for their edification.

Outline

The Corinthians are Bound Together in Fellowship with Christ, but Are Divided between Apostles (α, 1:1–17)

God "sent" (ἀπέστειλεν) "Paul" (Παῦλος) as Christ's ambassador to proclaim to his elect in Corinth the power of the Spirit and salvation through Christ in the message of the cross, in order that its impact might not be lost in mere rhetoric (1:1, 17). Because of the message the audience received from their "apostle" (ἀπόστολος, 1:1), they were "fulfilled" (ἐπλουτίσθητε, 1:5) in all things and now await the "revelation" (ἀποκάλυψιν) of their Lord (1:7). Yet divisions have arisen among them with some saying, "I am with Paul" (ἐγὼ Παύλου), and others, "I am with Apollos" (ἐγὼ Ἀπολλῶ) as if "Paul" (Παῦλος) were crucified for them, or as if anyone but Christ were at the root of their hope in future glory (1:10–13).

The Corinthians Remain Dependent on the Human Wisdom that God Is Destroying (β, 1:18—3:3)

Their divisions prove that they did not understand the message of the cross, through which God is dissembling the wisdom of the world and electing the weak and lowly of the world, rather than the powerful. This true wisdom and power of the cross are hidden to worldly powers and made evident only through the Spirit to spiritually mature believers who have begun to let go of human conventions of power and status. But because the Corinthians rely on these human concepts they remain spiritually immature, are unable to understand the gifts of the Spirit, become arrogant and divided against one another in competition for power, and so demonstrate that they are still just like ordinary ("fleshy"), unspiritual people (3:3).

Paul and Apollos are Co-Workers and the Corinthians' Divisions Could Disqualify Them from Salvation (α´, 3:4—4:21)

Paul (Παῦλος) and Apollos (Ἀπολλῶ) are both apostles who act as co-workers in Corinth to build the audience into God's temple that stands on the firm foundation of Christ (3:5–6). God will destroy whoever breaks down his temple, but this will not be known until the day of the Lord "reveals" (ἀποκαλύπτεται) it (3:13). In the meantime, the Corinthians should not boast in either "Paul" or "Apollos" (ἐγὼ Παῦλος, ἐγὼ Ἀπολλῶ, 3:4, 7). Such divisions only demonstrate that they are not qualified to judge in spiritual matters. As it stands, the diverse styles of Paul and "Apollos" are an example to the audience that they should not boast in people but in God since, whether from Paul or from Apollos, in Christ all things belong to them (4:6). But their spiritual immaturity and dependence on the worldly conventions is so strong that they already view themselves as "fulfilled" (ἐπλουτήσατε, 4:8), beyond that which their apostles proclaimed. As such, Paul now writes and sends Timothy to remind them of how to live in Christ and imitate their "weak" and "foolish" (μωροί) founder (4:10, 21).

Conclusion to Section A

So immense were the problems at work in the community at Corinth, Paul could have chosen a number of different topics to place in the bridge portion of this ring set. But the selection of wisdom/foolishness and power/weakness is appropriate at this early part of the letter because these encapsulate the core disease at play in Corinth rather than mere symptoms. The audience in Corinth is suffering from spiritual delusions. They believe they have become empowered with knowledge to an extent that also enables them to judge their apostles and fight among one another for supremacy in this "spirit-filled" community. Paul's oration on the cross and God's power and wisdom serves to undercut their position. As a pivot in the section, it builds on the cause of the divisions mentioned in the α set—the audience cling to worldly power and have misunderstood the cross—and anticipates the warning in the α' set—that if they remain "fleshy" and continue to divide God's temple, God will break them. Arrogance and boasting are consistent themes throughout Section A (1:1—4:21) and serve as the most demonstrable symptoms of the Corinthians' spiritually debilitating disease.

A pattern appears in this section. In all three pivotal units of the three ring sets (1:4-9; 2:6-13; 4:1-5) Paul underscores Christ's imminent judgment on the day of the Lord to emphasize a sense of urgency and remind the audience in Corinth of the incredibly high stakes involved in their present actions and communal life as the people of God who have been elected and sanctified to prepare them for the judgment. In fact, the pivotal β ring set (1:18—3:3) of the section recreates the audience's narrative of worldly power. In his unfolding plan at the end of the age, God is currently eliminating human conventional wisdom and replacing it with the wisdom of the cross.

The α' ring set builds off of the concluding units of the β set (1:18—3:2) that indict the Corinthians for spiritual immaturity and return to the initial α ring set (1:1-17) argument regarding the community's divisions over Paul and Apollos. Repetition of the phrases "I am with Paul," and "I am with Apollos" (among others), denote 1:1-17 and 3:4—4:21 as parallel ring sets. The focus and content of both are also complementary.

The development from the α (1:1-17) to α' (3:4—4:21) ring set is nothing short of dramatic for Paul's rhetorical plea to the audience. He is Christ's "apostle," "sent" to them by God's will for their sanctification (A, 1:1, 17). "Apollos" is also an apostle, but his God-given task is to nurture the group Paul had started. The diverse gifts that "Paul" and "Apollos" use to build the community are meant to teach the Corinthians not to be arrogant (A', 3:21; 4:6). God gives spiritual gifts to the apostles to preach the gospel, and gives faith to his elect to hear it. But this sanctification, spiritual empowerment, and even the church's growth, are gifts received from God, and are not from the Corinthians themselves or from the apostles. As such, the Corinthians should refrain from judging their apostles and causing divisions in the body of believers that God bound together in the Spirit to redeem and justify them in preparation for the imminent judgment (1:4-9, 30-31).

Breaking down the church with divisions has a doubly negative impact on their salvation. First, it separates them from the sanctification, redemption, and justification that they receive as incorporated members of Christ's body in the Spirit. Salvation comes because they are joined to Christ, not because they, as individuals, hold the Spirit. Second, dividing God's temple has the terrible consequence of God's retribution.

So the Corinthians have been "filled" with knowledge and grace from the Spirit as they await the "revelation" of their Lord Jesus Christ (A, 1:5–7), at whose arrival the work of each will be "revealed" by fire (A´, 3:13). But their insistence on judging the apostles ahead of schedule betrays the fact that they are still spiritually immature. They misunderstood the Spirit in terms of human wisdom, deluded themselves into thinking they were already "fulfilled," and go on to judge and divide against themselves and their apostles (A´, 4:8).

To preserve their salvation at this critical time, Paul is sending Timothy (4:17) and writing to remind them that they are his beloved children who should imitate his example of a "foolish" and "weak" member of Christ, in order that they can become empowered by the gospel and grow wise through the illumination of the Spirit (4:18–21).

6

Sexual Immorality and Injustice, 5:1—6:20

Section B, Ring Set α

ANALYSIS OF UNITS

HAVING ADDRESSED THE MATTERS of disunity and spiritual immaturity in the primary section, the central section now moves to instruct the Corinthians on how they are to live as the sanctified elect in Christ while also living in Roman Corinth. The indictments of the Corinthians' spirituality actually lay the rhetorical groundwork for Section B, which stands as the heart of the letter. Since Paul has demonstrated that the Corinthians are divided and spiritually immature like "ordinary" people who do not have the Spirit, they will have little defense against his stark accusations and instructions.

Unit A, 5:1–13: Sexual Immorality and Arrogance in the Community

a: 1/ In fact, there is report of sexual immorality (πορνεία) among you. And this very kind of sexual immorality (πορνεία) is not even found among Gentiles—someone is sleeping with his father's wife! 2/ And you are arrogant! Should you not rather grieve, in order that the one who does this work is sent from your midst? 3/ Although absent in body, I am yet present in spirit, and I have already, by the name (ὀνόματι) of the Lord Jesus, judged the one who has wrought this thing, in the same way I would if I were present.[1] 4/ I will be at your next meeting in spirit, where we must,[2] by the power of our Lord Jesus, 5/ hand over this very one (τοιοῦτον) to Satan for the destruction of his flesh, so that the Spirit[3] may be preserved on the day of the Lord.

b: 6/ Your boast is no good. Do you not know that a little leaven (ζυμοῖ) leavens the whole loaf? 7/ Clean out the old leaven (παλαιὰν ζύμην) to be unleavened (ἄζυμοῖ) [Passover] bread—so that you may be a fresh lump of dough—

c: since our Passover Lamb, Christ, was sacrificed [for us].[4]

b′: 8/ So let us celebrate, not with old leaven (ζύμη παλαια)—nor with the leaven (ζύμη) of evil and wickedness—but with unleavened (ἀζύμοις) sincerity and truth.

a′: 9/ Earlier I wrote to you in a letter that you are not to associate with sexually immoral people (πόρνοις)—10/ That did not mean all immoral, or greedy, or insatiable, or idolatrous people of this world—For then you would need to get out of this world altogether! 11/ Now I write to say that you must not to associate with anyone named (ὀνομαζόμενος) as a brother or sister who is immoral, or greedy, or idolatrous, or hateful, or drunken, or fraudulent; you should not even eat with such people (τοιούτω). 12/ For who am I to judge (κρίνειν) those who are outside? Should you yourselves not judge (κρίνετε) those who are within? 13/ God will judge (κρινεῖ) those who are outside. "Cast out the wickedness from your midst!"

---

1. Following NAB, NRSV, I take the phrase "in the name of the Lord Jesus" to belong to what precedes. Cf. NA[27], CEB.

2. I take the infinitive παραδοῦναται as having an imperatival force. Given that Paul will be with them spiritually, the imperative in English must receive a first person plural pronoun for the subject.

3. Although some translate τὸ πνεῦμα as "his spirit" (e.g., NAB), the internal evidence is persuasive to view the holy Spirit as the referent here. See Garland, *1 Corinthians*, 174.

4. It is difficult to translate v. 7 for a modern audience without clarifications. I add the term "Passover" to connect the important image of "unleavened" in v. 7a with the Passover Lamb of v. 7b. Although the witnesses that include "for us" are likely glosses, I include the words in brackets to convey to a modern audience Paul's main point of moral purity as an obligation on the believer that reflects the sacrifice of the Christ event.

Beyond What Is Written

Immorality and Arrogance in the Body of Christ (a), 5:1–5

The *a* element contains a concentric microstructure.[5] In the central lines, the audience should not be arrogant, but rather grieve over the "work" of sexual immorality because Paul is, in fact, "present" in spirit (*y*, 6:2–3a). The proper response is to judge the man who has "wrought" this deed as though Paul were "present" with them at their next meeting (*y'*, 6:3b).[6] Also, the proposed tribunal of the *x'* line (5:4–5) addresses the audience's poor response in the *x* line (5:1–2a). That the audience are arrogant regarding "this very kind" of sexual immorality "among" them that is not found "among" the Gentiles (*x*, 5:1) is paralleled by Paul's command that they, in the name of the Lord Jesus, hand over "this very one" to Satan in anticipation of the impending judgment "on" the day of Christ's return (*x'*, 5:4).[7]

This *a* element (5:1–5) offers further evidence of the audience's spiritual immaturity, in addition to their misunderstanding of the cross (1:18—3:2) and their divisions (1:10–17; 3:3—4:21). Their spiritual immaturity is cyclically involved with a spiritual arrogance that is divisive and destructive. Earlier they were "arrogant" towards one another and in factions, but now they are "arrogant" enough to condone immorality not even seen among the Gentiles. Just as they misunderstood the cross as foolishness (1:18—3:3) and questioned Paul's authority in respect to their own wisdom (4:18),[8] so too do they misunderstand their sanctification in Christ and arrogantly assume that their spiritual blessings will make them immune to future judgment.

Paul responds by rebuking their arrogance (5:2) and demanding that they, as one body, denounce the perpetrator, and expel him from their church (5:4–5). The two emphatic aspects of the command are the immediacy of

---

5. a: (*x*) 1/ In fact, there is report of sexual immorality *among* you. And *this very kind* of sexual immorality is not even found *among* Gentiles—someone is sleeping with his father's wife!

(*y*) 2/ And you are arrogant! Should you not rather grieve, in order that the one who does this *work* is sent from your midst? 3/ Although absent in body, I am yet *present* in spirit,

(*y'*) and I have already, by the name of the Lord Jesus, judged the one who has *wrought* such a thing, in the same way I would if I were present.

(*x'*) 4/ I will be at your next meeting in spirit, where we must, by the power of the Lord Jesus, 5/ hand over *this very one* to Satan for the destruction of his flesh, so that the spirit may be saved *on* the day of the Lord.

6. *Pace* Chow, "Patron," it is unlikely that Paul is concerned here about a dowry issue. The repetition of "sexual immorality" in parallel with prostitution presumes Paul is more concerned about what he views as extreme sexual activity that the community is tolerating; see Harris, "Discipline."

7. The words "among" and "on" both translate the Greek preposition ἐν.

8. Fee, *First Epistle*, 135.

the required response and the audience's unanimous action as one body. The expulsion is imperative since the community has allowed the man to bring immoral pollution into the sacred body.[9] Based on OT eschatology, Paul may very well fear that the entire community may be implicated in this one man's sin while he remains with them.[10] In this case, their "arrogance" refers not to an outright affirmation of his actions, but the mere acceptance of his presence. Paul has already judged him as though present, but the church, as a united entity, act as Christ when they cast the perpetrator from Christ's body (their church).[11] The Spirit that is to be preserved refers to the Holy Spirit, who is housed in the united body of the church.[12]

You Are Unleavened Bread, as Christ Was (b, c) 5:6–7

The *b* element (5:6–7a) supports the admonition in the *a* element with an analogy from the domestic sphere. Their boast in the man's actions and presumption of their own immunity to his sin or God's judgment is harmful because such an act permeates and affects the whole group, just as a little leaven leavens an entire ball of dough. The Corinthians must cast out this man so that they can be like a fresh ball of dough that is free of leaven. As those sanctified by God in Christ they are already like the unleavened bread that is set aside for God alone in sacrifices at the Temple in Jerusalem (Lev 24:5–9), and so must return to a renewed state of fresh, unleavened dough by casting out the one who wrought the immoral acts. He threatens the sanctity of the community and their relationship to God the same way a little leaven would endanger the sanctified state of the bread that is to be offered in the Temple.

The pivotal unparalleled *c* element (5:7b) adds Christ's exemplary sacrifice to support their tribunal's actions against the sexually immoral person. Since Passover was immediately celebrated with the use of unleavened bread, Christ's act on the cross "required the new bread" (i.e., his body) "to be purified from leaven."[13] Christ's crucifixion was an act given entirely to God and, as such, is itself a sanctified, unleavened, sacrificial offering that

---

9. Witherington, *Conflict*, 153.
10. Rosner, "Responsibility," 470–73."
11. Although Paul may have been influenced by expulsion processes seen in contemporary Jewish groups such as Qumran (see Keener, *1–2 Corinthians*, 50), Fitzmyer, *First Corinthians*, 231, points out that the declaration for expulsion would also bring parallels to Roman law that demanded exile from the region for actions that were contrary or harmful to society.
12. Fitzmyer, *First Corinthians*, 239.
13. Keener, *1–2 Corinthians*, 50.

serves as an example for how the Corinthians—who are sanctified in Christ as God's church, baptized in his name, and through him receive spiritual blessings and the Spirit—are also to remain in relationship to one another and to God. Such a high quality of sacrifices to God is demanded in Lev 22:17—23:8. It is notable that the stipulations regarding acceptable offerings (22:17-31) are found adjacent to the command for Passover bread to be unleavened (23:3-7). They are God's special people and, as such, must remain as untouched by the leaven of immorality as Christ, the glorious risen Lord.

Celebrate with Sincerity and Truth (b'), 5:8

In the *b* element the audience heard that their boast in the little "leaven" is no good since such activity leavens the whole loaf. They should cast out the old "leaven" in order to renew themselves and be like the "unleavened" bread that is offered in the Temple and consumed after Passover, as well as the example of Christ on the cross. Now, in the *b'* element, they hear that they, as a worshiping body, should celebrate not with the old "leaven" of sexual immorality and their arrogant response, but with a "leaven" of sincerity and truth that will renew them in the word of the gospel that proclaims God's power in Christ rather than arrogant human wisdom. This "unleavened response" is an acceptable offering before God that appropriately celebrates and confirms their spiritual blessings and sanctification in Christ to maintain them as a blameless sacrifice in preparation for the Lord's day of judgment. The audience's true identity, Paul reminds them, is reflecting the unleavened state of their Lord Jesus.[14]

Associations and Purity (a'), 5:9-13

The *a'* element returns to the issue of the sexually immoral person, his stepmother, and the community's arrogance.[15] The audience is not to associate with any brother who is named as immoral, and should not even eat with such a person. They must cut him off from the worship of the community as a unit. Paul clarifies from a previous directive that the Corinthians are not to understand his concern for their purity to mean that they cannot associate with any unclean party—for to do so they would need to "get out" of the world altogether (6:10).[16] Rather, they should focus within and judge

---

14. Ibid., 51.
15. Fee, *First Epistle*, 221.
16. This letter is thought by some to be found partly in 2 Corinthians 6:14—7:4;

their own members' actions. Paul exclaims that he has no interest in judging those who are "outside" the community because God will judge those who are "outside" (6:13). To purify themselves, the audience is told that they cannot get "out" of the world but they can "cast out" the wickedness that may precariously spread like leaven through the whole group, a point which both clarifies his last letter and excoriates those who mocked those instructions and may also have affirmed the man's behavior.[17]

The *a´* element (5:10–13) also develops the initial *a* element (5:1–5) and pulls together the entire unit. Anyone who is "named" as a brother and is found to be a "sexually immoral person"—or have any other kind of wickedness—must be set apart from the community (5:9–13). The community must, in the "name" of the Lord, judge and expel the "sexually immoral person" who is committing "sexual immorality" by sleeping with his stepmother (5:1–5). A person who does "such things" certainly brings the leaven of sinfulness into thecommunity that is supposed to be as unleavened as their Lord Christ (5:7). Those who are so arrogant as to accept this behavior (5:2) should not mock Paul as one who is intent on "judging those outside" the community (5:11). Paul's authority as apostle, founder, and father of the church, allows him to "judge" the sexual immorality of this person and exhort the community to do the same for the sake of their own sanctity. God will "judge" the non-elect, but the elect's duty is to maintain the unity and sanctity of the Temple of God's Spirit by judging and expelling immoral persons (5:12–13). Here Paul merges identity and ethics to exhort the Corinthians to live in a manner that reflects the purity of Christ's own body.[18]

In sum, this initial A unit engages the issue of sexual immorality and the purity of the church as Christ's body and God's Temple of his Spirit. At the center of the unit, the community is exhorted to be free of leaven (evil) as Christ, their Passover sacrifice, was free of any evil (5:7b). The outer core elements (5:6–7a, 8–9) support Paul's judgment of the sexually immoral person with the analogy to leaven. The temple of God's Spirit cannot have any type of ailment that will spread throughout the body. In the bracket

we, however, consider it to be a lost letter that is no longer extent. See Fitzmyer, *First Corinthians*, 243; Milinovich, *Now*, 13–15.

17. Fee, *First Epistle*, 221, points out that the first letter's ambiguous wording to separate from sinners seemed incomprehensible and emboldened the Apollos faction to uphold their theology of "power in the Spirit" against Paul.

18. Schnelle, *Apostle*, 205: "We should not underestimate the influence of pagan ethics and the social conduct related to it. In the ancient world, religious identity was always connected with social identity, that is, group identity (family, city), and so Paul expects the Corinthians not only to adopt a new faith but to change their whole pattern of life."

elements (5:1–5, 10–13) Paul first judges the man and exhorts the community to follow in kind in Jesus' name, and then concludes the unit by defending his original letter against the arrogant ones who had mocked him and affirmed the immoral person's behavior (5:2, 9).

Unit B, 6:1–8: The Wrong People's Court

a: 1/ Why do any of you dare to bring a lawsuit against another to be judged by (ἐπί) the unjust (ἀδίκων) and not by (ἐπί) the sanctified?

b: 2/ Do you not know that the sanctified will judge the world? But if the world is to be judged by you (ἐν ὑμῖν), should you not then be competent enough to judge trivial cases?[19]

c: 3/ Do you not know that you will judge angels? So why not human matters (βιωτικά)?

c′: 4/ So if you have meager human matters (βιωτικά) for trial, why then do you set in authority those who have no credibility with the church?

b′: 5/ I say this to your shame: is there not one among you (ἐν ὑμῖν) who is wise—who is able to arbitrate between his brothers' cases?

a′: 6/ But brother takes brother to court, and this before (ἐπί) the faithless. 7/ So you are already abject failures if you have lawsuits against one another. Why not be wronged (ἀδικεῖσθε)? Why not be defrauded? 8/ But instead you do wrong (ἀδικεῖτε), and you defraud, and this against a brother!

The Sanctified Will Judge the World (a, b, c), 6:1–3

Judgment, a key theme in the letter to this point, now takes on a civic meaning in addition to theological. Up to now, Paul has maintained that he was accountable to no human court. Only the spiritual person is able to discern things because of spiritual knowledge, but the unspiritual person—such as the Corinthians are accused of being—is not able to judge anything. Now, in the B unit, Paul admonishes the Corinthians' tendency to sue one another before Roman civic courts rather than bringing the case before the church.

The *a* element addresses the issue outright, asking how anyone in the community could dare to take a brother to civil court rather than before the sanctified in the church itself.[20] The problem is multifarious. The civic au-

---

19. So Fee, *First Epistle*, 230.

20. There is some disagreement as to whether the text refers to only one particular case (possibly in relation to the incestuous man in 5:1–13), or a larger problem of

thorities have already been judged as incompetent regarding God's wisdom because they rely on human conventional wisdom, as shown by their execution of Jesus (1:18; 2:6–13). Their authority is already waning and will be fully eclipsed when Christ returns to judge and subordinate them to his Father. Also, if a spiritual person has total wisdom and the unspiritual person has none, then how can they ask an unspiritual person to judge these allegedly spiritual people? The other side of the problem is that these so-called spiritual brothers are taking one another to court, and thus investing an unspiritual worldly authority with spiritual honor. As the *a* element impugns, these jurists have transferred the authority that God has given his elect to those associated with the rulers who are fading away. All of these issues are compounded by the central issue of the Roman litigation system's proclivity to favor wealthy and high-status for property disputes. The sum of these theological issues, wrapped together with the judicial system's embodiment of the corrupt and unjust worldly system that is fading away, likely contributed to Paul's view of these outside courts as unacceptable for the elect.[21]

The problem is exacerbated in the *b* and *c* elements (6:2–3) that ask if the Corinthians are even aware that the sanctified are able to judge the world because of the spiritual blessings God has given them. A logical riposte follows their ignorant behavior: if the world is to be judged by them, then should not even the least of them be able to judge such trivial human matters? A second question in the *c* element asks if they know that the elect are determined to judge angels in the new age, not alone humans. If none of them can arbitrate a human defendant, how can they do so with angels at the judgment? Their "wisdom" once again has diminishing returns and is endangering the blessings promised to them.[22]

Is There No One among You Wise Enough to Arbitrate? (c′, b′), 6:4–6

The pivotal *c′* element (6:4) demonstrates a progression from the *c* element (6:3) within the unit's ring formation. If the elect are to judge angelic and

---

numerous cases throughout the community. Given Paul's tone and the use of language (esp. in 6:6–8), I consider this to be more than one event, such that the community demonstrates itself yet again to misunderstand the initial message Paul preached to them.

21. Winter, "Litigation," 561–65.

22. According to Keener, *1–2 Corinthians*, 53, the community's knowledge of their future role could have come from the synagogue core's knowledge of such promises for Israel in Dan 7:22; Wisd 3:8. Fee, *First Epistle*, 234, also points to the tradition in Jewish Apocalypticism regarding fallen angels (*1 Enoch* 1–36).

"human" powers, they should be able to arbitrate their own meager "human" lawsuits before the sanctified, rather than shame the community before those outside the church (6:4). Or, even worse, they choose to defraud other members of Christ's body through Roman systems after receiving the spiritual knowledge of God's will in the gospel and threaten to bring back the leaven of worldly corruption from a local central image of Roman injustice. The ring progression continues to support Paul's argument in the b' element: if the world is to be judged "by you" (the elect, 6:2), should there not be one "among you" wise enough to arbitrate matters between church members (6:5)?

Better to Be Defrauded (a'), 6:6–8

The a' element concludes and sums up the argument in 6:1–8 in a concentric micro-structure.[23] The central lines are lexically parallel questions: why not be wronged, and why not be defrauded? The second offers a more specific form of "wrong" from the first. The plaintiffs likely feared not being able to collect from a Christian defendant without the authority of the city rule. After all, a civil judge had the local police at his disposal; the church did not. But the bracket x and x' lines (6:6–7a, 8) underscore other consequences. If brother sues brother before the faithless, then they are already an abject failure since, in a brother v. brother case, at least one brother is wronged and defrauded. Since wealthy individuals were more likely to pursue and win cases (often against poorer and weaker defendants), the issue opened the door to corruption and social injustice. A trial among the church could (hopefully) level the playing field.[24] Their acquisition of ordinary people to arbitrate between them demonstrates their inability to judge matters with spiritual wisdom, even in the most human of cases.[25]

The a' element sees a development from the initial a element (6:1–2a). The audience might as well be "wronged" without the civil courts because with them they still "wrong" a brother, and thus act no better than the

---

23. a': (x) 6/ But *brother* takes *brother* to court, and this before the faithless. 7/ So you are already abject failures if you have lawsuits *against* one another.
(y) *Why not be* wronged?
(y') *Why not be* defrauded?
(x') 8/ But instead you do wrong, and you defraud, and this *against* a *brother*!

24. Mitchell, "Courts," 575–81; Winter, "Litigation," 562–68.

25. Keener, *1–2 Corinthians*, 52, and Witherington, *Conflict*, 163, consider that the scandal of defrauding a brother arises from the unbalanced standards of treatment for different status levels in Roman courts. They also presume that the "new rich" in Corinth would seek to gain more property through lawsuits.

"unjust" whom they set over themselves in authority, when in fact, they should be preparing to judge angels. That the Corinthians in element *a* take each other to court to be judged "by" the unjust rather than "by" the sanctified (6:1–2) is developed in that their actions already prove them to be abject failures. Taking a brother to be judged "by" the faithless proves that this church is essentially unqualified to judge angels in the new age (6:6–8). It also confirms Paul's earlier point that they lack true spiritual wisdom (2:14—3:3).

Unit A´, 6:9–20: Sexual Immorality Has No Place in Christ's Body

a: 9/ Do you not know (οὐκ οἴδατε) that the unjust will have no share in God's kingdom? Do not be deceived: neither sexually immoral people (πόρνοι), nor idolaters, nor adulterers, nor pederasts and their partners, 10/ nor thieves, nor greedy persons, nor drunkards, nor slanderers, nor robbers will inherit God's kingdom.

b: 11/ Now, you yourselves did these very same things. But you were washed, you were sanctified, you were justified in the name of our Lord (κυρίου) Jesus Christ, and by the Spirit of our God!

c: 12/ "Everything is lawful to me," but (πάντα μοι ἔξεστιν, ἀλλ') not everything is beneficial.

c´: "Everything is lawful to me," but (πάντα μοι ἔξεστιν, ἀλλ') not if I am overcome by this thing. 13/ "Food is for the belly and the belly is for food," but God will destroy both.

b´: Now the body is not for immorality but for the Lord (κυρίῳ), and the Lord (κύριος) is for the body. 14/ Now God raised the Lord (κύριον) and he will raise us by his power.

a´: 15/ Do you not know (οὐκ οἴδατε) that your bodies are parts of Christ? So is it right to join a part of Christ with a prostitute? Of course not! 16/ Do you not know (οὐκ οἴδατε) that one who joins with a sexually immoral person (πόρνης) is made into one body? For it is said, "the two will become one flesh." 17/ Now the one who joins himself to the Lord is one Spirit. 18/ Flee sexual immorality (πορνείαν)! Anyone who commits sin does so outside the body, but the one who commits sexual immorality (πορνεύων) sins against his own body. 19/ Do you not know (οὐκ οἴδατε) that your body is a temple in which there is the Holy Spirit, whom you have from God, and you are not your own? 20/ For you were bought for a price! So glorify God in your bodies!

Beyond What Is Written

Former and Present Lives of the Audience (a, b), 6:9-11

The A′ unit offers a more general perspective to the issue of sexual immorality seen in the A unit (5:1-13).[26] Having stated in the B unit that the elect are to settle disputes within the church rather than have the unjust sit in authority over them, the A′ unit further explains why: the unjust have no share in God's rule (i.e., kingdom). The list of those who are disqualified from God's kingdom in the *a* element (6:9-10) include three that were mentioned earlier (sexually immoral, wicked, greedy, and idolatrous people, 5:9-13), but now adds adulterers, homosexuals (or pederasts),[27] their partners,[28] slanderers, and robbers. The groups essentially share, from the view of Paul's Jewish Apocalyptic heritage, the trait of disrupting God's created order.[29] Pharisaic tradition treated uncleanliness as more of a substance than a theory, and therefore much more threatening. Given the analogy with leaven in 5:7, Paul was extremely worried that such individuals would permeate the group, affecting them and their salvation negatively.

This list is punctuated by the *b* element (6:11), which indicts the audience for once being included among these categories. These elect in the audience once lived like the unjust who have no knowledge or hope. But they received the gospel, confirmed their election in the baptism in the name of Christ, and were established together in him (1:4-9). Hence, having witnessed their receipt of the gospel, Paul can say that they were washed

---

26. Many scholars group 6:9-11 with 6:1-8, viewing the commands in 6:10 as an affirmation of the speech against lawsuits in vv. 1-8. However, the lexical connections denote that 6:9-11 properly belongs with the rest of the discussion found in 6:12-20. In addition, the break at 6:8 allows 6:9-20 to act as a proper parallel to 5:1-13. Several parallel terms, such as πορνεια, connect 5:1-13 and 6:9-20. Also, stylistically speaking, 6:9-11 shares the diatribe and dialectical style found in 6:12-20; Collins, *First Corinthians*, 242, notes this connection, although he maintains 6:1-11 as a unit.

27. On the translations and problems that arise with these peculiar terms, see Fee, *First Epistle*, 242-45; Keener, *1-2 Corinthians*, 54-55. It is notable that the NT does not normally address homosexuality, per se, but more pederasty, the sexual engagement of youths by adult males. Based on the words that Paul chooses here in the present text, the exact characterizations remain unclear.

28. "Partners" here translates ἐρομένος, the passive love-partner within a pederasty relationship. It is important to note that Greeks distinguished between a young man who partnered with a pederast and a call-boy or prostitute. According to Scroggs, *Homosexuality*, 32-36, the ἐρομένος ("beloved") was a young man of pubescent or postpubescent development who engaged in sexual and professional relationships with an older man who served as both mentor and sexual partner. The ἐρομένος gave sexual pleasure to the older partner, but was expected not to enjoy the encounter himself (ibid., 40-42).

29. An analogous situation can be seen, e.g., in the angels who bring disorder to the world in *1 Enoch* 3-7.

from their previous unclean lives through baptism. They were sanctified in Christ and set apart to be God's own church—his Israel. They were justified in that, while they were once separated from God in their unjust ways (6:9), they now have a new relationship with God that is without blemish.[30] These three saving aspects of washing, sanctifying, and justifying were brought to the elect by the name of Jesus and by God's Spirit—both of which point to baptism as the demarcation between old life and new. The traits the audience received remind them that they did not earn or acquire these traits on their own (also 4:20); rather, they were all received through Christ, who became for these "lowly ones" God's wisdom, holiness, righteousness, and redemption (1:31). The harsh reminder of their past serves to underscore their responsibilities in the present: whatever the Corinthians had been before their baptism, they are something entirely new now in Christ, and God's Spirit demands a new way of life.

"Everything Is Lawful to Me" (c, c´), 6:12–13a

In the central elements (6:12–13a) of the unit, Paul responds to slogans of the libertine faction in Corinth. The slogans likely arose from a misunderstanding that the Spirit gave believers immunity from any and all customs or rules, as in 5:1–5. In the c element (6:12) Paul cites their slogan that "everything is lawful to me," but retorts that, although everything is possible to a believer, it does not mean that everything a believer does is beneficial.[31] This elliptical retort relies on the audience to recognize that doing what is possible is not always in everyone's best interest.

The second citation in the parallel c´ element (6:13a) repeats their slogan but develops the retort by stating that such freedom can be negative if the thing you feel empowered to do ends up ruling over or controlling you. The repetition of the pronoun "me" emphasizes the egocentricity of the slogan and its proponents.[32] Those who declare to be above the law are not concerned enough to view even the effect of their actions on others as a possible check to their desires.

---

30. Barrett, *First Epistle*, 142, among others, considers baptism to be in view behind the verb "to wash" (λυεῖν).

31. Keener, *1–2 Corinthians*, 57, points out that Paul uses the vocabulary and rhetorical strategy of a moral philosopher when he cites an opposing slogan and asserts his own as more "beneficial" to the group.

32. R. F. Collins, *First Corinthians*, 242.

Next, Paul responds to another Corinthian slogan ("food for the belly," etc.), which analogizes a sexual appetite.[33] As before, Paul's response serves to characterize the libertines' slogans as illogical and self-destructive. Even if the Spirit makes them powerful enough to be above the human customs and the cosmic order, they must still keep their desires in check with their new freedom, lest their desires overcome them and nullify whatever freedom they had attained with Christ.[34]

The Lord Benefits the Body (b'), 6:14

The analogy of the slogan to sexuality is addressed immediately in Paul's counter-example in the *b'* element (6:13b–14). The body is not for "immorality" but for the Lord, and the Lord is for the body. How the body is for the Lord will be addressed shortly but, for now, Paul explains why the Lord is relevant to the Corinthians' bodies. Just as God raised Jesus, so too will he raise the elect through his (Christ's) power.

There is a development from the *b* element (6:11) to aid the interpretation of the text. The "Lord," in whose name the elect in Corinth were washed, sanctified, and justified by the Spirit of "our" God and separated from their previous unjust lives (6:11), is now in the *b'* element purposed for their future salvation. They are separated from their past and sanctified in the present "in the name of the Lord" so that God might also raise "us/we" who are members of Christ, the glorious "Lord" Jesus (6:14). The elect then should seek what is most beneficial to the body—the Lord Jesus Christ, by whose power God will raise them—rather than their own desires.

You Were Bought for a Price (a'), 6:15–20

The *a'* element concludes the unit with a dense micro-ring structure.[35] The initial *x* line (6:15) builds on the previous statement that God will raise

33. See also Barrett, *First Epistle*, 145.

34. Witherington, *Conflict*, 168.

35. a': (*x*) 15/ Do you not know that *your bodies* are parts of Christ? So is it right to join a part of Christ with a prostitute? Of course not!

(*y*) 16/ Do you not know that *one who joins with* a sexually immoral person is made *into one* body? For it is said, "the two will become *one* flesh."

(*y'*) 17/ Now the *one who joins himself* to the Lord is one in spirit with him. 18/ Flee sexual immorality! Anyone who commits sin does so outside the body, but the one who commits sexual immorality sins *against* his own body.

(*x'*) 19/ Do you not know that *your body* is a temple in which there is the Holy Spirit, whom you have from God, and you are not your own? 20/ For you were bought for a

those who are joined to Christ—i.e., the members of the community. As such, they should be wary of the company they keep. The audience should know that, based on the teaching from Scripture (Gen 2:24), one who "joins him/herself with" a prostitute becomes "one" body with them (y, 6:16). The y' line (6:17–18) reminds the audience that they have "joined" themselves to Christ to be "one" Spirit with him. As such, they must flee the sexually immoral person that they were warned of in the y line because his/her sins symbiotically affect, in a self-destructive and violent manner, not only themselves but also the body to which they are attached.[36] Like leaven, their sin affects the other believers in the body of the church and Christ, with whom the believers have been "joined" to him in "one" Spirit.[37]

Just as the central lines stress the unified body the believers share in Christ, the bracket lines of the element stress how each individual must care for "your own" body. The x line (6:15) asks in general, if "your bodies" are joined to Christ, then would they join him or herself to a sexually immoral person (presumably in an illicit manner), or take Christ to a brothel? Clearly not. The x' line (6:19–20) reminds the audience that "your bodies" are the temple of the Holy Spirit, and thus they are not their own. Since they have been redeemed and sanctified by Christ, they now are conscripted to house God's presence.[38] They were bought for a price, and so they must live so that "your bodies" glorify God rather than bring shame to the Lord who redeemed them. The examples of the Spirit, Christ, and the temple (6:17–18) immerse Paul's argument in eschatological hues. The union seen with the church in Christ now will bring ultimate salvation in union with him in the future resurrection. Likewise, the formation of the church as the Temple of the Spirit in the present presumes a sanctified state and prepares them to be in God's presence in his kingdom (6:9–10).[39]

This final element completes the ring with lexical connections to the a element (6:9–11). The repetition of the inquisitive phrase, "do you not know," points to major matters that the Corinthians are acting as though they do not understand. They are acting as though they "do not know" that immoral persons, which they once were, do not enter the kingdom of God (6:9). Likewise, they are acting as though they "do not know" that their bodies are members of Christ and are joined to Christ as one Spirit. Lastly, it is

---

price! So glorify God in *your bodies*!

36. Fisk, "Violation," 554–57.

37. According to Byrne, "Sinning," 614–16, sexual immorality impacts both the spiritual and physical aspects of one's body. This would be so in both the individual sinner and the corporate body of Christ.

38. Fitzmyer, *First Corinthians*, 270.

39. See R. F. Collins, *First Corinthians*, 248.

as if they "do not know" that their bodies, bound to Christ, are a temple for the Holy Spirit (6:15–19). This temple is under God's protection, and any harm to it will be met with God's destructive response (see 3:5–10).

All of these things are necessary for them to know, because they have been elected and sanctified by Christ's power for future glory in the resurrection (6:14). But they jeopardize this glory when they return to their previous ways of life and join themselves to "sexually immoral people" who cannot inherit God's kingdom (6:9–10, 18). Therefore, they must flee "sexual immorality" (6:19), including all of the "sexually immoral" activities they participated in before they were washed, sanctified, and justified in Christ's name (6:9–11). They must flee their past, lest it overtake their present and nullify their future.

INTERRELATION OF UNITS

Outline

The pivotal B section engages topics regarding how the community is to relate to the outside world now that they are sanctified. The initial ring set of this section engages three topics: a believer who is in a sexual relationship with his stepmother, court cases before the corrupt Roman judicial system, and sexual immorality in general. The overarching ideological problem to all of these is that some Corinthians believe the Spirit has empowered them to overcome all common conventions, and yet retain a sense of pride in conventional, imperial power. They have the worst of both worlds. Paul now moves to show them that responsibility to the Spirit and the communal body of Christ is true freedom. Giving in to one's desires only adds a new master and constrictions to their life and could nullify their present and future glory, even as it stains their present holiness.

Sexual Immorality Is Like Leaven that Must Be Removed from the Community to Preserve Its Purity (A, 5:1–13)

Previously, Paul had instructed the Corinthians not to associate with any "sexually immoral person" (πόρνοις, 5:9) and, since there are many "sexually immoral persons" (πόρνος, 5:11) in the world, some in the community had mocked him for such an outrageous demand. But after hearing of "sexually immorality" (πορνεία, 5:1) in which a member is sleeping with his stepmother, Paul writes to correct and admonish their arrogance. The apostle is present to judge the man by the "power" (δυνάμει, 5:5) of Jesus and exhorts the community to assemble and judge the man in the "name" (ὀνόμαζομενς, 5:11) of their Lord and cast him out. He is like leaven and must be removed so that the loaf can be renewed and stand before the Lord as an acceptable offering.

The Corinthians Disqualify Themselves as Future Judges When They Try Cases before Non-Believers (B, 6:1-8)

Paul rebukes the audience for some members who have taken one another to court before pagans rather than addressing the matter before the Christian community. Pagan authorities do not have the proper wisdom to judge accurately, as shown by the rampant injustice in their system and their farcical judgment of Christ. He reminds them that the sanctified will judge the world and angels, but if they show themselves now to have no one among them competent enough to deal with such minor cases, they may well disqualify themselves from their future role and authority.

Sexual Immorality cannot Be Conformed to Christ, Who Died for the Elect (A´, 6:9-20)

In the A´ unit, Paul confronts the libertine Corinthians' slogans (6:12) by comparing their views to sexual immorality with life in Christ. "Sexually immoral people" (πόρνοι), as the audience members once were, cannot inherit God's Kingdom (6:9). Yet, having been washed, sanctified, and justified from their previous lives by the "name" (ὀνόματι, 6:11) of Jesus and the Spirit, now they can hope to be raised by his "power" (δυνάμεως, 6:14) in the new age. Given this incredible hope for future glory, the community should not seek to rationalize a path back to their sinful lifestyles. The past and future cannot overlap. Just as one cannot join a "sexually immoral person" (πόρνης, 6:15) to Christ, so too should those who are joined to Christ refrain from "sexual immorality" (πορνεία, 6:15-18).

Conclusion

Rhetorically speaking, the central B unit offers its bracket units a sufficiently persuasive eschatological context and reminder of what the community risks in the midst of the tense issue of sexual immorality. It builds on the community's "judgment" of the sinful man in 5:1-13, which in itself shows a precedent for proper judicial procedures for the church community. So

5:1–13 sets up 6:1–8 by showing that the Corinthians are able to judge one another without the help of outsiders, and 6:1–8 confirms the need for the Corinthians to take the judgment of the man seriously since they will (hopefully) judge angels at the eschaton.

The unit anticipates the command to refrain from contact with those who will not inherit God's kingdom and who exhibit the behavior associated with the believers' "old life." It also lays the groundwork for Paul's first demonstration of the community's new identity as members of the body of Christ and God's temple.

There is considerable development from the A to A´ unit that ties together the arguments regarding sexual immorality into a singular oration on sexual ethics and responsibility to the larger body of believers. Paul earlier wrote to the Corinthians to refrain from contact with sexually immoral persons (A, 5:10–13) and now demands that they exile the sexually immoral member (A, 5:1–5) because he associates them with traits of their old life (A´, 6:11). Like a small bit of leaven in a loaf of bread, this one person's actions could lead many more of them to relapse, such that they join these "sexually immoral" persons who will not inherit the kingdom of God (A´, 6:9). Their arrogance about his immoral actions is proof that he has already had a negative effect on them. In the meantime, they should recognize their new identity as members of the one pure and blameless body of Christ, to whom they would not dare join a "sexually immoral person" (A´, 6:19–20). Since the stakes are so high, it is best that they put their arrogance aside and follow the general principle to flee sexual immorality (A´, 6:18).

Furthermore, they are empowered to judge the sinful man "in the name of Jesus" (A, 5:3) because they were washed, redeemed, and justified "by the name of our Lord Jesus" and "by the Spirit" (A´, 6:11), and now comprise his sanctified and pure body on earth; therefore, they are empowered to judge their own members (A, 5:4–5), and preserve the blameless state of the paschal lamb (A, 5:9), who will return and dispense to them the authority to judge over peoples and angels (B, 6:3).

Just as Paul is able to be present with the community "by the Spirit" to convict the man with "the power of the Lord Jesus" to help the Corinthians purge the immorality from their corporate body (A, 5:4–5), so too will God preserve their bodies and raise them by "his power" (A´, 6:14). The members must remain pure because those who join to Christ become one in Spirit with the one who sanctified, washed, and justified them (A´, 6:11) to make them an eschatological sign as the earthly temple of God's holy "Spirit" (A´, 6:20).

7

Marriage, the Family, and the World, 7:1–40

Section B, Ring Set β

ANALYSIS OF UNITS

Having already addressed the divisions in the church and their libertine issues with sexual immorality, Paul must now address the other side of the morality issue that was creating divisions in the community. How are the lives of the sanctified elect, who have been washed from, and are to refrain from, sexual immorality (6:9–20), to live among the conventions of marriage, divorce, and other family matters? Paul has just admonished the libertine division of the church and now turns to correct and instruct the ascetic division that may have asserted the slogan that a man should not touch a woman (7:1). Now Paul must moderate between those two positions to correct their misunderstanding of the Spirit and the gospel that he preached in terms of how they navigate life in the world as God's sanctified.

Unit A, 7:1–9: Concession to Marriage

a: 1/ Now, about those things which you wrote—it is good (καλόν) for a man not touch a woman. 2/ But because of sexual immorality, each (ἕκαστος) man must have (ἐχέτω) his own wife, and each (ἑκάστη) woman must have (ἐχέτω) her own husband.

b: 3/ To his wife a man is obligated to hand himself over, and likewise (ὁμοίως) the woman to her husband.

b′: 4/ It is not the woman but her husband who has authority over her own body; and likewise (ὁμοίως) it is not the man but his wife who has authority over his.

a′: 5/ Do not defraud one another, except for a time arranged in agreement—in order to be free for prayer. But then return to one another again, in order that Satan might not tempt you through your lack of self-discipline. 6/ I say this as a concession, not a command. 7/ Now I wish that all people were like me. But each (ἕκαστος) has (ἔχει) his own gift from God—one has this, and another has that. 8/ Now, I say to the unmarried and to widows, it is good (καλόν) for them to remain as I am. 9/ But if they lack self-discipline, they must marry. For it is better (κρεῖττον) to be married than to burn.

Correct Conduct and a Concession (a), 7:1–2

In the A unit's opening element, the text turns to address the letter the Corinthians had sent to Paul.[1] Paul takes up first whether marriage is acceptable for God's sanctified elect, given its sexual obligations. It is apparent that one group, in hyperbolic contrast to the libertine contingent seen in 5:1—6:20, had taken a decidedly ascetic response to their acquisition of the Spirit.[2] It is not clear whether the two sides were using their spiritual qualities (knowledge and power for libertines; purity and sanctification for ascetics) against one another in jockeying for spiritual authority of the community in the absence of Paul and Apollos.

Paul begins this section by agreeing with the ascetics' assertion that "a man should not touch a woman."[3] But, although he considers the slogan

---

1. See chapter 2 regarding this lost letter and lead up to 1 Corinthians.

2. This outline of the two groups behind 5:1—7:40 seems most accepted. However, there is also a chance for a third group of members influenced by the Cynic perspective that bemoaned marriage as a distraction but celebrated sex as an organic necessity that should be expressed with prostitutes or non-committal sexual relationships (Keener, *1-2 Corinthians*, 63; Fitzmyer, *First Corinthians*, 274). Goulder's view that the ascetics represent a conservative Jewish group is less likely ("Sofia," 174–81).

3. Scholars and modern translations differ on whether the phrase "correct not to touch a woman" is Paul's own words or a slogan of the Corinthian ascetics that Paul is addressing. Collins, "Unity," 424, and Phipps, "Attitude," 127–30, argue Paul cites the Corinthians' slogan but disagrees with it. To a degree, the point is moot; see Fitzmyer,

Marriage, the Family, and the World, 7:1-40

correct in principal, he adds a practical caveat: because of the propensity for temptation and sexual immorality, each elect member must have a single spouse. The imperative (must), rather than subjunctive (should), underscores the importance of the issue. So, should Christians get married or remain married after baptism? In an ideal world, in Paul's view, the answer would be "no." But the elect do not live in an ideal world. They are inevitably surrounded by opportunities for temptation while this age is passing away. In the meantime, then, they should get married as a concession to ward off sexual immorality.[4]

Marital Obligations (b, b'), 7:3-4

The *b* element (7:3) unpacks how the husband and wife from the *a* element are to "have," or live with, their spouse. As seen in 5:1-2, "to have" a person can be a euphemism for sexual activity. This possession is presented here as a transfer of one's self to his/her spouse. Each, by law and custom, is obligated to engage in sexual activity within a marriage—primarily to provide an heir and, if possible, the honor of numerous children.[5]

The *b'* element (7:4) develops the *b* element (7:3). That the man hands himself to his wife, and the woman "likewise" to her husband (*b*, 7:3), explains that the result of this transfer is that the husband now has authority over his wife's body, and "likewise" the wife now has authority over her husband's body (*b'*, 7:4). Since custom requires transfer of possession of one's body to his/her spouse in a sexual manner, Paul concedes that this activity is preferable to the alternative of burning with lust.

At this point, Paul steps outside contemporary expectations of marriage duties and rights. A woman was often viewed as her husband's property, but rarely vice versa. Yet Paul demands husbands and wives to recognize their spouses' authority over their bodies, regardless of gender.

First Corintihans, 275; Caragounis, "Fornication," 543–59. Whether the slogan originated from Paul or the Corinthians, the apostle agrees with the phrase in principle and offers a difference only as a concession to difficult circumstances. His subsequent exhortations to imitate his celibate lifestyle in 7:9–13, 34–39 also show Paul's feelings and the ascetics' to be indistinguishable.

4. MacDonald and Vaage, "Unclean," 534: "If Paul was prepared to announce and personally strove to embody the new creation in Christ displayed through a sex-free life, it seems that the apostle was equally unprepared to enact this vision collectively. For whatever reason, there remained in his thinking a telling gap between what was imaginable for the house church as a discrete social body in the context of the ancient Mediterranean city."

5. Witherington, *Conflict*, 174.

The threat of immorality was significantly real for Gentile converts. Although a few pagan writers spoke against sexual relationships outside of marriage (e.g., the Peripatetics and Musonius), the majority approved or did not bother to comment.[6] In fact, Plutarch simply advises wives to bear with the knowledge that their husbands were with other women.[7] Romans at times married for social mobility—status, business, or to have a legal heir—rather than romance, and it was not uncommon for a man to have mistresses and prostitutes for personal and sexual relationships in addition to his wife.[8]

In many cases, the wife's role in the relationship was diminished. Custom limited wives' speech in their households, even with their own husbands; and husbands were expected to speak for their wives in public. In addition, many marriages in Rome arranged a man with a wife half his age, presenting an initial imbalance in personal experience, knowledge, and physicality that would be perpetuated for the remainder of the relationship.[9] Convention presumed that men were more rational than women, and thus more apt to speak and control family and business matters.[10] Even more progressive philosophers such as Musonius, maintained that the woman was naturally weaker, inferior to, and to be ruled by, her male counterpart.[11] Her highest purpose in life was to please her husband. Physical and autonomous superiority from cultural conventions allowed men to visit brothels and engage mistresses without significant complaint from their voiceless and powerless wives.

In light of these points, Paul's words challenge the audience with a powerful image and question: can a twenty-something, voiceless woman have authority over her forty-something, powerful husband? In Paul's view, the answer is necessarily affirmative. It is the husband's duty to his wife and her authority over him that will keep the man away from sexual immorality and make possible Paul's concession for marriage.

---

6. Yarbrough, *Gentiles*, 57.
7. Ibid.
8. Bruce, *1 and 2 Thessalonians*, 82; Ward, "Musonius," 286–88.
9. Witherington, *Conflict*, 170.
10. See, in particular, Kroeger, "Women"; Meeks, *Urban*, 23.
11. Yarbrough, *Gentiles*, 56.

Marriage, the Family, and the World, 7:1–40

Concession for Marriage Explained (a´), 7:5–9

In the *a´* element, Paul again tries to agree with the ascetic group in principal, but also moderates their position for practical purposes.[12] The central line (7:7b) of the element concedes that God has not given the gift of celibacy to all believers, and so, despite Paul's preference (7:6–7a, 8), it is not practical for all believers to try to be celibate. The bracket lines (7:5, 9) offer concessions to married and widows: the former are to abstain only for a time (7:5), and the latter may remarry (7:9). In both cases, the concession is offered to avoid temptation for sexual immorality.

Looping back to the initial element of the unit (7:1–2), Paul admits that his concession in the *a* element arises due to the threat of immorality (as seen in 5:1–13; 6:9–20). Paul equally concedes, however, that although married couples should not defraud one another of their rightful possession, they may agree to arrange a time of abstinence (as owners may do) in order to pray. However, they should return to one another's possession as obligated because, just as Paul conceded that people must marry to avoid immorality (*a*, 7:1–2), so too must he concede that they remain intimate, lest Satan tempt and overcome their lack of discipline (7:7).

The repetition of the phrase "each has" in the *a* and *a´* elements solidifies the connection as more than thematic. "Each" must "have" a spouse because of sexual immorality; and, since "each has" his own gift from God and may not have the charism of celibacy, couples should return to one another to avoid temptation from Satan. Furthermore, that it is "correct" for a man not to touch a woman is affirmed in that it is "good" for a widow to remain unmarried like Paul. But they may marry because, just as it is conceded that the young should marry to avoid sexual immorality (*a*, 7:2), so too should widows marry because it is "better" than burning with lust (*a´*, 7:9).[13]

---

12. a´: (*x*) 5/ Do not defraud one another, *except for* a time arranged in agreement—in order to be free for prayer. But then return to one another again, in order that Satan might not tempt you through your *lack of self-discipline*.
    (*y*) 6/ *I say* this as a concession, not a command. 7/ Now I wish that all people were like me.
    (*z*) But each has his own gift from God—one has this, and another has that.
    (*y´*) 8/ Now, *I say* to the unmarried and to widows, it is good for them to remain *as I am*.
    (*x´*) 9/ But *if* they *lack self-discipline*, they must marry. For it is better to be married than to burn.

13. Along with the concern for immorality, it is possible that Paul wished to quell a fanatical trend in the community regarding eschatology and gender. MacDonald, "Holy," 162–72, argues that some of the ascetics may have felt that in receiving the Spirit and becoming a part of God's new creation, they were, in fact, already transported into God's kingdom and were de-gendered into an androgynous state of equality.

In the end, though, Paul would prefer that all be like him and abstain, like the ascetics do. But it is unfair to demand this of all the elect because God has not blessed everyone equally, and only some are able to negotiate abstinence successfully in the midst of constant temptation. The rest might succumb to these tests and engage in sexually immoral acts—thus threatening the sanctity of the community with worldly leaven and forfeiting their inheritance of the kingdom (5:1–9; 6:9–11). For these reasons, Paul concedes, it is acceptable for the elect to marry in the passing present age.

Unit B, 7:10–16: Remain Married, Unless It Is Impossible

a: 10/ And to the married I command—not I, but the Lord—a woman must not be divorced (χωρισθῆναι) from her husband. 11/ But if she does divorce (χωρισθῇ), she must remain unmarried or be reconciled to her husband—and a man must not leave his wife.

b: 12/ Now, to the rest, I—not the Lord—say, if any (εἴ τις) brother has (ἔχει) a wife who is a non-believer (ἄπιστοί) but she agrees to live with him, he must not leave (μὴ ἀφιέτω) her.

b′: 13/ And if any (εἴ τις) woman has (ἔχει) a husband who is a non-believer (ἄπιστοί), but he agrees to live with her, she must not leave (μὴ ἀφιέτω) her husband. 14/ For the non-believer husband is sanctified by his wife, and the non-believer wife is sanctified by her husband—for otherwise the children are unclean, but now are sanctified.

a′: 15/ But if the non-believer demands divorce (χωρίζεται), the believer must be divorced (χωριζέσθω). A brother or sister must not be enslaved to such circumstances—God has called us for peace. 16/ For how do you know, o wife, if you will save your husband? Or, how do you know, o husband, if you will save your wife?

Further, some members may have become convinced that this new state of sanctified androgyny precluded them from sexual relationships, even within marriage. These points could explain Paul's concern about some ascetics (male and female) "defrauding" their spouses of protection from immorality (7:5) when said spouses did not share such feelings about the Spirit and still required sexual contact within their marriage. R. F. Collins, *Divorce*, 27, notes that both men and women members may have been pursuing abstinence.

Concession to Divorce (a), 7:10–11

The B unit moves to address the issue of divorce. Paul cites a logia of Jesus to refute divorce altogether, possibly because members were using it in their internal disputes. Paul admits that the forbiddance to divorce is from Jesus, but adds that he is able to interpret Christ's command within its new, Greek context. As a Pharisee, this is not out of character for Paul. If divorce does occur, then the divorced must remain unmarried or be reconciled to her husband. And, in the same way, a man should not let go of his wife on account of his new life in Christ.

So why was divorce occurring in Corinth? Several possibilities arise. First, the believer may want a divorce because they found their spouse's sexual or religious demands unacceptable. Second, the non-believing spouse may want out of the marriage because 1) they viewed this new faith community as strange and contrary to Roman customs (even seditious), or 2) they rejected the believer's sexual expectations. It should not be forgotten that Christians were already considered problematic or killed in some parts of the Empire (e.g., 1 Thes 3:1–5; Acts 17:1–15; Mark 13:9–13), even in Corinth (Acts 18:1–17). It is very possible some spouses considered the believers' new faith as *impietas*—a breach of devotion to national, local, and familial loyalties. Any of these factors could have triggered a case of divorce.

Argument for Spouses of Non-Believers to Remain Married (b, b´), 7:12–14

The *b* element (7:12) returns to those who are married with the directive, "now, to the rest," and expresses Paul's additional interpretation of Christ's logia: if a believer has a non-believing wife who agrees to stay with him despite his new life, he must not leave her.[14] In the same way, a sister who has an unbelieving husband who agrees to stay with her must not leave him.

Having heard in the *b* element (7:12) that believers should not leave their non-believer spouses, the *b´* element (7:13–14) explains why. A brother or sister should not leave an understanding non-believer spouse because the latter is sanctified by the former—as are the children.[15] As explained earlier, two who are joined together become one flesh (6:19–20 // Gen 3:9). The believers are joined to Christ and are sanctified in him. Their

---

14. Elliott, "Marriage," 224, notes that "the rest" refer to those married to non-believers.

15. MacDonald and Vaage, "Unclean," 545, point out that Paul and the Corinthians presume the children of mixed marriages will be sanctified in some manner.

non-believer spouses, in being joined in flesh to the believer in marriage, are then also mystically connected to Christ and indirectly sanctified. Their children, who are the products of their joined flesh, are also sanctified in this symbiotic relationship.[16] The terms "unclean" and "sanctified (clean)" are placed in sharp contrast around the idea of one's call.[17]

Concession to Divorce Non-Believer Spouses (a′), 7:15–16

The a′ element ties back to the a element (7:10–11) with the repetition of the term "divorce" and concessions to divorce for the believers. Although the Lord Jesus commanded against divorce in the a element, and although unbelieving spouses are sanctified by the believers whom they join and who are joined to Christ by baptism, if the non-believer chooses to divorce the believer, then the believer must be divorced.[18] The strong term "enslaved" underscores how the bonds of marriage may be too heavy and suffocating for a believer if their non-believing spouse's demands are considered out of line for a sanctified member of Christ's body.[19] God has called his elect to peace, so they should not try to stay married when the non-believer seeks divorce, nor should the church demand that the believer remain married to the non-believer based on Christ's logia alone.[20]

So why were some members refusing to divorce, even when the non-believer demanded it? First, some members may have been citing Jesus' logia regarding divorce to preclude any type of separation, even with non-believers. Second, there seems to be a presumption among the Corinthians that they could save their non-believing family members through carrying on with the marriage, perhaps also in hopes of further evangelization. Third, and most likely, a woman might refuse a divorce in order to maintain a relationship with her children since the father normally took full custody of the children under Roman law.[21]

A concern for their children within mixed marriages is addressed immediately with anticipation. The force and order of the directives implies that some in the church felt that this indirect sanctification of spouses warranted that the believer must stay in the relationship in order to sanctify,

---

16. For an excellent study on this passage and its difficult history of interpretation, see MacDonald and Vaage, "Unclean," 526–46.
17. R. F. Collins, "Unity," 425.
18. On the relation to Jesus' commands, see Neirynck, "Sayings," 141–76.
19. Garland, *1 Corinthians*, 291.
20. Vawter, "Divorce," 537.
21. Keener, *1–2 Corinthians*, 65.

Marriage, the Family, and the World, 7:1–40

and thus save, their non-believing spouses and children. But it is not guaranteed that a believer can save their spouse by their marriage relationship alone. So, Paul explains, one must divorce if forced to do so, but should then remain unmarried.

Unit B´, 7:17–24: Remain as God Called You

a: 17/ As the Lord (κύριος) assigns to each (ἑκάστῳ), as God has called each (ἕκαστον), so too must one walk. And such do I command in all of my churches.

b: 18/ If one is circumcised (περιτετμημένος) when he was called, he must not hide it; if one was called with a foreskin (ἀκροβυστίᾳ), he must not be circumcised.

b´: 19/ The circumcision (περιτομή) is nothing and the foreskin (ἀκροβυστία) is nothing. Only keeping God's commandments matters.

a´: 20/ Each (ἕκαστος) is to remain in the state in which he was called. 21/ If you were called as a slave, it is not to be a concern. But if you are able to, by all means, seek to be free.[22] 22/ For the slave who is called in the Lord (κυρίῳ) is the Lord's (κυρίου) free person; likewise the free person who is called is Christ's slave. 23/ You were bought for a price: do not try to be slaves to people. 24/ Each (ἕκαστος) in the situation he was called, brothers and sisters—in this one must remain, as from God.

Paul's Universal Command: Walk as God Called You (a, b, b´), 7:17–19

In the *a* element Paul commands—as he does in all of his churches—for the Corinthians to walk in the manner they were when God called them. Each must live in a manner acceptable to God's will and in accordance with the peace for which they were elected. This section underscores a principle that supports his previous arguments in the specific issues of marriage and divorce.[23]

In the *b* element, Paul outlines this directive with conditional examples: if one was circumcised when called, then he must not hide it; likewise, one who has a foreskin when called should not seek to be circumcised. The

---

22. Dawes, "Freedom," 694, argues that the grammar calls for an emphatic sense in this verse.

23. Fitzmyer, *First Corinthians*, 205.

phrase "keeping God's commandments" usually refers to observance of the Torah. Yet here Paul uses the phrase in a more general sense of keeping God's will, such that one can fulfill the spirit of the Torah without being circumcised.[24]

The *b´* element (7:19) explains the logic behind the directive of the *b* element (7:18). One should not cover his circumcision or seek to be circumcised after his call because circumcision and foreskin are nothing compared to keeping God's will. Based on the content of the unit, one may understand God's commands to include not just OT scripture, the prophetic gospel message about Christ, and the ongoing voice of the Spirit in worship, but also God's assignment of the elect to their lot in life. Being Jewish might affect your status in a Greco-Roman city, but what matters to God is obeying his commands. So, whether Jew or Gentile, the believers should accept their place from God without complaint.

Same in Appearance, but Transformed in Substance (a´), 7:20–24

The *a´* element contains a concentric micro-structure.[25] As a doublet to the example of Jew/Gentile in the *b´* element, this element explains the same rule with the slave/free contrast. The central line (7:22) declares a paradoxical inversion in that, because of the epoch-changing event of the cross, the elect, slave and free alike, have been bought at a price through Christ's sacrifice. As a result, the slaves have been bought from their earthly masters and given freedom in Christ while the freepersons subject themselves to Christ as their master. However, whether slave or free, all of the elect may remain as they are. Just as circumcision and foreskin are nullified in Christ, so too in him are the states of slave and free equivocated. Since they were bought, their lives are not their own (7:23; see also 6:19–20), and so they must live as their new Lord and master assigns. The second set of lines explains that a slave may become free, but believers, slave or free, must not become slaves to people (perhaps also in marriage; see above, 7:12). The phrasing that "each is to remain in this state," as when called—slave or free—is repeated

---

24. Thielman, "Law," 239.

25. a´: (x) 20/ *Each is to remain in the state* in which he was called.

(y) 21/ If you were called as a slave, it is not to be a concern. But if you are able, by all means, *seek to be* free.

(z) 22/ For the slave who is called in the Lord is the Lord's free person; likewise the free person who is called is Christ's slave.

(y´) 23/ You were bought for a price: do not *try to be* slaves of people.

(x´) 24/ *Each in the state* he was called, brothers and sisters—*in this* one must *remain*, as from God.

in both bracket lines (7:20, 24), but the latter underscores that each receives their state by God's will.

This element explains and completes the argument of the B′ unit (7:17–24) as a whole. Paul's commands for all his churches to walk as the Lord Christ assigns in the situation "God" calls "each" is clarified in that "each" must remain as he is because it is a direct command from "God." The "Lord" has the power to assign these statuses at election (*a*, 7:17) because the slaves are bought by the "Lord" for freedom and the free believer is indebted to the "Lord" (*a′*, 7:22–24). Since the states of Jew and Gentile are subordinated to keeping God's command in remaining as they are, and since the states of slave and free are equivocated for the elect in the cross and subsequent Lordship of Christ, they have no need to radically change their worldly status aspects. And, since God has called them to peace, they should remain as they are (7:24).

Paul's treatment of slavery must be delicate. On the one hand, Roman culture considered slaves the sexual property of their owners, and so their status in the pure body of Christ could possibly be compromised (5:1–13; 6:9–20).[26] On the other hand, Paul has no ability to manumit all of the slaves who receive the faith. The latter would certainly result in a violent reaction from the local authorities. So he wishes for them to seek freedom through legal manumission, if at all possible. Since there is no mention to the contrary, we must assume that Paul did not consider the sexual role that slaves would be forced to engage with pagan masters as a disqualifier from the community.

Within the context of the A unit, however, we can assume Paul did not allow Christian owners to use their slaves as sexual objects. Marriage is the only acceptable medication for burning lust. This is further reason why Paul must remind the masters of Christ's lordship over them. Whether or not they have the legal right under Rome's customs, their slaves are not to be used for sexual purposes any longer.

Unit A′, 7:25–40: Focus on the Lord as the World Fades Away

a: 25/ Now, about those yet to be married, I do not have a command from the Lord, but I give direction as one who has been shown mercy by the Lord to be faithful. 26/ So I think this is good (καλόν): because of the imminent calamity, it is good (καλόν) for a person to remain as he is. 27/ Are you bound to a woman? Do not seek divorce. Are you divorced from a woman?

---

26. For an excellent article on this otherwise commonly overlooked point, see Glancy, "Obstacles," 481–501.

Do not seek another woman. 28/ But even if you marry, it is no sin (οὐχ ἥμαρτες); and if a virgin (παρθένος) marries, she does not sin (οὐχ ἥμαρτεν). But they will have worldly afflictions, and I would want to spare you from that.

b: 29/ This is what I'm saying, brothers and sisters: the time is short. So from now on, those who have wives should live as though they do not have them, 30/ and those who are crying as if they were not crying, and those who rejoice as if they were not rejoicing, and those who are buying as if they held on to nothing, 31/ and those who use the world (κόσμον) as if they did not use it. For the present form of this world (κόσμου) is passing away.

b′: 32/ And I want you to be without worry. 33/ For the unmarried man is worried about the Lord's matters, how to please the Lord; but the married man is worried about the world's (κόσμου) matters and how to please his wife, 34/ and he is divided. Also, the unmarried woman and the virgin are worried with the Lord's matters in order that they might be holy in body and spirit—but those who marry worry about the world's (κόσμου) things, and how to please her husband. 35/ And I say this to benefit some of you, not to tie you up, but that you be properly devoted to the Lord without distraction.

a′: 36/ But if anyone thinks (νομίζει) he is acting indecently toward the virgin (παρθένον) to whom he has been betrothed, or if the time is right and it ought to be so, let him do as he wishes—he does not sin (οὐχ ἡμαρτάνει). Let them marry. 37/ But if he steels his heart steadfast—not having anxiety, but rather authority over his own will—and decides this in his own heart to keep the virgin as his betrothed, he will do well (καλῶς). 38/ So the one who marries his virgin (παρθένον) will do well (καλῶς), but the one who does not marry will do better (κρεῖσσον). 39/ A woman is bound in marriage for the time her husband lives. But when he dies she is free to marry whom she wishes—but only who is in the Lord. 40/ But she will be happier if she remains as she is, in my opinion. And I think I also have the Spirit of God.

Regarding Unmarried and Widows (a), 7:24-28

Just as Paul felt it best for a man not to touch a woman in the A unit, in the A′ unit Paul returns to what is best in marriage. The initial principle of sexual abstinence is correct because of the approaching calamity of Christ's return—namely, it is good for a person to remain as they are. He has no command from Christ for the unmarried or engaged couples, but he has been entrusted to opine on the topic. One married should not divorce, and one divorced should remain so; but if the unmarried chooses to marry there is no sin. Because, although the approaching calamity should necessitate vigilance of the elect in remaining as they are, the potential for immorality and its detrimental effect on the salvation of believers makes necessary the concession that they be allowed to marry without fear of sin.

Life in a World that Is Passing Away (b, b'), 7:29–35

The *b* element (7:29–31) builds on the idea of the calamity stated earlier and restates that the time is short. For this reason, just as the elect's worldly status aspects were nullified before in Christ, now, in light of his return, his elect should live in a way that is unconcerned with the regular patterns of their worldly lives, be it in marriage and commerce or the emotions of crying and rejoicing. All worldly matters are neutralized because the form of this world is passing away and the reign of Christ in the Spirit is initiated via the prayer of the church and their sanctification. In this elected state, believers should set themselves apart and await their inauguration to glory at Christ's return.

The *b'* element (7:32–35) supports and explains the principle of eschatological life seen in the *b* element with a focused interest on marriage. The reason why Paul says that believers should live as though they are not married is because the time is short, the world and its customs are fading, and he does not want them to worry in vain about worldly matters (7:34). The view that marriage is a distraction from higher thinking was found in some contemporary pagan scholars.[27] His initial statement, that they should be free from worry, is half correct: anxiety over Christ is admirable. But married believers who focus on their spouses and the "world's" matters are anxious in vain because "the world" they are using is passing away. They should instead be concerned about what their Lord, who has bought them as his own, desires for them. This element then explains the *b* element, but also supports the initial thesis of the unit that the unmarried should remain as they are.

Better to Remain Unmarried and Widowed (a'), 7:36–40

The closing element contains a micro-ring structure.[28] The central lines of the element (7:37, 38) offer ideal and exceptional ways of life. One may mar-

---

27. Such as in Antipater, Hierocles, and Epictetus; see Yarbrough, *Gentiles*, 41. See also a lengthy discussion on the topic in Deming, *Marriage*, 53–61.

28. a': (x) 36/ But if anyone thinks he is acting indecently toward the virgin to whom he has is betrothed, or if the time is right and it ought to be so, let him do as *he*

ry without sin and "do well," but ideally he should be able to steel himself and "do better" by remaining unmarried and without anxiety. The bracket lines (7:36, 39–40) offer that a man who wishes to marry may do so without sin, and a widow may remarry another believer whom she wishes. As a seal of authority on all of the instructions he has given so far regarding marriage, and in anticipation of a presumed resistance in the audience, Paul declares that he has God's Spirit, and thus the authority to interpret and teach regarding these matters (7:40). The defensive tone presumes that some of the ascetics in the audience would view Paul as compromising too much from the ideal sanctified state.

The a' element restates the concession of the a element, but adds a preference. A young man or virgin "do not sin" if they marry, but "do well" if they remain unmarried (a, 7:25–29), just as a young man or widow also "do well" and may marry without sin. *However,* those who steel themselves with discipline to remain unmarried "do better" (a', 7:36–40). In this regard, Paul is demanding a fair amount from the community. Roman law viewed marriage and childbearing as each individual's duty to the Empire.[29] To remain unmarried and childless by choice would be viewed as *impietas* and further stigmatize members in the group that already refused traditional patron gods and customs. But his comments are based on an eschatological principle—life in the end times should be focused on the Lord, not on the things of a world that is passing away. Therefore, believers do best to remain as they are.

---

wishes—he does not sin. Let them marry.

(y) 37/ But if he steels his heart steadfast—not having anxiety, but rather has authority over his own will—and decides in his own heart to keep the virgin as his betrothed, he *will do well.*

(y') 38/ So the one who marries his virgin *will do well,* but the one who does not marry *will do better.*

(x') 39/ A woman is bound in marriage while her husband lives. But when he dies she is free to marry whom *she wishes*—but only who is in the Lord. 40/ But she will be happier if she remains as she is, in my opinion. And I think that I also have the Spirit of God.

29. Witherington, *Conflict,* 174.

Marriage, the Family, and the World, 7:1-40

INTERRELATION OF UNITS

Outline

Concession to Marriage (A, 7:1-9)

Paul responds to questions and agrees in principle with the ascetics' position that it is "good" (καλόν) for a man not to touch a woman, such that he considers it "good" (καλόν) for unmarried and widows to stay as they are. But he offers as a concession, not a "command" (ἐπιταγήν) that, due to the temptation for immorality, one may marry and "give" (ἀποδιδότω) themselves over to another (7:4-6). The spouses' "authority" (ἐξουσιάζει) over each other's bodies protects them from burning and temptation. Likewise, although Paul prefers for unmarried and widows to remain like him, he feels it is "better" (κρεῖττον) for them to marry than to burn with the rest (7:9).

Paul Recommends to Stay Married, Unless Impossible (B, 7:10-16)

Believers should not immediately divorce their non-believer spouses. The marriage may remain where spouses live in agreement. Since believers should not be "enslaved" (δεδούλωται) to marriage that is abusive, and because God "called" (κέκληκεν) the elect for peace (7:15), the members should divorce if the non-believer demands it.

Remain as You Were When God Called You (B´, 7:17-24)

The believers' status at the time of their "calling" (κλήσει, 7:18) remains central to their life and is to be viewed as God's will. Whether Jew or Gentile, slave or free, the believer should remain as they are when "called" (ἐκλήθη, 7:18-24). Although a slave should seek manumission if possible, they should recognize that "slaves" (δοῦλοι, 7:21-23) are free in Christ, and the free who are "called" (κληθείς, 7:22) become Christ's "slaves." Since they were all bought for a price, they must not become "slaves" to people (δοῦλοι, 7:23). In light of 6:9-20 and 7:1-9, Christian masters should not sexually abuse their slaves. Instead, they must follow the command of their new master Christ and remain faithful to their wife alone.

Beyond What Is Written

Focus on the Lord as the World Fades Away (A´, 7:25–40)

Paul "concedes" (ἐπιταγήν, 7:25) that, because of the coming calamity, it is correct for the believers to remain as they are, whether married or single. The time is short, and the world and its conventions are fading away. During this time, Paul prefers for Christians to be concerned with remaining holy in "body" (σώματι, 7:34) and spirit, rather than attending to marital duties. And so an unmarried Christian who has control over his desires and chooses not to marry does "well" (καλόν, 7:26). One who does marry does "well" (καλῶς, 7:38) and does not sin—but the one who refrains from marriage does "better" (κρεῖσσον, 7:38). Paul has no command regarding these matters, but offers instruction according to his understanding of the faith with which the Lord had entrusted him.

Conclusion

The pivotal and parallel B (7:10–16) and B´ (7:17–24) units focus on the negative theme of slavery and positive theme of "election" or "calling" to put forward an over-riding principle for the problems that Christians deal with in their lives outside the community. It is within the tense topics of divorce, slavery, and status that Paul outlines a guideline for the Corinthians' reference in any future situations: do not be "enslaved" to other people (or your own desires), and try to remain in the same status as when "called" since God has "called" the elect to peace. That is, God calls them to have peace in their sanctified lives from worldly concerns and also have peace with him in the hope of future glory.

The use of these terms in the B´ unit shows a development in Paul's argument from their use in the B unit. That the community is not to allow any brother or sister to be "enslaved" to a non-believer in marriage (B, 7:10–16) is developed and explained in that the "slave" who is called to the Lord is a freeperson in Christ, and the freeperson who is called is a "slave" to Christ (B´, 7:17–24). So, the pivot units argue, the believers' allegiance is to Christ first, even superseding that of marriage to a non-believer, because they either gain their freedom from him or lose it under him.

That God has called the elect to peace, such that they should not be compelled to remain unmarried when a non-believer divorces them, is balanced by the B´ unit that directs the audience to accept their place in life as when they were "called"—whether circumcised or Gentile, slave or free. Because each of the elect are bought for a price, the meaning of circumcision and status of freedom are nullified in the Lord. In all cases, they are not to be slaves to imperial custom, culture, or other people, but only to Christ. They are also to remain in the peace in which God has called them in Christ.

Thus the central units argue that, while baptism does not (and cannot) affect one's social status, it does nullify the social statuses within the community itself. This encompasses the major cultural institutions of marriage, slavery, and ethnocentrism. The distinctions that are made in these categories in the outside world (married, divorced; slave, free; Jew, Gentile) are now nullified through baptism and the "peace" that God has brought to the elect. Because he has bought them for a price with Christ, the believers can no longer be "enslaved" to social conventions or outside judgments. Nor should believers view one another with worldly standards. While God conquers the cosmos in Christ, he calls the elect to reconciliation without enmity. In political terms, God has colonized the world and its foolish rules but has made a treaty with the elect, to the effect that the elect can no longer be dominated (or "enslaved") by the rules of a corrupt society. As such, the elect should view one another no longer as "slave" or "free," "married" or "unmarried," "conqueror" or "colonized." Regardless of their social status outside the church, all are equivocated to the same inherent status, namely, that they are all in treaty with God.

The bracket units are forwarded on the themes of the Lord's command and Paul's concessions as an authoritative interpreter of the Christian tradition. Since he agrees with the ascetics in principle, but fears temptations for the community, he "concedes" (but does not "command") that the Corinthians should be married. That he is able to authorize marriage in the A unit is explained in the A′ unit when, in the absence of a "command" from the Lord regarding virgins, Paul states that he can give "concessions" as one who has been found worthy and entrusted by the Lord Jesus to speak to the elect on his behalf.

The audience is also encouraged to have authority over the bodies of their spouses. The unmarried are better-suited to keep their "body" and spirit holy for the Lord's return, and those who are unmarried should have "authority" over their desires (A′, 7:34–37). These points underscore marriage's role of protecting the elect from external sin by each spouse "having authority" over the other's "body" when the individuals cannot discipline themselves as Paul does.

Last, but certainly not least, Paul underscores in these units a preference regarding marriage that everyone should be like him. So he agrees in principle with the ascetics that it is "good" not to touch a woman, and it is "good" for widows to remain like him, just as it is "good" for virgins and all the sanctified to remain as they are in light of the coming calamity (7:26). But, since it is "better" to marry than to burn with lust, Paul "concedes" that a man or woman who marry do "well," in that they do not sin. But, he adds, in keeping with his agreement with the ascetics, the unmarried Christian does "better" by comparison (A´, 7:38).

In sum, Paul's primary preference in 7:1–40 is that the Corinthians be like him, living expectantly for the parousia, free of distraction from the world. But this is not possible for numerous reasons. So his next preference is that they live in peace—both with those inside and outside the community. He states this preference positively with the direction that they remain in life as they were called. This implies that, although baptism does radically change one's relationship with God, it is not intended to radically change one's life or status in society, with regard to marital or civic duties. A baptized person, then, is not precluded to a life of celibacy. One may remain sanctified in marriage. The integrity of sanctification and peace are the keys to Paul's teaching in 1 Cor 7. The former is not lost in marriage; and marriage can actually protect it. But when the marriage cannot continue with a non-believer, then peace must be sought, even if in divorce. These practical teachings are summed in a general rule of thumb that it is best to remain in the place of your calling.

8

Eating Disorder in Corinth, 8:1—11:1
Section B, Ring Set α´

ANALYSIS OF UNITS

HAVING ADDRESSED THE MATTERS pertaining to sexuality and relationships in the previous ring sets of this central part of the letter (5:1—7:40), Paul will conclude Section B with a discussion on Christian freedom and love for one's neighbor in the midst of the common practice of eating outside the community. The exact problems that required Paul's response are debated. What is clear is that one contingent of the Corinthian group (perhaps the libertines) continued to frequent Greco-Roman temples in the city for social gatherings and ate what was offered them, including meat sacrificed to the deities on these premises. This group believed their spiritual knowledge absolved them of any guilt for attending such services. They knew there was only one God, and there were no actual gods being worshipped at these sites. However, another contingent in the community considered such behavior to be scandalous. Paul now argues to mediate both sides of the issue by emphasizing the virtue of self-sacrifice and the duty of the free individual to work for the good of the whole.

Beyond What Is Written

Unit A, 8:1–6: God Is All in All

a: 1/ Now, concerning food offered to idols, I recognize that "we all (πάντες) have knowledge (γνῶσιν)." Now knowledge (γνῶσις) puffs up, but love edifies. 2/ If someone thinks that he knows (ἐγνωκέναι) something, he does not yet know (ἔγνω) what he must know. 3/ But if someone loves God, this one is known (ἔγνωσται) by him (αὐτοῦ). 4/ Now, concerning eating food that is sacrificed to idols, we recognize that there are no idols in the world and that there is no God but One (εἷς).

b: 5/ For although (εἴπερ) there are so-called "gods" (θεοί)—whether in heaven or on earth—

b′: and although (ὥσπερ), there are many "gods" (θεοί) and many "lords,"—

a′: 6/ For us there is one (εἷς) God, the Father, from whom all things (πάντα) have their origin, and toward him (αὐτοῦ) we move; and one (εἷς) Lord Jesus Christ—through whom all things (πάντα) originated, and through him (αὐτοῦ) we exist. 7/ But this knowledge (γνῶσις) is not with everyone (πᾶσιν).

The One God Is Known by Love and Knows those Who Love Him (a), 8:1–4

The opening unit begins with a micro-ring element.[1] The central line contends that one who thinks he knows something does not actually know what is most important. This is because, as the adjacent *y* and *y′* lines (8:1b, 3) explain, love is more important than knowledge in comprehending God and his will. Knowledge puffs up, but love builds up. "Knowledge" is superficial; love is substantive. The element is bracketed by the repeated phrase, "now concerning food sacrificed to idols," and the agreement that "we have knowledge" (8:1a, 4).[2] The repetition of the phrase underscores the fact that, although he agrees that there are no "gods" behind these sacrifices, Paul must address this issue and denounce those who eat idol meat because of

---

1. a: (*x*) 1/ Now, *concerning food* offered to idols, *I recognize* that "we all have knowledge."
(*y*) Now knowledge puffs up, but *love* edifies.
(*z*) 2/ If someone thinks that he knows something, he does not yet know what he must know.
(*y′*) 3/ But if someone *loves* God, this one is known by him.
(*x′*) 4/ Now, *concerning eating food* that is sacrificed to idols, *we recognize* that there are no idols in the world and that there is no God but One.

2. Horsley, "Gnosis," 32–33, argues that Jewish Hellenists who emphasized knowledge are at the root of the contention here. This particular form of Judaism was naturally opposed to Paul's apocalyptic Judaism.

118

how it has affected relationships between the church's members.³ That this one God can be known best through love will become a prominent theme as the argument develops.

The term "idol food," or "meat sacrificed to idols," is polemical and innately denounces the recipients of the sacrifices as non-gods.⁴ Meat was rarely eaten (and almost never by the poor), but meat that was sold at market often had been sacrificed to a Greco-Roman deity of some sort. This does not become as much of an issue, however, as does meat that might be consumed at a deity's temple during some sort of religious rite.⁵ The line that "we all have knowledge" likely is a slogan from the Corinthian letter to Paul that he now cites in his response. As he did with the ascetic faction in 7:1, he agrees with this group in principal, but disagrees with how they execute their slogan in daily life.⁶

Many So-Called "Gods," but Only One Creator of All Things (b, b´, a´), 8:5–7a

The central elements (8:5a, b) concede that there are many so-called "gods" that others in Corinth might worship or acknowledge. The many temples in Corinth certainly were used for sacrifices to various Greek and Roman traditional deities, including Aphrodite, Asclepius, and Isis (among others). Paul tacitly decries these "so-called gods," whether in heaven or earth. Jewish tradition recognized spiritual powers that affected events on earth and daily life. These were at times called "daemons." Although spiritual entities, they were not considered to be "gods" themselves. They did not take part in the creative process of the earth and they were not perfect. In fact, many were viewed as corrupt or malicious.⁷

In contrast to the many "gods" and "lords" in the central elements, the a´ element (8:6–7a) pulls the unit together by returning to the issue of knowledge and the One God.⁸ Although the non-elect have their many gods who are distilled of power by their sizable number, the elect have spiritual knowledge of "one" God (8:4), whom they can call Father (8:6) because of their fellowship with his Son, their "one" Lord Jesus Christ. The description

---

3. Brunt, "Rejected," 120–21.
4. Witherington, *Conflict*, 189.
5. Ibid.
6. On the letter and slogan, see Fitzmyer, *First Corinthians*, 338.
7. Arnold, *Powers*, 94–95.
8. On the presence of the "strong's" slogans in 8:1–9, see Fotopoulos, "Arguments," 619–21.

of "one" for Jesus and the Father presents them as singular and powerful sources of creation, in contrast to the many weaker "so-called gods" (8:5–6).[9]

Although Paul concedes in the *a* element (8:1–4) to the Corinthian faction's slogan that "we all have some knowledge" of the One God, in the *a´* element (8:1) he will add the caveat that "this knowledge" is not distributed in the same degree to all. "This knowledge" likely refers to all that is said about God and knowledge following the slogan, including that he is known best through love (8:2–3) and that he is the ultimate source of creation (8:6). "All things" includes the gifts the elect receive through Christ.[10] Paul's critique of the Corinthians' slogan is that, although they all have "knowledge" about God, their "knowledge" about living for him is incomplete without understanding the role of love in that relationship.

Unit B, 8:7b–13: The Weak Are Abused by the "Knowledge" of the Strong

a: 7b/ When some, who are so accustomed to idols up to now, eat meat sacrificed to idols, their conscience, being weak, becomes defiled. 8/ Now, food (βρῶμα) does not commend us to God: if we do not eat, we do not fall short; nor, if we eat, do we do better.

b: 9/ But see that your (ὑμῶν) freedom does not become an obstacle to the weak. 10/ For if someone sees you (σέ) who have knowledge (γνῶσιν) at table in an idol's temple, will not their (αὐτοῦ) weak conscience be emboldened to eat meat that is sacrificed to idols?

b´: 11/ So the weak member for whom Christ died perishes on account of your (σῇ) knowledge (γνώσει)! —the brother for whom Christ died! 12/ So when you who sin against a brother or sister and strike their (αὐτῶν) weak conscience you also sin against Christ!

a´: 13/ Therefore, if food (βρῶμα) scandalizes my brothers, I do not eat meat—ever—so that my brother might not fall.

Food Is Not Absolute, but Discretion for Others Is (a, b) 8:7b–10

The B unit builds on the final idea of the preceding unit, namely, that the Corinthians might all have knowledge, but the knowledge they have is

---

9. Giblin, "Monotheistic," 530, notes that Paul could also here mean, "no one deserves to be called God but One."
10. Ibid.

incomplete. Their so-called freedom has blinded them to the indirect consequences their actions have on others. Apparently citing an actual situation evolving in the community, Paul claims that some (the "weak"), having gone to such pagan rites their whole lives, do not share the same perspective or spiritual "knowledge" that enables the strong to eat idol food. The defiling of the conscience does not refer to being scandalized by viewing fellow elect members partaking in temple sacrifices. It refers more to the weak thinking it is acceptable to continue practices that naturally affirm the existence and power of this presumed deity, and the subsequent guilt they feel.[11]

Anticipating a sharp response, Paul interjects that he knows food does not determine salvation (8:8). Rather, it is what one does with the food in relation to a so-called deity that is of issue. In the *b* element (8:9) Paul warns the strong not to let their so-called "authority" through knowledge corrupt the weak. Doing so would embolden the weak to also eat idol meat, but, without the particular "knowledge" that the strong maintain, they may backslide into pagan customs of patronizing multiple deities.

The terms "strong" and "weak" likely come from the Corinthians' letter to Paul and are polemical in the "strong" group's favor.[12] Paul uses these terms in response to the letter, but likely does not himself view the groups in the same manner. Clearly, as he will present to the so-called "strong" group, their "strength" is a limited knowledge of Christian love that actually harms their "weak" brother. Although Paul agrees with their principle and presents himself as "strong," he is critical of them and actually sides with the "weak."

An Offense to a Brother Is an Offense against Christ (b´, a´), 8:11–13

The parallel *b´* element (8:11–12) underscores that the strong faction's "(your) knowledge," along with "their (your) freedom," embolden the weak to eat idol food and subsequently perish. An aspect the strong applauded as a spiritual strength in fact defiles their brother or sister, for whom Christ died, and therefore acts as an offense to Christ.

So how exactly does the weak member "perish"? What could be at work here is that, while the strong take part in the sacrifices like actors in a play, the weak see them and view their actions as affirming the common Greek practice of associating with more than one deity. The weak then also take part in the meal but also engage in the ceremonial and theological

---

11. On this view, see Gooch, "Conscience," 250. He also recommends reading "conscience" in 8:1–13 not as an internal moral compass, but as a type of self-consciousness or anxiety over guilt.

12. See Dunn, *1 Corinthians*, 60.

aspects inherent in such rituals. For instance, sacrifices at dining rooms in pagan temples were intended to create a relationship between the deity and the participants. Acting in this meal was an exchange and barter: the participant offered a sacrifice in order to receive a favor, or patronage, from the deity.[13] The believer "perishes" because his relationship with God, which is determined by grace through fellowship with Christ, is nullified by dependence on a secondary deity. The strong's "strength" is shown to be a horrendous liability.

Emphasizing the overall thrust of the unit, the *a'* element (8:13) returns to the issue of food in general. Even though Paul agrees with the strong that "food" has no bearing on one's salvation (8:7), he nonetheless would refuse any type of "food" if it caused another believer to stumble (8:13). He presents himself as a model of what true strength is: having an "authority" or right to do something, but refusing to do it in order to benefit others. His example will provide the foundation for the next major unit that follows.

Unit C, 9:1–27: Paul's Life as Example of Self-Sacrifice

a: 1/ Am I not free? Am I not an apostle? Have I not seen Jesus our Lord? 2/ Even if I am not an apostle to others (ἄλλοις), I certainly am to you. For you yourselves are my seal of apostleship in the Lord. 3/ My defense to those who would judge me is this: 4/ Do we not have the authority to eat and drink? 5/ Do we not have the authority to take along a wife as the rest of the apostles, and the brothers of the Lord, and Cephas? 6/ Or do Barnabas and I alone not have the authority to work?

b: 7/ Who has ever fought a war with his own resources? Who plants a garden and does not eat his own fruit? Or who shepherds a flock and does not eat of the milk of the flock? 8/ Am I speaking in human terms, or does not the Law (νόμος) say these same things? 9/ For in the Law (νόμῳ) of Moses it is written, "You shall not muzzle an ox while it is threshing." The ox is not a concern to God. 10/ Or what do all of us say? For it was written for us that the one who threshes and the one who plows by hope will have a share. 11/ If we sow spiritual things among you, should we not reap from you some material?

c: 12/ If others have a right to share with you, do we not even more? But we do not make use (ἐχρησάμεθα) of this authority; rather, we endure everything, in order that we might not give any hindrance to the gospel of Christ. 13/ Do you not know that the priest eats of the work of the temple, or that

---

13. Ferguson, *Backgrounds*, 147.

those who make the sacrifice at the altar share in that sacrifice? 14/ In the same way, the Lord arranges that those who proclaim the gospel should make their living from the gospel. 15/ And I have made use (κέχρημαι) of none of these things.

d: Now I do not write these things for myself, or for these things to be done for me. For I would rather die than that! No one will empty out my boast (καύχημα)!

d′: 16/ Now if I preach the gospel, it is no boast (καύχημα) for me—for the burden is imposed upon me. I'll be damned if I do not proclaim the gospel!

c′: 17/ For if I do this willingly, I am compensated. If I do it unwillingly, I am entrusted with a stewardship. 18/ So what is my compensation?— That by proclaiming the gospel free of charge I might not make full use (καταχρήσασθαι) of my authority.

b′: 19/ Being free from all things, I made myself a slave to all so that I might gain the masses. 20/ So, for the Jews I became a Jew, so that I might gain Jews. For those under the Law (νόμον) I became like one under the Law (not that I myself am under the Law (νόμον))—so that I might gain those under the Law (νόμον). 21/ To those without the law (ἀνόμοις), I became as one without the law (ἄνομος)—not that I am not without a law (ἄνομος) before God, but rather am subject to the Law (ἔννομος) of Christ—so that I might gain those without the law (ἀνόμους). 22/ I became weak for the weak so that I might gain the weak. I became all things to all people so that I might save anyone. 23/ And I do all things through the gospel, so that we might become sharers with it.

a′: 24/ Do you not know that in a foot race, everybody races, yet only one takes first prize? In the same way, run so that you win. 25/ And those who train abstain from everything to gain a material crown, but we do it to attain an eternal crown. 26/ So I do not run aimlessly, nor do I punch at the air. Rather, I control my body and pull it under subjection, lest we become like other (ἄλλοις) proclaimers who are disqualified.

Diatribe Regarding Paul's Apostolic Rights and Deferrals (a, b), 9:1–7

The rhetorical questions that open the pivotal C unit imply that Paul is a free apostle who has seen the Lord Jesus and received a commission from him to preach the gospel. That alone should qualify him as an apostle but, to buttress his argument, he contends that he is certainly an apostle to the

Corinthian church. They are, in fact, the seal of his apostleship (9:2) in that their reception of the Spirit from his preaching verifies that he was sent by Christ. Paul further contends that those who may judge him must recognize that he knows an apostle's rights, which include the benefits of commensality and companionship. If other apostles can receive these, why should not he, who is proven as an apostle to this community?

The *b* element (9:5–7) adds support with examples prevalent in an agricultural society. The audience knows that a soldier, a field hand, and a shepherd do not bring their own materials for work, but are paid with plunder, harvest, and milk, respectively. Next Paul points to the Law's prohibition against a muzzled ox as proof that an apostle should not be denied his wages. In addition to the other examples above, the Mosaic Law (Deut 26:4) mandates that he has the right to receive wages from the Corinthians for bringing the Spirit to them (1 Cor 9:10–11).

It is possible that some members of the community had offered Paul amenities during his time in the city, but he demurred because he worried this would entitle them to favors from him, or hold him in debt to them in some way.[14] The terms "strong" and "weak" may have developed in the community along status-oriented lines, and those who sought patronage over Paul claimed to be the "strong."

Proclaiming the Gospel to Others (c, d), 9:8–15

Yet the *c* element (9:11b–15a) develops further in a micro-ring structure that Paul does not make full use of his absolutely clear apostolic rights that were outlined in the *a* and *b* elements (9:1–8) above.[15] The central *z* line (9:13) of the element gives an example followed by an emphatic response. Does not the priest of a ritual have a right to eat of his work at a temple? Of course! Even so, Paul has a right to "eat" and make use of the benefits suited to a working apostle. The next layer of lines contends that he endures all

---

14. Cf. Dunn, *1 Corinthians*, 60–62. D. Martin, *Slavery*, 77–80, also views the argument as a "fictitious defense" that molds a particular view of Christian leadership rather than responding to a situation of patronage in Corinth.

15. c: (*x*) 12/ If others have a right to share with you, do we not even more? But we do not *make use* of this authority;

(*y*) rather, we endure everything, in order that we might not give any hindrance to the *gospel* of Christ.

(*z*) 13/ Do you not know that the priest eats of the work of the temple, or that those who make the sacrifice at the altar share in that sacrifice?

(*y'*) 14/ In the same way, the Lord arranges that those who proclaim the *gospel* should make their living from the *gospel*.

(*x'*) 15/ And I have *made use* of none of these things.

things in his ministry so as not to hinder "the gospel of Christ" (*y*, 9:12b), even though Christ ordered that those who preach the "gospel" should make their living from the "gospel" (*y´*, 9:14). The thesis statement of the element is repeated in the brackets: Paul absolutely has a right to these benefits among the Corinthians, but he "has not made use" (*x*, *x´*, 9:12, 15) of them so that he does not hinder the message of the gospel. Continuing the diatribe against an invisible opponent, the *d* element (9:15b) defensively states that Paul does not write such things for himself, but rather proclaims the gospel only for others. He would rather die than be robbed of his boast in his ministry for others.

Recompense for Preaching the Gospel (*d´*, *c´*), 9:16–18

The *d´* element (9:16) confirms that Paul's goal in proclaiming the gospel is to benefit others, not himself. His boast is not in his own accomplishments, but rather in proclaiming the gospel to the elect whom God has called to be in fellowship with Christ, who died to buy back the elect from the power of sin so that they might be washed in baptism with the Holy Spirit to become sanctified, redeemed, justified, and enlightened with spiritual knowledge (1:4–9, 30; 6:15–20).

So his "boast" is that he brings the elect the opportunity to attain the glory of God in Christ through faith in the gospel. He refuses to be robbed of his "boast" because it is not a "boast" in himself. Paul's faith in Christ is what brings him salvation—but preaching the gospel that brings salvation to others is his recompense. The gospel he preaches is not the means of his salvation, but the means by which he proclaims the good news that he has already accepted in Christ.[16]

The *c´* element (9:17–18) develops further that Paul's boast is the fact that he does not make full use of his absolutely clear apostolic rights[17] that were outlined in the *a* and *b* elements (9:1–8) and reconnects to the argument of the *c* element (9:9–11). While in the *c* element (9:12–15a) Paul states that he does not "make full use" of his apostolic rights in order not to hinder the gospel of Christ, in the *c´* element (9:17–18) Paul clarifies that his true recompense in preaching the gospel without "making full use" of patronage is the ability to boast that he does it for others and Christ. To take hold of these benefits would mean that he is preaching for himself, and thus is just

---

16. According to Nasuti, "Dynamics," 257–59, Paul distinguishes himself from prophets such as Jeremiah who lamented their ministry as a burden. Paul instead rejoices and boasts in the opportunity to preach the arrival of a new age.

17. Fee, *First Epistle*, 417.

"doing a job."[18] But if he preaches the gospel for others without benefit, then he is truly "free" in that he is devoted and indebted to Christ alone (9:1). Whatever opinion the "strong" have of themselves, they can learn about true "freedom" from Paul's example of self-sacrifice. True strength is not accessing a benefit that is rightfully yours but, rather, in refusing to indulge in it. Such is the root and goal of the gospel.

Self-Discipline as a Key to Living the Gospel (b´, a´), 9:19–27

The b´ element (9:19–23) moves forward to present in a micro-ring Paul's polymorphic pastoral style as a model of Christian life for the "strong" to imitate.[19] Paul presents four major groups that have required his self-discipline and sacrifice to evangelize: 1) Jews, 2) law-observant Jewish Christians or God-fearers, 3) Gentiles, and 4) "the weak" (seen earlier in 8:1–13).[20] The center-most lines address the objects of Paul's evangelization and their respective relationship to the Mosaic "Law." He is willing to observe the "Law" and allude to it in his preaching of the gospel to God-fearers and newly-converted Jews who still view their traditional customs as necessary for salvation (9:20b). Likewise, he is willing to act like the "lawless" Gentiles when he preaches to them (9:21), perhaps meaning that he preaches Christ in a manner that pagans would understand (as seen in Acts 13 or the Thessalonian correspondence). In both cases, Paul's point is that, although he is a Jew who is not under the Law, but also not lawless before God (only subject to the Law of Christ), he does not allow the Law or his background

---

18. Ibid., 420.

19. b´: (x) 19/ Being free from *all things*, I made myself a slave to *all* so that I might gain the masses.

(y) 20/ So, for the Jews *I became* like a Jew, so that I might gain Jews.

(z) For those under the *Law* I became like one under the *Law* (not that I myself am under the *Law*)—so that I might gain those under the *Law*.

(z´) 21/ To those without the Law I became like one without the Law—not that I am *without a law* before God; rather, I am subject to the *Law* of Christ—so that I might gain those *without the Law*.

(y´) 22/ *I became* weak for the weak so that I might gain the weak.

(x´) I have become *all things* to *all* people so that I might save anyone. 23/ And I do *all things* through the gospel, so that we might become sharers with it. (This structure is also noted by Garland, *1 Corinthians*, 427.)

20. These four categories are debated points, and I veer from the majority in my allocation of the second and fourth groups. Many scholars view the first two groups as referring to Jews, and the third to Gentiles. The identity of the fourth group has led to strong debate, with suggestions such as those who are theologically weak (Fitzmyer, *First Corinthians*, 354), non-Christians (Garland, *1 Corinthians*, 432–37), or Christians who still felt obliged to follow Jewish dietary customs (Barrett, *First Epistle*, 215).

Eating Disorder in Corinth, 8:1—11:1

to become a deterrent to his audiences—the focus must be on Christ as the center of his message.

The next layer of lines contains the verbs that are implied in the center of the micro-ring. In the y line, Paul claims that he "becomes" (or acts) like a Jew in order to win Jews to the gospel. Examples include his travels to preach in synagogues and his strict concern for maintaining ritual purity when visiting Jerusalem (Acts 21). Paul states even stronger in the parallel y' line that he "becomes" weak (*not* "like the weak") in order to gain the weak to the gospel. In both cases, Paul implies that he veers from his regular lifestyle and instead defers to the sensitivities of his audiences so as not to offend them or affect their reception of the gospel. The center must be Christ, not himself. That Paul becomes "weak" further embodies a modeling of Christ in reflecting the weakness of the cross. Thus his previous affirmation of the "weak" is not poor leadership; it is, in fact, proper pastoring because it encourages others to reflect the weakness of the cross in their daily lives with one another.

The bracket lines of the element establish the thesis and conclusion of the micro-argument. Although free from "all things," Paul has subjected himself to being a slave to "all" in order to win or gain the masses to the gospel. The lowering of oneself from the status of a citizen to that of a slave is the equivalent of death or non-existence.[21] Paul has essentially forfeited his own life and well-being in order to "gain" more (x, 9:19). This gain is explained in the final line in which Paul has become all things for all people in order that he might save anyone (x', 9:22b–23). Paul eliminates himself from his message so that he does not affect the audience's reception of the Spirit in the gospel.

Whereas in the b element "the Law of Moses" demands that an apostle have rights to food and other benefits (9:7–11), the b' element presents "the Law of Christ" as the example for self-sacrifice (9:19–23). So whereas the "Law of Moses" gives Paul the right to receive benefits for preaching the gospel, the "Law of Christ," i.e., Christ's example of power through weakness and self-sacrifice to benefit others, compels Paul to demur from his rights for the sake of others (9:12).

The a' element (9:24–27) completes this pivotal C unit as a whole as it argues that, while Paul might not be considered qualified to preach the word by "others" (preachers and Corinthians alike), he should be to the audience because he sowed the Spirit among them successfully, and, even more so, because he did not make full use of his apostolic rights. In the example of Christ, following the Law of Christ, he trained himself so as not

---

21. D. Martin, *Slavery*, 82–84.

to hinder the gospel, but offered a full demonstration of Christ's example in self-sacrifice. As such, he is even more qualified as an apostle of Christ than the "others" (a´, 9:27) who preach and also take advantage of the benefits. In the C unit as a whole, Paul presents a lesson on strength to the "strong." If they truly wish to be "strong" they must become like the "weak" Paul, so as to discipline themselves and strive to love their fellow believers.[22]

Unit B´, 10:1–19: Look at Israel's Example

a: 1/ For I do not want you to be unaware, brothers, that all (πάντες) our ancestors were under the cloud and all went through the sea. 2/ And all (πάντες) were baptized into Moses in the cloud and in the sea. 3/ And all (πάντες) ate the same spiritual food, 4/ and all (πάντες) drank the same spiritual drink. For they all (πάντες) drank from the same spiritual rock that followed. And that Rock was Christ (Χριστός).

b: 5/ But a majority of them did not please God (θεός) and their ruin was scattered over the desert. 6/ And these things happened as an example for us (ταῦτα δὲ τύποι ἡμῶν), so that we do not become fanatics for wickedness, as they desired wicked things. 7/ Nor should you become idolaters like them, as it is written, "The people ate, and drank, and rose up in idolatrous debauchery." 8/ We must not lust after idols, as they lusted after idols, and twenty-three thousand of them fell (ἔπεσαν) in one day.

c: 9/ We must not tempt the Lord[23] as they tested him—by (ὑπό) serpents they perished (ἀπώλλυντο)!

c´: 10/ We must not murmur as they murmured—by (ὑπό) the hand of the destroyer they perished (ἀπώλοντο)!

b´: 11/ Now, these things happened as an example for us (ταῦτα δὲ τυπικῶς ἡμῶν), and were written for our instruction—for we who stand at the end of the ages! 12/ So the one who considers how he stands must be careful that he does not fall (πέσῃ). 13/ You have encountered merely natural temptations. God (θεός) is faithful, so that you will not be tempted beyond your power; rather, he will test you so that you pass and empower you to endure.

a´: 14/ Therefore, my beloved, flee from idolatry! 15/ Consider what I said and judge for yourselves what I say now: 16/ Is not the cup of blessing with

---

22. Fee, *First Epistle*, 422.

23. *Pace* NA[27], I find the support of the variant Χριστον to be heavily influenced by the Western tradition. I instead prefer the reading κυριον, which has admirable attestation (א B C P 33).

which we bless a sharing of Christ's (Χριστοῦ) blood? Is not the bread we break a sharing in Christ's (Χριστοῦ) body? 17/ Though we are many, we are one bread and one body because we all (πάντες) partake from one bread. 18/ Consider Israel according to the flesh! Are not those who eat of the temple sacrifice sharing together at the altar? 19/ So what am I saying? For what is idol food and what are idols to us?

Israel's Baptism and Fall in the Desert (a, b), 10:1–8

Pulling away from the self-example of Unit C (9:1–27), in Unit B´ Paul returns more directly to the issue of idol meat, using ancient Israel's example as a type from whom the community can learn. Paul recalls God's miraculous grace in rescuing the Israelites in the Exodus from Egypt, and presents the passage through the sea as a type of baptism.[24] After which, they all ate manna (spiritual food) and drank water from a rock (spiritual drink), who was, in fact, Christ, who followed them. Their baptism and life with God seemed secure.

The *b* element (10:5–8), however, begins purposefully with a strong "but." Despite the incredible grace bestowed on the Israelites, Scripture explains that problems arose: many did not please God, and they were struck down in the desert (Exod 32–34; Num 14:28–38). These events are mentioned in Scripture, Paul explains, so that the audience might learn from them and not make the same mistakes. The element closes with imperatives and an example. The Corinthians are instructed not to give in to their desires or lust after idols. The example of Israel, who ate, drank, danced lustfully after idols, and then fell shows the consequences of such behavior. Corinth's members, who are also God's sanctified people, now stand at a turning point in a desert of their own: baptized, followed by Christ, and now also tempted—just like Israel.

These two initial elements together warn the audience that election does not promise salvation. After all, the Israelites were sanctified, and they all ate of the same spiritual food and drink, yet that was not sufficient to keep some of them from falling prey to their own desires. In the same way, the "strong" (perhaps some being libertines) cannot expect their spiritual transformation in baptism and the sharing of the Eucharist to give them a free pass to continue eating idol meat at temples.[25]

---

24. Hays, *Echoes*, 87: "Paul has a disconcerting habit of adducing scriptural prooftexts whose pertinence to his argument is not immediately evident."

25. See Hays, *Echoes*, 91.

Beyond What Is Written

Central Exhortation: We Must Not Test the Lord (c, c'), 10:9–10

The central *c* element (10:9) holds the unit's key exhortation that the elect must not test the Lord. The Israelites were said to "test" God and murmur in the desert, and it proved fatal for many. In light of the B Unit (8:7–14), "testing the Lord" would refer to eating idol meat and corrupting the "weak," for whom Christ died (8:8–12). The parallel *c'* element (10:10) also warns against any type of "murmuring," or dissent against God, his plan, and the leaders he sets over his people. Given that the Israelites often murmured with regard to how Moses was leading them through the desert (Num 12–16), this line could be an implied refutation to those who have been questioning Paul's qualifications as their apostle and spiritual leader. Both offenses bring the same end for the Israelites: they perish in the desert, never to see the promised land.

The New Elect Must Learn from the Example of Ancient Israel (b', a'), 10:11–19

Following the pivotal exhortations for the community not to test the Lord but, rather, rally around Paul without dissent, the closing elements of the B' Unit engage more closely the practices of the audience in Corinth. While the *b* element (10:5–8) states that "these things happened" for "our" (the contemporary elect's) benefit and "were written" so they do not succumb to their desires to continue eating idol meat, the *b'* element (10:11–13) develops this further to say that "these things happened" and "were written" for the benefit of the eschatological people in Corinth who stand at the end of the age. Paul sees the Corinthians and himself as the pinnacle of God's plan, and thus anything that happened prior must be for educating those who must pass the final series of tests at the close of the age. Further, those who consider themselves to be standing firmly now in their election (i.e., the "strong") must watch that they do not "fall" (*b'*, 10:12) like the Israelites who also were baptized, and yet ate and drank with lust for idols and "fell" in the desert (*b*, 10:8).

The *a'* element (10:14–19) concludes this major section with a micro-ring structure.[26] At the center of the element (*z*, 10:17), the eschatological

---

26. a': (x) 14/ Therefore, my beloved, flee from *idolatry*! 15/ Consider what I said and judge for yourselves what I *say* now:

(y) 16/ Is not the cup of praise with which we praise a *sharing* of Christ's blood? Is not the bread we break a *sharing* in Christ's body?

(z) 17/ Though we are many, we are one bread and one body because we partake from one bread.

people who partake of the one bread in the Eucharist, although many persons, are united in the one Body of Christ, who is the glorious Lord and the nexus of all creation that is being renewed (8:5-6). This tenet of faith is flanked by rhetorical questions which demand the audience to recognize that this one bread they eat is the body of Christ, and this cup of praise, with which the eschatological people praise God, is a "sharing" in Christ's blood (*y*, 10:16), just as the Israelites who sacrifice at the altar "share" of the food together in God's presence (*y´*, 10:18). It is in the Eucharist, as the united body of Christ, that the elect find the presence of God most fully. Being one in Christ, the Corinthians are transformed to encounter God in a substantive manner as the elect whom he called, sanctified, and justified to be renewed into the creatures that he envisions them and empowers them to become (1:31; 10:12-13).

The bracket lines of the element (10:14-15, 19) return more forcefully to the matter of idol food. Following everything that Paul has stated earlier in the unit, he demands that they take counsel from the example of Israel and flee from idol food. The element closes with rhetorical questions that link back to the opening line, demanding the audience to ask what in fact idol food means to them in light of what has been said about their spiritual ancestors in the desert.

The *a´* element (10:15-19) also connects back to the *a* element (10:1-4) to focus on Christ's prominent role in their place as ancient Israel's eschatological successors. In the *a* element, "all" of the audience's spiritual ancestors were baptized by Moses, and they "all" ate of the same food and they "all" drank from the same drink, which came from Christ. But the audience, God's eschatological people, "all" share in one bread, one body, who is Christ (*a´*, 10:17). The audience is also warned by the example of their Israelite ancestors because, while "Christ" followed them in the desert, they still fell (*a*, 10:4). Yet, these things happened to give the elect at the end of the age a better opportunity to succeed in God's plan for salvation.

Now, for the eschatological people, including those in Corinth, Christ is not outside, but inside as well. He is not merely following them through the desert; rather, they have been bound in Christ by the Spirit to become God's righteousness, redemption, wisdom, power, and glory (see 1:30). They are not merely moved from one territory to another, but rather, from human existence to an eternal place in God's presence, and from the present corrupt age to the renewed age of God's kingdom.

(*y´*) 18/ Consider Israel according to the flesh! Are not those who eat of the temple sacrifice *sharing* together at the altar?

(*x´*) 19/ So what am I *saying*? For what is *idol food*, and what are *idols*, to us?

Beyond What Is Written

Unit A´, 10:20—11:1: Do Not Do What You Can, but Do What Is Right for All

a: 20/ No. Rather, what non-believers[27] sacrifice, they sacrifice to demons, not to God. I do not want you to become (γίνεσθαι) intertwined with demons. 21/ You cannot drink of the Lord's cup and the cup of demons, and you cannot share (μετέχειν) in the Lord's table and the table of demons. 22/ Should we try to test the Lord? Are we stronger than he is? 23/ "Everything is lawful," but not everything is beneficial (συμφέρει). "Everything is lawful," but not everything edifies.

b: 24/ Do not seek your own benefit, but seek that for others (ἑτέρου). 25/ Eat any meat that you buy at the market without any judgment (μηδὲν ἀνακρίνοντες) by your conscience. 26/ For the earth and all its fullness belong to the Lord.

b´: 27/ If a non-believer invites you, and you wish to go, eat everything that is given to you without any judgment (μηδὲν ἀνακρίνοντες) on your conscience. 28/ But if someone says to you, "This is idol food," do not eat it, in deference to the one who warned you, and because of the conscience— 29/ I am speaking not of your conscience, but of the other's (ἑτέρου).

a´: Now "why should my freedom be limited by someone else's conscience?" 30/ Or, "if I thank God for what I share (μετέχω), why am I despised for the food for which I give thanks?" 31/ In reply, whether you eat or drink—or whatever you do—do everything so as to glorify God. 32/ Become (γίνεσθε) blameless before Jews, Greeks, and God's church— 33/ just as I strive always to please everyone in all things, not seeking my own benefit (σύμφορον) but that of the many— so that you might be saved. 11:1/ Become (γίνεσθε) imitators of me, as I am of Christ!

You Can Not Have Fellowship with Both Demons and Christ (a), 10:20–23

The opening element of this A´ unit (10:20—11:1) responds immediately to the questions that closed the B´ unit (10:1–19). What concerns Paul is not that idols are real. —They are not. Rather, his concern is with the elemental forces that, although not divine, maintain a supernatural presence around pagan altars and temples. In Paul's view, these elemental powers trick pagans into thinking that gods are truly present and then gain strength from

---

27. "Non-believers" is added to clarify the general pronoun "they" in the Greek.

the sacrifices that are inadvertently made before them.[28] Finally, Paul's main contention against attending pagan temple rites is not the food itself, or that there are other gods, but the fact that those who attend these rites share in the presence of demons.

Sharing here is not merely a problem because of proximity. The action of taking food within these rituals created a relationship between the participant and the supernatural force to whom the sacrifice was made.[29] In this case, the demons become patrons to those who receive the sacrifice and become bound in a relationship with the other participants at the temple. For Paul, this is unacceptable behavior for the elect. To share in this food means that they have decided God is not almighty and require the aid of other elemental powers. They are, to a degree, co-opting God's authority over the earth.

The final lines of the element are clearly directed toward the so-called "strong" group. Their attempts to continue at the temples, in light of the B′ unit's example (10:1–19), is dangerously close to falling in the same pattern of testing God as Israel in the desert. They might be "strong," the next rhetorical question implies, but they are certainly not stronger than God, who has saved them by choosing the weak and lowly of the world to be his elect (1:18—2:5). Underscoring a connection between the demographics of the "strong" group and the libertines addressed in 5:1—6:20, Paul again repeats the slogan that "everything is lawful" for a baptized member who is free from their previous lives because of the Spirit. But he again repeats that just because one *can* do something does not mean that they *should*. Not every action benefits or edifies others (10:23).

Guidelines for Benefiting Others Pertaining to Idol Food (b, b′), 10:24–29

Having addressed the issue of idol meat negatively and mocked the "strong" and their slogans, Paul now offers positive guidelines for everyday situations involving meat. In the *b* element (10:24–25) he states plainly that they should seek the benefit of others, not merely their own gain. They may eat any meat that is bought at the market. Even though this meat was likely sacrificed to some Greek deity, it is not a part of a formal rite at a temple. It is not partaken in the presence of demons and, as long as it is eaten at home, does not offend any of the so-called "weak" who do not see the member eating it. They may do this without "judgment by their conscience" because the

---

28. On daemons and temples, see comments above in Unit B (8:7b–12).
29. Ferguson, *Backgrounds*, 147; and see above in the section regarding 8:1–6.

meat itself is not a problem. After all, creation (and everything in it) belongs to the Lord (10:25).

But, the *b′* element (10:27–29) warns, there are other situations to watch. If invited to a non-believer's house to eat, they should eat everything that is given to them without "judgment by their conscience," for the same reasons they may do for any meat bought at the market (*b*, 10:25).[30] But, if someone informs them that this meat was in fact idol meat, then they should defer to the greater good and not eat it. The identity of the anonymous informant could be a host who is sensitive to Christian and Jewish monotheistic sentiments,[31] or it could be another believer who is also at the event and who is more anxious about the food's origins. In either case, Paul's point is that one should defer to, rather than offend, the conscience of the informant; and he goes so far as to clarify this point with an additional parenthesis.

Partake and Do Everything to Glorify God (a′), 10:29b—11:1

Having addressed the guidelines for common food situations the audience might encounter, Paul now anticipates a strong rejection of his demands. The question, "Why is my freedom limited by someone else?" (whether it appeared in the Corinthians' letter, or whether he merely conjectured it from their ideology) embodies the "strong" group's presumed response to Paul's instruction. He then counters the nature of the true problem, and links back to the *a* element (10:20–23) of the unit. One who partakes of idol food at a ritual "shares" fellowship and patronage with demons (*a*, 10:21-23). The problem with idol food then is not one's innate freedom. Rather, since one is giving thanks to God for this food, if they know it is idol meat sacrificed in the presence of demons, how can they "share" and give thanks for food that symbolizes a relationship with a supernatural entity other than the one almighty God (*a′*, 10:30)? To do so would be blasphemy, and endangering to their salvation and that of others. There is no "strength" in such an action—merely foolishness.

The element, unit, and ring set close with final exhortatory principles. Paul demands that they do everything to glorify God, whether with food or anything else. They should not "become" intertwined with demons and relationships with other elemental powers (*a*, 10:20). As God's elect, they should "become" blameless before all people—Jews, pagans, and especially

---

30. According to Gooch, "Conscience," 250–51, "judgment by their conscience" here refers to the principle that one must not be a stumbling block to others" in v. 32.

31. See Witherington, *Conflict*, 227.

their own community of God's church. After all, this is their rightful identity that they are to pursue, even though they live in a non-believing world (6:12–20). They can do this best by becoming imitators of Paul, who demonstrates Christ's self-sacrifice in his ministry (2:1–5; 9:1–27). Just because they have complete freedom does not mean that their actions are "good" (10:23). They should instead glorify God by seeking the "good" of others. This service and love toward others, not their spiritual knowledge or freedom, is what will solidify their relationship with God and their salvation.

INTERRELATION OF UNITS

Outline of Units and Sub-Sets

To this point, the units in the ring sets corresponded directly to one another. However, in situations where multiple units converge, it is possible to have two or more units form a sub-set in which lexical terms in the outermost units demonstrate cohesion that transcends the singular unit delimitations.[32] In this case, the A and B units form sub-set A, the C unit is itself sub-set B, and the B´ and A´ units form sub-set A´. The A (8:1–13) and A´ (10:1—11:1) sub-sets are delimited by the repetition of the important terms "edify" (οἰκοδομεῖ), "food" (βρώσεως), "conscience" (συνηδείσιν) and "watch" (βλέπετε). The B sub-set is marked by Paul's self-defense and terminology peculiar to chapter 9.

Idol Meat in Corinth, Sub-set A (Units A, 8:1–7a, and B, 8:7b–13):

Paul writes regarding "food" (βρώσεως) sacrificed to idols (8:4) because, although the "food" (βρῶμα) they eat cannot affect their relationship with God (8:7b), it can affect their relationships with fellow believers when the "food" (βρῶμα) scandalizes others and affects their conscience (8:13). When the strong exercise their freedom to eat idol meat the weak can be harmed because their "conscience" (συνείδησις) is "built up" (οἰκοδομηθήσεται) to eat idol food (8:10). As a result, the weak experience regret or a desire to backslide to pagan customs. This scandal of harming a brother's or sister's "conscience" (συνείδησιν) is equal to sinning against Christ (8:12), who

---

32. This is an acceptable variation on the methodology proposed by Lambrecht and Heil (see chapter 1) in that it is an organic development of observing lexical connections within the text. Given that the unit structures are fluid within the realm of performance, so too may larger formations of the progressing lexical repetitions develop larger patterns within the argument as it is performed.

died to save the "weak" as well as the "strong." Paul encourages the "strong" to "watch" (βλέπετε) that their alleged rights do not hinder the weak (8:9) and to recognize that comprehension of the One God is incomplete without love. Knowledge puffs up (8:1–3), and so one can only attain a complete relationship with God through love that "builds up" (οἰκοδομεῖ) the body of Christ to God's glory (8:3).

Paul's Example of Freedom through Self-Denial, Sub-set B (Unit C, 9:1–27):

The apostle presents himself as an example of denying one's own rights and benefits in order to serve and save others. Paul has many apostolic rights, but he denies these so as not to hinder the gospel in his proclamation to diverse groups. His boast is not in his authority or power in these rights, but in his ability to deny himself in order to provide salvation to others.

Ancient Israel as Example, Sub-set A´ (Units B´, 10:1–19, and A´, 10:20—11:1):

While the Corinthians argue that their so-called freedom should not be hindered by another's weak "conscience" (συνείδησιν, 10:28), they must "watch" (βλέπετε) that they do not fall to temptation (10:12) like their spiritual ancestors of Israel who also ate spiritual, God-given "food" (βρῶμα, 10:3). Paul agrees that everything is lawful, but not everything "builds up" (οἰκοδομεῖ) the body of Christ (10:23). So the Corinthians should be mindful and "watch" (βλέπετε) that they, by serving the needs of others, act in a manner that glorifies God. This consists not in taking full advantage of one's so-called spirit-empowered "rights," but in acting in a manner that does not bring judgment on the "conscience" (συνείδησιν) of other believers.

Conclusion

In the central B sub-set (Unit C, 9:1–27) of this ring set, Paul relinquishes his apostolic rights so as not to burden his communities, but rather, that he might receive the fullest recompense for his work. His focus is always on gaining more, whether Jew or Gentile, to the gospel. He adapts to his audience in order to diminish his own impact on the people, so that the gospel might win over all, despite his own limitations. As such, he offers an example to the Corinthians who claim to be "strong" and demand to continue eating meat sacrificed to idols at temples.

The unit/sub-set is placed strategically as a digression of sorts to demonstrate Paul's leadership by example. This pattern has been seen previously in this letter in 2:6–13 (within 1:18—3:3) and 4:1–5 (within 3:3—4:21). In each case, Paul presents himself as a model for a particular spiritual trait that the audience should follow: spiritual wisdom (2:6–13), deferring to the Lord's judgment (4:1–5), and now love for one's brother or sister in Christ (9:1–27).

The "weak," for whom Paul admonishes the strong in the A and A´ units, are one of the groups whom Paul himself claims to serve by denying his own rights for their benefit and salvation (9:20–23). While Paul's "brother" apostles take advantage of their rights, he encourages the Corinthians to exert caution. Believers should defer to their weak "brothers" since harming a "brother" is equivalent to sinning against Christ. The "rights" that the Corinthians claim do not make all of their actions ipso facto "right." True "freedom" is found in discretion. Paul claims to be "free" not because he has rights, but because he chooses to decline them. It is the "power" to defer one's rights that shows one to be truly "free"—both with regard to others and one's own desires.

The bracket sub-sets emphasize the root purposes of the church are to provide edification and spiritual nourishment. Whereas food is normally seen as nourishment for a "body," here "food" is a major issue that divides God's sanctified church in Corinth. The issue has flared up and requires Paul's comment because the "strong" in the audience have argued that their freedom should not be hindered by the "conscience" of the weak. Paul offers that they can eat meat from a market—but not at a temple—out of respect for the other's "conscience." He even goes so far as to say that they should defer to the concerns of a conscientious host who informs them of some food's sacrificial status (10:25). Since a believer's scandalized "conscience" can be moved to eat meat and return to earlier pagan practices, Paul warns the "strong" that any actions that harm the conscience of their brother or sister are a direct offense against Christ.

Paul agrees that "food" in itself cannot condemn the audience. But neither can their election guarantee the Corinthians' absolute indemnity. After all, the Israelites ate spiritual "food" but fell in the desert due to the temptation to idolatry. If the "strong" cause their "weak" brothers and sisters to stumble in their faith because they insist on upholding their own freedom to eat idol "food," then they have sinned against the body of Christ by severing its holy members.

Beyond What Is Written

Paul's demand that the Corinthians should "watch" that they do not fall (10:7) is clarified by the earlier admonition that they should "watch" that their authority does not scandalize a fellow believer (8:9). In short, Paul wants the audience to do all things for the edification of their community. Yes, the Corinthians have rights and knowledge, but not every action "edifies" (10:23). A negatively affected conscience can be "edified" to patronize with demons and idols. Instead, Paul focuses not on knowledge as the center of the Corinthians' relationship with God, but love. Love for others is what truly edifies the body of Christ and binds one into a renewed relationship with God. So whether Jew or Greek, strong or weak, believer or non-believer, love is the true standard by which the Corinthians should govern their actions and relationships outside of the community.

INTERRELATION OF RING SETS

Outline

"Everything Is Lawful," but One Believer's Sins Affect the Whole Body of Christ (α, 5:1—6:20)

This ring set conveys Paul's responses to three major issues in the church at Corinth: (1) a man who was living with his stepmother; (2) prostitution, sexual immorality, and backsliding into other pagan practices (perhaps even some form of idolatry); and (3) Christians were suing one another before pagan officials. Feeling empowered by the Spirit, some Corinthian members responded to challenges with the slogan, "Everything is lawful to me" (πάντα μοι ἔξεστιν, 6:12). In terms of sexuality and food customs they state that "'food' (βρώματα) is for the belly and the belly for 'food'" (βρώμασιν, 6:13). But Paul rejects their slogans and counters that not all things bring unity or edify the whole, and God—not the elect—is the ultimate arbitrator of both food and the belly.

Paul warns the audience not to backslide into their former lives of "idolatry" and sexual immorality since "idolaters" (εἰδωλολάτραι) and the sexually immoral cannot inherit the kingdom (6:9–11). So they must also guard against the threat of leaven in their holy community by "judging" those who backslide and threaten their holiness. They should not worry about "judging" outsiders, nor ask Paul to judge them—God will judge those outside the community. But they should take care to "judge" (κρίνετε, 5:4-5, 13) those in the community who act like those who are outside. Likewise, they should be able to "judge" (κρινέσθαι, 6:1) cases between brothers rather than sue before pagan civic authorities. They will, after all, "judge" (κρίνεται, 6:4) angels and people at Christ's return (6:1–8). Surely, then, they can have the faculties to guard the sanctity of Christ's body through deliberate juridical processes.

Believers Should Remain as They Were Called and Seek Peace (β, 7:1–40)

Paul responds to particular questions regarding marriage and divorce, but also puts forward guidelines for daily life. He concedes that marriage, although not ideal for the sanctified, is necessary at times for avoiding sexual immorality. So he encourages members to stay married when they can; but if a divorce is forced upon them, then they must divorce. This directive aims at peace, to which the elect have been called by God. They should remain as they were called— whether married or single, slave or free, Jew or Gentile— in order to remain in peace. But they should also not permit themselves, or other Christians, to be enslaved by non-believers.

"Everything Is Lawful," but those Who Are in Christ must Love and Seek the Benefit of Others (α´, 8:1—11:1)

Here we again hear the Corinthians' slogan, "Everything is lawful to me" (πάντα ἔξεστιν) and again Paul retorts that "not everything unifies or builds up" (οὐ πάντα οἰκοδομεῖ, 10:23). They should instead seek the good of others, not themselves. The major problem here is that the "strong" feel that they should be able to eat food that is sacrificed before "idols" (εἰδωλοθύτων, 8:3–5) at temples. After all, they claim, "food" (βρῶμα) does not affect one's relationship with God (8:8). And, they ask, why should their freedom be "judged" (κρίνεται, 10:29) by those with a weak conscience? But Paul retorts that, out of respect for his brothers and sisters, he would not eat any "food" (βρῶμα) that caused a fellow believer to stumble (8:13). As the example of Israel in the desert teaches, those who partake in spiritual "food" (βρῶμα, 10:3) may still perish. And, although they are free to eat anything at their own homes without judging their own conscience, they should defer to conscientious hosts and the concerns of their fellow believers when eating in public (10:27–28). Their so-called "knowledge" and "freedom" are trumped by the demand that they love one another.

Beyond What Is Written

Conclusion to Section B

The topic of how the Corinthians are to behave in relation to the outside world, now that they have been made into God's sanctified church in Christ, sets apart the B Section as a cohesive argument. The problems necessitating Paul's comments fall into four basic categories: 1) sexual immorality (5:1–13; 6:9-20); 2) lawsuits before civic authorities (6:1-8); 3) domestic issues, such as marriage, abstinence, divorce, slavery, and status shifts (7:1-40); and 4) partaking in idol meat at temples (8:1—11:1). Paul responds to these problems in three separate ring sets and, due to the repeated terms that connect the units into one cohesive argument, all of the principles that he puts forward in these individual sets give guidelines for the audience's daily life in a corrupt and fading cosmos.

In the α ring set (5:1—6:20), Paul instructs the Corinthians to keep the body of Christ holy and unleavened by excising any leaven, i.e., a brother or sister who remains too connected to the world (and thus their old lives). Leaven of this sort (be it sexual immorality or attachment to money and power through corrupt imperial courts) threatens the sanctity of the whole community. The β set (7:1-40) reminds the audience that they have been called to live in peace; and so they should not let themselves, or a brother, or sister be enslaved in a relationship that compromises their holiness. The α´ set (8:1—11:1) encapsulates these principles in two key guidelines: 1) actions demonstrate true freedom and authority when they are grounded in selfless love and concern for others and edify the whole body or act for the common good; 2) the Corinthians should imitate Paul just as he imitates Christ (11:1). If the Corinthians succeed in executing these guidelines for sanctified life, then they will remain holy in mind and spirit (7:24-28), as God has established them to be (1:4-9), as they await the return of their Lord Jesus Christ.

The β ring set's placement (7:1-40) presents largely domestic issues within a very apocalyptic light that intensifies the overall urgency and purpose behind Paul's exhortation. The Corinthians have been called to peace. As such, if married, divorced, widowed, single, slave, or Gentile—they should remain so. But if they must marry, or must divorce, then they should do so as is seen necessary. And if they can find legal manumission, then they should, by all means. But the place in life in which they are called is presented as, for the most part, divinely initiated. Therefore, being at peace with others and being at peace with God's intentions for one's salvation are significantly interrelated.

This β set, although often isolated from its setting, is rhetorically and lexically connected to its adjacent ring sets and inherently imbedded within its overall rhetorical context. Following the clear admonishment of the libertines in the α ring set (5:1—6:20), it serves to quell any exuberance from the ascetic pro-Pauline group. It also sets up the discussion about the domestic issue of eating meat and acting for the benefit of one's fellow believer, particularly by advancing the standard guideline of maintaining peace within one's relationships with others. Such a guideline is organically developed in the exhortation to love and seek the benefit of others in the α´ set (8:1—11:1). The β set also reminds the audience that they should avoid falling back into their old habits because the world is fading away as a result of the cross. To claim a right to sexual freedom or eating meat at temples seems a dangerous gamble when the judgment is so near and the stakes include nothing less than their own salvation.

There is remarkable lexical and rhetorical coherence between 5:1—6:20 and 8:1—11:1. Since "idolaters" cannot inherit the kingdom, and since the audience have been washed, sanctified, and justified from their previous lives in "idolatry" (α, 6:9, 11), Paul must strongly warn the so-called "strong" members that their consumption of "idol meat" may well lead other members to partake in food before "idols" in temples (8:10–13). This would in turn harm their conscience and thus afflict those for whom Christ died. This offense against Christ is severe enough to draw a didactic parallel. The Israelites were saved from slavery by God, but they then fell in the desert after worshipping a golden calf "idol" (10:3). Their example in Scripture is meant to teach the Corinthians to take a better path, which involves following Paul's example of Christ (9:19–23).

The repetition of the slogan, "Everything is lawful to me," addresses two different existing situations in the community that parallel one another. In the first use of their slogan (6:10) Paul decries their sense of sexual freedom; and in the second (10:23), the selfish irresponsibility of their actions and empowerment as a complete misuse of the Spirit they received in fellowship with Christ (1:4–9). In both cases, Paul challenges the slogans as short-sighted, selfish, and incomplete. In truth, although everything is possible or lawful, not every action edifies the community (6:12–13; 10:23–24). In the former, it is not their body alone, but Christ's body, that they affect: he redeemed them, and they belong to his corporate body that is shared by other believers (6:15–20). In the latter, they are called not to seek their own benefit, but that of others, since their knowledge of God can only be complete when they learn to love as he does (8:1–7; 10:20–31).

In the α set, a Corinthian slogan compares sexual desires to food that is necessary to eat: "food for the belly and belly for the food" (6:13). This view organically coheres with their later slogan that "food" does not affect our salvation or relationship with God in the α´ set (8:8). Paul challenges these views in their respective sets, but presents his total argument as the product of the development from the α to α′ sets. First, he counters that God is the arbiter of both the food and the belly, thus pointing out that "food" or desires can never be consumed outside of a moral category, or outside God's jurisdiction (6:13). He later points out that food is truly within a moral category when its deliberate consumption harms the conscience and salvation of other members, for whom Christ died to redeem them from idolatry and their sins (8:10–13). So food in itself is not bad, but when one's self-centered desires lead one to consume things (sex or food) that offend and harm others, then one's actions with that food can negatively affect their relationship with God as well. Israelites are put forward as a concrete example of the consequences such actions bring (10:1–19)—and the entire Section B serves as a strong warning not to follow down that same path. They are instead called to learn from it and embrace their identity as those who now stand at the end of the age (10:11).

9

Order in Worship and the Church, 11:2—14:40

Section A′, Ring Set α

INTRODUCTION

HAVING ADDRESSED HOW THE sanctified Corinthians should live among non-believers in the B section (5:1—11:1), Paul now returns to problems that are similar to how the letter started, namely, with internal dissent, factions, and theological misunderstandings. In the initial α ring set (11:2—14:40) of the letter's third and final section, Paul confronts misunderstandings and indiscretions in the church's worship practices while also reengaging the issue of church (dis)unity.[1] The result is a large arc of arguments on what it means to be a church that worships God as Christ's unified body. Although the Corinthians await a future realm of glory and are already being prepared to enter God's mysterious presence, it is apparent that their transformation is not yet complete. While they await a new world with absolute freedom and authority, they are still political tenants of Rome who live in Corinth.

---

1. Many recent scholars (e.g., Agosto, *1 y 2 Corintios*, 78) have criticized the arbitrary division between chaps 11 and 12 and prefer to view all of 11:2—14:40 as a discussion on order in worship, or as an oration on how the factions manifest themselves in the practice of worship (e.g., Margaret Mitchell, *Rhetoric*, 258).

And even when they receive their long-awaited authority in the resurrection, they will always be subject to God's will and order in creation.

Regarding 11:3b–15 and 14:34–35 as Interpolations

Based on the findings of this study with regard to lexical repetitions and performative structure, I have come to agree with several recent scholars to exclude 11:3b–15 and, further below, 14:34–35, from the letter's original structure. These texts appear to come from later correctors who inserted statements that limited the efficacy of women's participation in the liturgy.[2] The placement in 11:2–16 and 14:26–40 makes sense, since these would be the opening and closing units of what would otherwise comprise didactic and authoritative apostolic instruction on proper procedure within the church.[3]

I came to this conclusion after no short span of time and for the following objective reasons: (1) the overall structure of 11:2—14:40 coheres around 12:31b—13:13 as its pivot when 11:2-34 is collapsed into one unit (11:2-3a, 16-34); (2) the internal inconsistencies of these passages with

---

2. The position that 11:3b–15 is a later interpolation has been argued by at least seven separate scholars: Cope, "1 Cor 11:2–16," 435–36; Watson, "Voice," 520–36; Walker, "Women," 94–110; Trompf, "Attitudes," 196–215; Mount, "1 Cor 11:3–16," 313–40; and Munro, "Strange," 26–28. The list of scholars that views 14:34–35 as an interpolation is decidedly larger, including (along with the scholars mentioned above) Agosto, *1 y 2 Corinthios*, 109–11; Barrett, *First Epistle*, 330–32; Cleary, "Women," 78–81; Conzelmann, *1 Corinthians*, 246; Fee, *First Epistle*, 699–708; Furnish, *Theology*, 12; Hays, *1 Corinthians*, 245–49; Horrell, *Social Ethos*, 184–98; and Horsley, *1 Corinthians*, 196, among others.

3. Alfred Loisy, *Remarques sur la littérature épistolaire du Nouveau Testament*, 112, cited in Murphy-O'Connor, "Interpolations," 159, was the first to present 11:3–16 as an interpolation, but there was little following. Three quarters of a century later Walker, "1 Cor 11:2–16," 99–100, renewed the issue. He pointed to textual issues in 11:3 and 11:17 that call the content in between into question, and considered the discussion of women to break the contextual arguments about food and meals in 10:1–31 and 11:17–34. He further argued "this matter" in v. 17 appropriately refers back to the command set forward in 11:1 and moves forward the call to imitate Paul into his directives on living in accord with the eucharist. Lastly, idem, "Vocabulary," 75–88, he deduced that several terms are non-Pauline. Trompf, "Attitudes," 199–200, is persistent in demonstrating the lexical and theological connections between 1 Cor 11:3–16; 14:34–35 and texts from the Pastorals. See also Merkle, "Arguments," 527–48, who crystalizes a similar line of thought and argument from creation that is found in both 1 Cor 11:3–16 and 1 Tim 2:13–14. It is also notable that scholars (e.g., Lowery, "1 Cor 11:2–34") are at pains to explain the rhetorical connection or line of thought that connects the discussion on women to the eucharist in 11:17–34.) On 14:34–35, the dubious MS witnesses are of central concern to those who view the text as an interpolation. Most convincing on this is Fee, *First Epistle*, 699–708.

other Pauline texts; (3) the coherence of these texts with later works and/or interpolations; and (4), although well-crafted to fit their contexts, demonstrations within the particular units show 11:3b–15 and 14:34–35 are unnecessary to their particular ring formations, and, in fact, appear to be later intrusions.[4]

First, it should be recognized that the whole of 11:2—14:40 develops more clearly and coherently without 11:3b–15 and 14:34–35. In its present setting, the text of 11:2—14:40 falls into an eight-part schema:

A (11:2–16) // A′ (14:26-40): Gender and Order
(αἰσχρόν, "shame," ὑποτάσσω, "submit")

B (11:17–34) // B′ (14:14–25) no significant lexical connections

C (12:1–13) // C′ (14:1–13) no significant lexical connections

D (12:14–31a) // D′ (12:31b—13:13) no significant lexical or thematic connections

Under this paradigm, the initial concern is with head coverings (not the abuse of the Eucharistic meal) and the central units are, though important, not rhetorically or aesthetically parallel. While the A and A′ units share the key terms of "shame," "submit," "if anyone thinks," and "all the churches," half of those may be due to the interpolators' agenda. There are, however, no significant lexical correlations between the remaining pairs: 11:17–34 and 14:14–25; 12:1–13 and 14:1–13; 12:14–31a and 12:31b—13:13.[5] Of particular concern is how 12:14–31a, which is to act as a primary pivot unit that aids its parallel unit, has no thematic or significant lexical connection to the discourse on love in 12:31b—13:13.

The revised text presented here demonstrates a seven-part ring set that is more coherent with Paul's ultimate concerns of disorder and unity in the letter:

---

4. It is reasonable to note that I did not seek to argue for these points when I began investigating the ring formations in this letter. In fact, I sought to offer concrete lexical evidence that 14:34–35 belonged in the text. But, while pursuing the ring formations, the evidence became clearer to me that these were in fact interpolations. So I sympathize with those who are skeptical about these revisions. My hope is that the arguments for all of the units presented here will help to assuage your concerns and perhaps contribute further objective evidence to the conversation about the role of women in worship that must continue to be addressed across all denominations of Christianity.

5. Based on the criteria presented in the opening chapter, this study requires that there not only be lexical connections, but also that the words that are repeated have some particular significance to the author's argument or thought. See Blomberg, "Structure," 4–8; Douglas, *Thinking*, 11; Milinovich, *Now*, 24.

Beyond What Is Written

A (11:2-3a, 16-34) // A′ (14:26-33, 36-40): Order at Worship
(εἰ τις δοκεῖ, "if anyone thinks," 11:16; 14:37; πασαί ἐκκλησία τοῦ θεοῦ/ ἁγίου, "all the churches of God/ the sanctified," 11:17; 14:33).

B (12:1-13) // B′ (14:14-25): The Body's Diversity Grows the Community
(ἕτερος, "other," 12:4-10, 14:16-17, 21; ἄλλους, "different," 14:19; φανερώσις, "manifestation," 12:7; 14:25; πίστις/ ἄπιστοί, "faith, non-believer," 12:9; 14:22-24)

C (12:14-31a) // C′ (14:1-13): The Body's Diversity Edifies Each Part
(αποστολος [αποκαλυπσις], προφετης, διδακη/σκος, "apostles [revelation], prophecy, teaching," 12:28-29; 14:6; περρισούω, "abound," 12:23-24; 14:12; ζηλοῦτε, "zealously pursue," 12:31a; 14:1, 12)[6]

D (12:31b—13:13): Love Is the Key to Cohesion and Transformation
The oration on love and spiritual transformation acts as the physical and rhetorical center of Paul's argument.

The A (11:2-3a, 16-34) and A′ (14:26-33, 36-40) units admonish the community for divisions and challenge any dissenters to Paul's demand for order. The units in the body of the ring set—B (12:1-13), C (12:14-31a), C′ (14:1-13), and B′ (14:14-25)—develop the image of the community as a single body made of diverse parts. The central D unit (12:31b—13:13) is shown to be not merely a rhetorical "digression," but rather the pivotal unit around which the entire ring set turns and develops Paul's argument for unity within the church and worship.

These thematic and rhetorical parallels are affirmed by lexical repetitions that connect the multi-layered ring. The C and C′ units are connected by the repetition of "abound" (12:23-24; 14:12), "pursue" (12:30; 14:1, 12), and the triad "apostles/revelation, prophets/prophecy, and teachers/teaching" (12:28, 30; 14:6). The B and B′ units both emphasize the terms "manifest" (12:1; 14:25), "other" (12:8-11; 14:19), "different" (12:9-10; 14:21), and "faith" (12:9; 14:22-24). And the A and A′ both share the phrase "all the churches of God/the sanctified" (11:16; 14:33) and the rhetorical challenge

---

6. While the term "apostle" does not appear in the B′ unit, the aural connection between apost- / apok-, when combined with the supporting repetition of the two terms prophecy and teaching, offers sufficient lexical correlation between major terms to connect the two units. See Milinovich, *Now*, 99-106. Also, while the term prophet/prophecy is ubiquitous in this ring set, it is only combined with teaching and apostleship in these two units.

Order in Worship and the Church, 11:2—14:40

"if anyone considers to disagree" (11:16; 14:38).[7] These formidable connections are too rich and imperative to the overall message to be merely coincidental. Rather, they demonstrate an organic and effectively persuasive argument regarding the united nature of the community and necessary order—in structure, activity, and substance—in the worship assembly. These points alone can effectively bring the Paulinicity of 11:3b–15 and 14:34–35 into serious question.

Next, the content of the opening and closing units of the existing text in 11:2—14:40 presumes gender to be the major issue. However, the true causes of concern to Paul to this point in the letter have been not gender roles but division in the community, pneumatic abuses, and overall disorder. The revision of units 11:2–3a, 16–34 and 14:26–33, 36–40 adhere to that theme and retain the true focus of Paul's argument to covenantal and liturgical disorder.

So, although the later redactors did a fine job of recognizing the inherent ring structure and utilizing the existing terminology to build their interpolations, the revised text presented here is demonstrably more organic and coherent with Paul's overall concerns in the community. The introduction of gender roles merely offers a new snipe to hunt in an already problematic context for writing the letter, as evidenced by the numerous theories and studies that have sought a solution and explanation to the letter's sudden interest in gender in these two sections.

Dissimilarity with View of Women in the Undisputed Pauline Letters

Second, as is often noted (even by those who maintain the originality of the texts) the content and message of 11:3b–15 and 14:34–35 do not find significant parallels in other undisputed Pauline letters. In fact, we more often find the opposite. A key example is in Gal 3:28: "There is no Jew nor Greek, there is no slave nor free, there is no male nor female; for you are all one in Christ Jesus." But there is also the larger context of Paul's ministry to be considered.

Paul had many women co-workers whose ministerial activities would have required speaking within the context of worship. Phoebe, a deaconess, read the letter to the Romans to the churches of Rome (Rom 16:1, presumably within their house churches!) and also funded Paul's ministry as his *patrona*.[8] Prisca is mentioned as a co-teacher with her husband Aquila (Rom

---

7. These terms are exclusive to their respective units within this ring set.
8. Borg and Crossan, *First Paul*, 48. Perry, "Phoebe," 15–19, demonstrates that Paul's

147

16:3; 1 Cor 16:19; 2 Tim 4:19; also Acts 18:2, 18, 26).[9] The wealthy Euodia and Syntyche appear to be major leaders in the church at Philippi (Phil 4:2). And Paul even greets a woman named Junia whom he describes as "prominent among the apostles" (Rom 16:7), a rank that he considered the highest in the church (himself included), and would certainly entail preaching the message of the gospel in a church context.[10] The comments in chaps 11 and 14 in question are in no way compatible with how well Paul speaks of his female co-workers and his expectations of their ministries, which appear to include speaking, teaching, and leading communities (including both men and women).[11] It is also notable that, of the twenty-seven people that Paul names in his letter closures, ten are women; and of the eleven people who are especially praised or singled-out for the contributions to leadership and ministry, five are women.[12]

As one who has argued for the Paulinicity of these passages in the past, I can attest to the painful amount of rhetorical and logical gymnastics one must go through to adapt these passages to Paul's overall theology. These apologies for the texts include 1) contextualizing Paul's particular situation to Corinth,[13] 2) relativizing his words to be "progressive" for his time,[14] 3) attributing the statements in 11:4–9 and 14:34–35 to a misogynistic group

commendation of his benefactor to the Roman churches shows her to be a Gentile of high-status who is so appreciated among the Christian churches that he is able to call her "sister" and "deacon." As such, Phoebe was a walking representation of Paul's gospel to the Gentiles.

9. Kurek-Chomycz ("Tendency," 118–27) provides an excellent overview of such scribal biases against women ministers, even including the early witness of P[46].

10. On all of these, see the appendix in Keener, *Women*, 238–57. Despite the surmounting evidence of Paul's appreciation for women's ministry in the church that Keener himself presents, he still accepts 14:34–35 as authentic.

11. Beavis, "Egalitarianism," 47, 49: "An accurate historical account of Christian beginnings continues to include what Jane Schaberg calls 'struggles regarding egalitarianism,' not a perfectly realized social reality conforming to modern feminist ideals, but real efforts of women and men to coexist as equals, under a variety of conditions and understandings of the reign of God." Beavis' article is instructive in its correction to some theorists' objecting that the early church was in fact not egalitarian or concerned with gender equality. She adds "the use of fictive familial language by the *basileia* movement does not mean that the patriarchal family was the model for proto-Christianity any more than the language of [the kingdom of God] means that it was modeled on the Roman empire, except insofar as the *oikos* of God was a reaction *against* the traditional family as the *basileia* was an implicit repudiation of the Roman regime" [emphasis hers]. See also D'Angelo, "Women Partners," 65–86.

12. Borg and Crossan, *First Paul*, 50.

13. Wire, *Women*, 149–52; Witherington. *Conflict*, 284; Margaret Mitchell, *Rhetoric*, 260–62, 281.

14. Keener, *Women*, 88.

in Corinth that Paul indirectly quotes,[15] and 4) contouring the meaning of the word "woman" to be more exclusive and particular to the wives and husbands disagreeing in public.[16] The last argument has gained ground of late, but its proponents have yet to explain a significant obstacle. How can Paul say in 14:34–35 that wives cannot speak against their husbands, or that women are naturally inferior to men, when he consistently names Prisca ahead of her husband Aquila, thus denoting that the former was a more prominent teacher than her husband? While the revised text provided here may seem "radical," it actually requires less hermeneutical gymnastics than explaining the existing text in chapters 11–14.

Similarity to View of Women in Deutero-Pauline Literature

Third, although the lines in question do not sound like Paul, they do share many common ideas and terms with the later letters that are attributed to Paul. There is little question that 11:3b–15 and 14:34–35 share more in common with parts of 1 Timothy and Titus than with the view of women that is presented in Paul's undisputed letters.[17] For example, spouses of both genders are said to have authority over their partner (7:1–9), women are given the freedom to divorce an unbeliever when it is necessary (7:11–14), and widows are encouraged to live alone without a male authority in their lives (7:21–23). These views of women found in 1 Corinthians are much more in line with Gal 3:28.[18]

---

15. Shoemaker, "Unveiling," 60–63; Flanagan, "Put Down, 10–12." Against this view, however, one can point out that all other generally agreed upon indirect quotations of the Corinthians (1:11, 12; 2:15; 6:12–13; 7:1; 8:1–4; 10:23; 15:12) have distinctive markers of some sort (e.g., a strong ἀλλά, or a contradictory tone) that 11:2–16 and 14:33–37 lack.

16. Schussler-Fiorenza, *Memory*, 226; Dunn, *1 Corinthians*, 151. I also held this opinion in previous research and even earlier drafts of this chapter.

17. The debate regarding the authorship of the Pastoral Epistles has increased from a foregone conclusion toward the negative. While I appreciate those who have argued for Pauline authorship (and there are very good arguments for seeing 2 Timothy as authentic), I remain unconvinced that 1 Timothy or Titus could be penned by the apostle.

18. Garland, *1 Corinthians*, 258–60, points out that Paul's instructions in 7:1–9 provide more protection and respect to women's needs that did many of his contemporary philosophers, and Witherington, *Conflict*, 175, considers "his egalitarian treatment of the rights of each partner [to be] remarkable and [amounts] to a serious qualification of the status quo." Bassler, "Widows' Tale," 24: "When Paul himself presented his lifestyle as a Christian social alternative (1 Cor 7:8–9, 25–38) the effect was revolutionary: a choice was offered that would free women from the subordination that was then part of marriage."

The undisputed Paul honors female co-workers who read his letters to congregations in the church, teach, host dinners, and act as apostles. The disputed Paul and these questionable sections demand women to remain silent in the church. The undisputed Paul sees men and women as equal and united in Christ. The disputed Paul and these sections view them as secondary and devoted to their male counterparts.[19]

Consider these examples: 1 Timothy forbids women to teach or to have "authority" over men. She should instead "keep silent" and "learn in submissiveness." The logic behind this is that Adam was formed first, then Eve (1 Tim 2:8, 11 // 1 Cor 11:4–9). The majority, if not all, of the blame for humanity's fall is also placed on Eve (2:13).[20] The commands for silence and submissiveness are telling. The vocabulary is not entirely non-Pauline, but its usage is not found in such a manner anywhere else in the undisputed letters. In fact, even Ephesians (a debated letter itself) directs both men and women to be subordinate to one another in marriage and does not confine submissiveness to women alone (Eph 5:20–25).[21]

Other connections can be seen in the ideological focuses of the texts. In no other place does Paul put such attention on what Christian women can or cannot wear, yet both 1 Cor 11:3–15 and 1 Tim 2:7–11 view modest apparel on women as a form of worship by which they are able to give glory to God. Both of these texts also underscore women's role in childbearing as a key to their relationship with God, Christ, and humanity (1 Cor 11:12; 1 Tim 2:15).[22] These three texts also base their arguments for what women can or cannot do in the present on the stories of Genesis 2–3. Women are inferior to men, and must not have authority over them, because a) they are created from men (1 Cor 11:4–9; 1 Tim 2:13) and b) they are susceptible to deception and thus will inevitably lead men toward destruction (1 Cor 14:34–35; 1 Tim 2:10–14).

---

19. In a helpful excursus, Collins, *I & II Timothy*, 72–75, outlines how the view of women in the Pastorals (particularly 1 Timothy and Titus) is decidedly different from that found in the undisputed letters. For instance, while the undisputed letters mention nearly a dozen women as co-workers and ministers of Paul, the Pastorals make no mention of any specific female minister.

20. For additional side-by-side examples with Deutero-Pauline works, see Trompf, "Attitudes," 206. For a very accessible discussion on this topic, see Crossan and Borg, *First Paul*, 48–58.

21. Heil, *Ephesians*, 243–51, among others, notes how this particular demand by the author would be viewed as wildly progressive amongst the husbands and wives within the intended audience of first century Ephesus.

22. The emphasis on childbearing could be due to ascetic women who had decried marriage and family life. See Karris, *Pastoral Epistles*, 67–69.

In addition to socio-theological, there are also grammatical similarities between 1 Tim 2 and the contested passages in 1 Cor 11 and 14. (1) The awkward infinitive construction βούλομαι οὖν προσευχέσθαι in 1 Tim 2:10 bears particular resemblance to οὐκ ὀφείλει κατακαλύπτεσθαι in 1 Cor 11:7.[23] (2) The specific meaning of the verb ἐπιτρέπω for "permitting women to have authority over men" is found only in 1 Tim 2:12 and 1 Cor 14:34. Both texts echo and utilize the creation story of Eve in Gen 2–3 to argue that a woman who holds authority over a man is unnatural and leads to destruction.[24] (3) The texts in 1 Tim and 1 Cor 11 also share the particular phrase "what is proper for a woman [to do]." The peculiar verb πρέπω ("to seem right, proper") only occurs in the Pauline corpus in 1 Cor 11:3; Eph 5:3; 1 Tim 2:10; Titus 2:1. The term is even more striking in its context since elsewhere Paul uses καλόν for the same sense (1 Cor 7:1–9, 24–40).

The debated sections of 1 Cor 11:3–15 and 14:34–35 then cohere more with the Deutero-Pauline perspective which blames women for original sin, commands more of them than men in maintaining a modest appearance (1 Tim 2:9), and limits their ministerial faculties to childbirth (2:15). As such, I agree with the significant number of scholars who, for these reasons, prefer to excise 1 Cor 14:34–35 from its context. Furthermore, I echo the vocal minority that, on these same grounds, both 11:3b–15 and 14:34–35 should be considered interpolations to the original text.

Coherence within the Revised Units

Fourth, the revised sections 11:2–3a, 16–34 and 14:26–33, 36–40 may be shown to be inherent ring formations that pre-exist later Deutero-Pauline intrusions. The repeated terms and phrases "praise you" (11:2, 17, 22), "have/possess" (11:16, 22), "this matter" (11:16, 22), and "the churches of God" show 11:2–3a and 16–17 to be addressing the same situation that is then connected within an elemental micro-ring formation (*a*, 11:2–3a, 16–22) to its parallel line in 11:20–22. As will be explained in further detail below, "this matter," for which there is no precedent in God's other churches and for which Paul refuses to praise the Corinthians (11:16–17), is revealed to be "this matter" of the Corinthians' abuses at the Lord's Supper (11:21). Such unjust abuse seems to warrant the level of scorn seen here more than simple head coverings.[25]

---

23. Zamfir and Verhoye, "1 Timothy 2:8–10," 277–79.

24. On both these points, see Perriman, "Eve," 130–33.

25. Fishbane, *Interpretation*, 48, demonstrates how some ancient scribes recognized the inherent ring formation and adapted their comments to the follow the existing

As for the later text in 14:34–35, the textual problems and reasons for its exclusion are well-known, but there are also objective lexical criteria to show 14:26–33, 36–40 to work as a coherent unit. Without that later intrusion, v. 33b goes appropriately with v. 33a: "For God is peace, as in all the churches of the sanctified." This verse then joins vv. 36–38 to form the *b′* element that develops the earlier concern in the *b* element (14:27–32) about proper order in worship with the repeated terms "God" (14:28, 33, 36), "prophet" (14:29, 32, 36), and "spirit/ual" (14:32, 37). Without the interpolation, the revised central element retains the focus of proper order for prophets and spiritual participants during worship.

Process, Motive, and Consequences of the Interpolations

This part of the explanation can only be speculative. It appears likely that an interpolator utilized the terms from the earlier direction that prophets and tongues-speakers are to "remain silent" while another is "speaking in the church" and that the spirits of the prophets "must be subordinate" to the prophets when communicating the directives that women "must remain silent" and must not "speak in church" but "must be subordinate" to their husbands. The interpolator was sensitive enough to maintain the common term "shame" (11:7–10; 14:35) in both sections to add an additional connector between the initial and ultimate units in the ring set.

Having this major Deutero-Pauline ideal in place in the final unit of the ring set on worship, another pair of Paulinist views of women, namely, women's modesty and men's authority over them, were then added to the beginning of this discussion. Although further work is warranted for an in-depth redactional study of 11:2–16 and 14:26–40, brief observations may be made at this time.[26] First, the interpolator was able to make "this matter" of 11:3a, which refers to the Lord's Supper, refer instead to women's modesty and secondary status to men in relation to Christ in worship. Second, the interpolator was able to make women's silence in church as mandatory as basic group procedures like speaking one at a time (14:28–30). And third, the interpolator was able to leap-frog Paul's main interest in Corinth's abuse of the Lord's Supper in order to promote his own social ideology by making gender roles in worship the first and last concerns of the massive argument. So we should reconsider referring to these individuals as "pastors" or "stewards" of a tradition. They were more cultural activists than stewards.

structure in Ezek 31:1–18.

26. The redaction-critical questions behind these texts will be engaged in more depth in a future article.

Order in Worship and the Church, 11:2—14:40

ANALYSIS OF UNITS

Unit A, Disunity and Disorder at the Lord's Supper: 11:2–3a, 16–34

a: 2/ I praise you for everything of mine that you remember and for holding fast to the tradition I gave to you. 3/ But I want you to know that 16/ if anyone considers to debate this matter, consider this: we have no such custom, nor do any of God's churches. 17/ So of these reports I do not praise you: you do more harm than good when you come together (συνέρχεσθε). 18/ First, when you come together (συνερχομένων) there are divisions among you. And for the most part, I believe it. 19/ For there must be division among you in order that your "honored" ones might shine more among you. 20/ So, when you come together (συνερχομένων), it is not to eat the Lord's supper. 21/ For each takes his own meal when you arrive to eat, and some go hungry while others get drunk! 22/ Don't you have your own houses (οἰκίας) where you can eat or get drunk? Do you so despise the churches of God that you shame those who have nothing? What am I telling you? That I should be praising you? In this matter, I certainly do not praise you!

b: 23/ For I received from the Lord (κύριος), which I also handed on to you, that the night the Lord (κύριος) Jesus was handed over, he took bread (ἄρτον), 24/ and after giving thanks he broke it and said, "This is my body (σῶμα), which is for you. Do this in memory of me." 25/ In the same way, he drank from the cup (ποτήριον), saying, "This cup is the new covenant in my blood (αἵματι). Do this, as often as you drink, in memory of me. 26/ For whenever you eat this bread (ἄρτον) and drink this cup (ποτήριον) you proclaim the death of the Lord (κύριος) until he returns.

b´: 27/ So whoever eats this bread and drinks this cup of the Lord (κύριος) unworthily is liable to the body (σώματος) and blood (αἵματι) of the Lord (κύριος). 28/ Each person must examine himself and then eat the bread and drink from the cup. 29/ For the one who eats and drinks without discerning the body (σῶμα) eats and drinks judgment upon himself. 30/ It is for this reason that many of you are sick, and infirm, and dying! 31/ Now if we discerned ourselves, we would not be judged. 32/ But, since we are now judged, we are disciplined by the Lord (κύριος) so that we are not condemned with the world.

a´: 33/ So, my brothers and sisters, when you gather together (συνερχόμενοι), wait for the others before you eat. 34/ If someone is hungry, he must eat at home (οἴκῳ), in order that you do not gather together (συνέρχησθε) into judgment. I will give direction on the other matters when I arrive.

Beyond What Is Written

Admonishment of the Community for Abuses (a), 11:2–3a, 16–22

That Paul has "heard" of this problem regarding the community meal (likely from Chloe's people) implies that the Corinthians did not discuss it in their letter and, perhaps, did not want Paul to know about it at all. The central lines of this micro-ring element denounce the Corinthians' meetings as futile and misguided.[27] The initial term "first of all" shows the matter to be a primary concern to Paul. The problem is that there are divisions "among you" (*y*, 11:23b–24) when they gather. The parallel *y'* line (11:25) deduces sarcastically that there must be contentions "among you" so that those who think highly of themselves "among you" can show off to the rest. The problem, though, is that such arrogant actions abuse others, cause division rather than edify, and make a mockery of their worship. As in 5:1–5, Paul repeats the phrase "among you" to emphasize that the problem does not have an external cause but rests solely on the shoulders of the community.

The bracket lines reveal points of contact to tie together the rich element. Paul wishes to "praise" them for everything in the tradition that he taught that they hold and remember (11:2). But regarding "this matter" (11:3, 22), the divisions at the gathering for worship and the abuse of the Lord's Supper, Paul twice refuses to "praise" them (11:17, 22). The "churches of God" "have" no such custom (11:16), and so Paul mockingly asks if they mistreat those who "have" nothing because they secretly despise the "churches of God" (11:20).[28] After all, do they not "have" houses where they can eat and drink lavishly without offending everyone? As the central lines denote, and as Paul likely knows, it is the public forum of the worship that entices some of the wealthy in the community to show off all the more.

---

27. a: (*x*) 2/ I *praise* you for everything of mine that you remember and for holding fast to the tradition I gave to you. 3/ But I want you to know that 16/ if anyone considers to debate this matter, consider this: we have no such custom, nor do any of *God's churches*. 17/ So of these reports I do not *praise* you: you do more harm than good *when you come together.*

(*y*)18/ First, when you come together there are *divisions among you*. And for the most part, I believe it.

(*y'*)19/ For there must be *division among you* in order that your "honored" ones might shine more among you.

(*x'*) 20/ So, *when you come together*, it is not to eat the Lord's supper. 21/ For each takes his own meal when you arrive to eat, and some go hungry while others get drunk! 22/ Don't you have your own houses where you can eat or get drunk? Do you so despise *the churches of God* that you shame those who have nothing? What am I telling you? That I should be *praising* you? In this matter, I certainly do not *praise* you!

28. Margaret Mitchell, *Rhetoric*, 264: "In particular, the celebration of the Lord's supper has occasioned and reinforced separations within the community on economic and social grounds."

Order in Worship and the Church, 11:2—14:40

In contrast to their high spiritual opinions of themselves, the Corinthians' meals are not a sharing in the Lord's Supper because the wealthy get drunk while the poor go hungry. It appears that the Corinthians' spirituality is again betrayed by their lack of social consciousness. Fraternal organizations of this type in the Greco-Roman world frequently encouraged members to bring their own food. However, most of those groups maintained homogeneous memberships in terms of status.[29] There were rich groups and poor groups, but Christianity was unique in that it ran the gamut of social categories. As it stands, their divisions nullify the communal, and thus also covenantal, aspects of the meal.[30]

The Tradition of the Lord's Supper (b), 11:23–26

The second element in this unit presents the tradition of Christ's words at the last supper with his disciples in a micro-ring format.[31] The scope of the element is immense. The meal remembers the new covenant that was made in Christ's blood on the cross, celebrates a new relationship with God in the present, and looks forward to Christ's return in the future. The words of the tradition likewise explode the Corinthians' social and political locations: they are transported from the Greek isthmus to Jerusalem in order to witness the ritual meal that solidifies their new covenant relationship with God that Christ's death introduces on their behalf.

The initial line offers the setting for the mini-narrative tradition in which the Lord, on the night he was betrayed, celebrated a Passover meal with his disciples. The central lines present the parallel aspects of this covenant meal. First, Christ broke the bread, gave thanks, and offered the bread as his own body, which is "for you," and asks them to "do this in memory of me" (*y*, 11:24). In the same manner, he took the cup, saying this cup is "the

---

29. According to Keener, *1–2 Corinthians*, 96, seating arrangements would also be an issue at a house church since guests were often placed around a table in descending order.

30. Grosheide, *First Epistle*, 267.

31. b: (*x*) 23/ For I received from *the Lord*, which I also handed on to you, that the night *the Lord* Jesus was handed over,

(*y*) he took bread, 24/ and after giving thanks he broke it and said, "This is my body, which is for you. *Do this in memory of me.*"

(*y′*) 25/ In the same way, he drank from the cup, saying, "This cup is the new covenant in my blood. *Do this*, as often as you drink, *in memory of me.*

(*x′*) 26/ For whenever you eat this bread and drink this cup you proclaim the death of *the Lord* until he returns.

new covenant in my blood." This also is to be done in worship "in memory of me" (*y′*, 11:25).³²

The meal, although a Passover, has connections to ancient covenant procedures, which consisted of 1) a reading of the contract (Exod 19:1—23:32), 2) a sacrifice in which the blood was used to seal the parties in the contract's stipulations (Exod 24:1–8), and 3) a meal between the parties to signify their new relationship together (Exod 24:9–11).³³ Christ's offering of his body and blood at the meal is a down payment of his sacrifice on the cross that will retroactively seal his disciples in the new covenant with God that they are presently experiencing in the covenant meal.³⁴ This new covenant refers to the prophecy in Jer 31:31–34 that God would re-establish with his people Israel.³⁵ The Corinthians and all the sanctified who celebrate this meal are those who receive the fulfillment of that promise.

The final line's emphasis on Christ's death points out that "in my memory" does not refer to the person of Christ alone, but, in particular, to his dying on the cross that serves as a ransom for the elect and seals them with the blood of a perfect sacrifice in a new covenant relationship with God (see 5:7–8). This death is what they are to proclaim until "the Lord" returns because it is good news for the elect.

Self-Examination Is Necessary to Engage in the Covenant Meal (b′), 11:27–29

The b′ element also contains a micro-ring structure.³⁶ The central line concerns the significant illnesses that are afflicting the Corinthians as the

---

32. Or, literally, "keep doing this in memory of me," as the grammar denotes a continuous action. So Fitzmyer, *First Corinthians*, 440.

33. Childs, *Exodus*, 501–11; Durham, *Exodus*, 338–48.

34. Grosheide, *First Epistle*, 271, and Chrysostom, cited in Bray, *1–2 Corinthians*, 113, see a connection to Exodus, but do not take it as far as it could go. Horsley (*1 Corinthians*, 161), however, sees the eucharist as "a sacrifice. . .by which God and the people were bound, by analogy, with the covenant ceremony in Exodus 24:5–8."

35. Fitzmyer, *First Corinthians*, 443.

36. b′: (*x*) 27/ So whoever eats this bread and drinks this cup of *the Lord* unworthily is liable to the body and blood of the Lord.

(*y*) 28/ Each person must examine *himself* and then eat the bread and drink from the cup. 29/ For the one who eats and drinks without *discerning* the body eats and drinks judgment upon *himself*.

(*z*) 30/ It is for this reason that many of you are sick, and infirm, and dying!

(*y′*) 31/ Now if we *discern ourselves*, we would not be judged.

(*x′*) 32/ But since we are now judged, we are disciplined by *the Lord* so that we are not condemned with the world.

catastrophic results of the community's actions at worship in the Lord's supper. It is possible that Paul views the illnesses as God's punishment for the community's abuses at the Lord's supper, similar to how God struck the Israelites with plagues in the desert traditions (1 Cor 10:1–19 // Exod 32:20–35). Paul offers a remedy to the afflictions in the adjacent lines by demanding that each Corinthian must "contemplate the Lord's body" before eating and drinking of the Lord's Supper at worship. In a play on words in the parallel y' line (11:31), Paul states that if the Corinthians "contemplate themselves," they can stave off being condemned (presumably, either by illnesses in the present, or eternal punishment in the future).[37]

The bracket lines merge the images and authority of the returning risen Lord with the Lord who offers his body and blood as an offering for the elect. Since the one who attends the meals at the church's worship is in fact eating and drinking into a new covenant relationship with "the Lord's" body and blood (11:27), they must take care to contemplate the meaning of the body and themselves as a member in this new covenant relationship, lest they take the "Lord's" meal unworthily and be liable to the body and blood of "the Lord" (x, 11:27).[38] As it stands, their present sufferings are intended to teach them the errors of their ways. It is better for them to be disciplined now than to be condemned with the corrupt cosmos at "the Lord's" return (x', 11: 32). In the process of his diagnosis, Paul claims a prophetic insight for the otherwise unknown cause of their present travails.[39]

The b' element affirms the theological weight of the b element with an exhortation for the members to observe their own consciences and actions prior to sharing in this covenant meal.[40] Whoever eats the "bread" and drinks of the "cup" offered at worship in Corinth in the b' element (11:27–29) shares in the same "bread" and "cup" of Christ's Last Supper with his disciples in the b element (11:23–26). Although worshipping in Corinth, the audience is transported to partake of the "body" of the divine savior who died for them (11:25). The remembrance is not merely cognitive, but is experiential and transformational. It is at the meal in worship that

---

37. Margaret Mitchell, *Rhetoric*, 265: "The Corinthians must discern the body, which means simultaneously the eucharistic body and the ecclesiological body of Christ."

38. Fitzmyer, *First Corinthians*, 445: "Bread and cup, body and blood of the Lord correspond to each other in an unmistakable way, and their implication should not be missed; they have become for Paul the real 'spiritual food' and 'spiritual drink' of 10:3–4. His words thus affirm the real presence of the Lord in the eucharistic food and drink."

39. Witherington, *Conflict*, 252.

40. The technical juridical language underscores the importance of this discernment. So Collins, *First Corinthians*, 438.

the Corinthians truly manifest themselves as Christ's body and affirm their relationship with God through Christ. Only as Christ's united body can they stand before God redeemed and blameless (1:30; 6:25).

This relationship with God is to be understood as covenantal and entirely renewed. The "cup" they drink is the "cup" that contains the blood of the new covenant. In ancient contract rituals, the life-force of the blood sealed the parties into the new relationship and its stipulations. So too does Christ's blood bind the elect to a renewed relationship with God who will raise them to glory because of their fellowship with his Son and acceptance of his Spirit.

For these reasons, they must evaluate themselves to be sure that they do not enter into God's presence with contempt for his mercy and this opportunity to share in a new relationship with him as a member of the blameless body of Christ. Self-reflection makes one aware of his/her flaws, the importance of Christ's sacrifice, and the magnitude of God's love and mercy for his elect, whom he has invited to a new relationship with him in a renewed creation. One is then required to examine "the body" (b', 11:29), which in this context can richly refer to both the individual believer's "body" and the corporate "body" of Christ, which was given up for the believers as a sacrifice, and to whom these believers are now fastened in fellowship and the Spirit (b, 11:24; see also 1:4, 9; 6:9–13; 11:27).[41] This discernment anticipates the future judgment and prepares believers for submission to their present Lord and future judge. In short, the Eucharist immerses the participants in the death and resurrection of Christ and "crystalizes the new life in [him] and the apocalyptic expectation of his return."[42]

The transcendent nature of the passage is emphasized by the parallel images of both the sacrificial and the risen Lord Christ. Paul expects the Corinthians to execute the ritual meal properly because he had received these instructions from "the Lord." By these words "the Lord" mediated a covenantal meal that brings the elect and God into a new relationship. The Lord's body and blood are offered to seal this relationship, and the elect are invited to partake in this same meal during worship so that they remember and proclaim the center of their faith, the cross, and look forward to the fulfillment of their faith in "the Lord's" return.[43] This is all the more reason why they should take care to discern themselves so that they partake of "the Lord's" meal worthily and do not offend "the Lord's" body and blood by

---

41. Horsley, *1 Corinthians*, 161.
42. Stambaugh and Balch, *Environment*, 59.
43. Garland, *1 Corinthians*, 551; Matera, *Theology*, 130.

bringing sin to the table of fellowship that is to be a renewed relationship with God (11:28).

The Corinthians' present afflictions are due to failures to discern and treat the Lord's Supper, and thus his body, with proper respect. In this case, Paul treats the Eucharist like a type of *pharmakon*, which can bring the consumer either health or toxicity.[44] The latter is the case for the Corinthians since they have eaten without regard for the whole body of Christ in those less fortunate than themselves. As such, they have consumed "their own condemnation."[45] However, the elect in Corinth may take heart in that they are being disciplined a little now by "the Lord" who died for them so that they might not be condemned with the corrupt world when "the Lord" returns to judge with God's authority (11:32).

New Instructions for the Community's Gatherings (a'), 11:33–34

Following the rich and difficult portions above regarding the community's abuses at the Lord's Supper, Paul concludes the unit by returning the discussion to their gatherings and offering concise instructions on how to proceed from here until he visits again. In the *a* element (11:17–22) Paul had warned the Corinthians that they did more harm than good "when [they] gathered" because they caused divisions from status and arrogance "when [they] gathered," to the extent that their "gatherings" had no effective spiritual association with the "Lord's Supper" (11:17–22).

Following the instruction and warnings in the central elements (11:23–26, 27–32), Paul closes the unit by explaining that "when [they] gather," they should wait for one another to eat, and all eat equal amounts. If some want a larger meal, then they should do so apart from the rest of the body. Continuing in their present manner brings judgment on their "gatherings" because it causes divisions and brings members to the Lord's sacrificial and covenantal meal in an unworthy state (11:33–34). Even worse, since the state of their practices has had no association with the Lord's Supper, they have not effectively been partaking in the Lord's covenantal meal that affirms their renewed relationship with God.

Furthermore, the divisions "among you," and contentions "among you" that arise because of the arrogant ones "among you," who wish to show off their wealth by eating and drinking in a manner that fowls the Lord's Supper (*a*, 11:18–19), precipitate in the illnesses and plagues now "among you" (*a'*,

---

44. D. Martin, *Body*, 190.
45. Ibid.

11:30) in the community.[46] If they wish for these meals to mean anything they must follow Paul's instruction and reform their current celebration practices, lest their present bodily afflictions become eternal condemnation at the Lord's return.

Unit B, 12:1–13: Many Spiritual Gifts, but One Spiritual Body

a: 1/ Now, concerning matters of the Spirit, brothers and sisters, I do not want you (ὑμᾶς) to be uninformed. 2/ You know that when you were pagans you were led astray with voiceless idols. 3/ Therefore, it is imperative that it be made known to you (ὑμῖν) that no one is able to say, "Jesus must be cursed," by the Spirit, and no one is able to say, "Jesus is Lord," except (εἰ μή) by the Holy Spirit (ἐν πνεύματι ἁγίω).

b: 4/ Now, there is a variety of gifts (χαρισμάτων), but the same Spirit (αὐτὸ πνεῦμα). 5/ And there is a variety of ways to serve, but the same (αὐτός) Lord. 6/ And there is a variety of works (ἐνεργημάτων), but the same (αὐτός) God who works (ἐνεργῶν) everything in all things. 7/ And to each (ἑκάστῳ) is given (δίδοται) the manifestation of the Spirit for a good purpose.

b′: 8/ For to one excellent speech is given (δίδοται) by the Spirit, wisdom to another according to the same Spirit (αὐτῷ πνεύματι); 9/ and to another faith by the same Spirit (αὐτῷ πνεύματι), and to another gifts (χαρίσματα) of healing by the one Spirit; 10/ to another great miraculous works (ἐνεργήματα), to another prophecy, to another discernment of the Spirit, to another speaking in tongues, and to another the interpretation of tongues. 11/ And all of these things are wrought (ἐνεργεῖ) by the one and the same Spirit (αὐτὸ πνεῦμα), who distributes to each (τῷ ἑκαστῳ) just as the Spirit wishes.

a′: 12/ For just as one body has many parts, and—as with every part of a body—all members are part of the one body, so too is Christ. 13/ For we (ἡμεῖς) are all baptized through the one Spirit into the one Body, whether (εἴτε) Jew or Gentile, whether (εἴτε) slave or free, and we are all given one Spirit to drink.

---

46. Soards, *1 Corinthians*, 248: "[Paul] is explaining that he perceives God to be at work disciplining the members of the Corinthian church. Whether or not he was right in his conclusions, he does not say that all sickness and death are the result of inappropriate behavior."

Reason for Explanation of Spiritual Gifts (a), 12:1–3

Having demanded in the previous unit that the Corinthians pursue order and equality, in the second unit of this large ring set Paul will exhort the community to recognize the reality of their unity. They are one body in Christ, although they are many parts; and they have a diversity of spiritual gifts, but the same Spirit who gives these gifts for their edification.[47]

The church worship service remains the presumed context for Paul's remarks. They are united because the Spirit binds them as members of Christ and animates their weekly worship and covenant meal. As such, this unit builds directly from the unit prior regarding proper church order. Now, however, the emphasis is on the underlying reasons for ordered unity rather than particular instructions of conduct (see 11:3–4, 26–34).

The initial element (12:1–3) continues the harsh tone of the previous units with an imputation that the Corinthians lack spiritual knowledge (see 1:17; 1:18—3:3; 3:7–21; 4:6–21). Whereas before Paul had claimed the Corinthians were acting like non-believers or regular people (esp. 3:3, 21), he now associates their spiritual ignorance directly with their pre-gospel background.[48] This line also implicitly reminds the audience of Paul's agency in their reception of the Spirit.

The description of the community as "lead astray" to "voiceless idols" underscores the dire situation in which the members lived prior to receiving the message of salvation and receipt of the Spirit. Paul's explanation cannot be seen as anything but patronizing and condescending, and the tone is intentional.[49] It is because of their pagan pedigree that Paul must explain to them this new Spirit of God. The animation they receive now from the Holy Spirit is not like any pagan ceremony in which worshippers fall into chaotic ecstasy or are misled by daemons to honor false, mute idols of stone.[50] The Spirit of God, the God of peace, animates worshippers in an ordered manner and serves as the sole source of liturgical praise.[51] If someone says in worship, "cursed be Jesus," it is not by the Spirit.[52] Conversely, someone cannot confess "Jesus is Lord" except by the power of the Spirit.

---

47. Agosto, *1 y 2 Corintios*, 93, finds a more simplistic, thematic structure in 12:4–30. However, the lexical evidence supports dividing 12:1–13 and 12:14–30.

48. Barrett, *First Epistle*, 278.

49. Witherington, *Conflict*, 256.

50. See above in Units A and B of the last chapter, and in Unit A of the present chapter.

51. R. Martin, *Congregation*, 9.

52. "Anathema" here could be due to groups (either Gnostics or conservative Jews) cursing the idea of the incarnation. See Barrett, *First Epistle*, 280.

Beyond What Is Written

Diversity of Manifestations from the Same Spiritual Source (b, b´),
12:4–11

The central elements of the unit engage the identity of the audience as both diverse and unified. Paul begins by switching terminology from "spiritual talents" (πνευμάτικων) to "spiritual gifts" (χαρισμάτων). The former was likely the term preferred by the Corinthians in their Spirit-status competitions.[53] By calling them "gifts" rather than "talents" Paul underscores that the manifestations of the Spirit are not of the Corinthians' own merits, nor to be used to grade one another's holiness. They are all gifts from the same source. The believer does not control the Spirit—the Spirit animates the believer to manifest their faith in a manner that affirms the faith of others, converts the non-believers, and edifies the community.

The rhythmic repetition of the key term "same" underscores the singular source of these Spiritual gifts in the community members. The element challenges the audience to ask how they can say their talents are better than another's if they are all gifts from the same source—same Spirit, same Lord, and the same God who works in all things (11:4–6).[54] The believers are not the authors of these spiritual manifestations. They are repeatedly placed as the objects who are given the manifestations of the Spirit by God, not for the individual's own good, but for the good of the whole community.

The *b´* element (12:8–11) continues this discussion by repeating and developing five key terms from the *b* element (12:4–7). This diversity of spiritual "gifts" (12:4) all come from "one and the same" Spirit (12:9), the "same" Lord Christ (12:5), and the "same" God who works all things in everything (12:6). Regardless of the miraculous "works" done by the believer (12:10), all things are "worked" by the one and "same" Spirit (12:11), not the believer. In fact, the believer's status as receiver, not author, of the Spirit's animation is painfully underscored to disabuse the audience of their spiritual pride. The manifestations of the Spirit "are given" by God "to each" believer for the benefit of the group (12:7). So the one who "is given" wise words does not speak well of his own accord; rather, "the same Spirit" who animates all of the other talents in the other believers distributes "to each" in a manner that is based on the wisdom of God and not on the merits of the receiver (12:11). This element also outlines the broad diversity found in these gifts: profound speaking, knowledge (12:8), faith, gifts of healing (12:9), miraculous works, prophecy, tongues, and the interpretation of tongues (12:10). All of these gifts are manifest within the context of worship. The diversity of individuals

---

53. Witherington, *Conflict*, 255.
54. Morris, *1 Corinthians*, 166.

and gifts by which the Spirit is manifest amplifies the unity that they share as those who are sanctified and baptized in one and the same Spirit.[55]

So for Paul, these gifts, although manifest in a variety, all unite the community through a common source (the Spirit), a common animator (God), a common agent (Christ), within a common context (worship) for the singular purpose of building up the community—the Body of Christ and God's Temple.

One Body in Baptism, though Diverse in Culture and Status (a´), 12:12–13

In the *a´* element Paul completes the unit by returning to the analogy of community as body that was seen earlier in the letter (6:15–19; 11:22–30) and connecting to the *a* element (12:1–3). No member can curse Jesus, and no member can proclaim Jesus as Lord, except by the Spirit (*a*, 12:3). All members form one body of Christ through the singular unifying presence of the Spirit and the shared experience of baptism (*a´*, 12:13). The audience recognizes that Christ, the diverse subject, is the church; and their gifts parallel other aspects of diversity in Christ's body.[56]

The conditional particles point to absolute aspects of faith and worship. No one can proclaim Jesus is Lord "except" by the illumination of God's Spirit (12:3); but all who have the Spirit can proclaim Jesus as Lord because, "whether" Jew or Gentile, or "whether" slave or free, all are bonded together into the body of Christ by the Spirit to call on his name (12:13).[57] So there is no cultural or status-oriented prerequisite for acquiring the Spirit. God's selection of the sanctified, manifest in one among a diversity of spiritual gifts, is as absolute as the singularity of the gift's origin. And his decision is manifest in the spiritual gifts that appear after baptism, which binds all believers into the body of Christ.[58]

The Spirit arrives to confirm the gift of faith that God has already bestowed on his elect. Paul must make known to "you" the importance of the Spirit in worship because "we" who are baptized and joined together as the body of Christ participate in worship by the animation of the whole and the distribution to each believer.[59] Worshipping in the Spirit with order

---

55. Furnish, *Theology*, 90.
56. Matera, *Theology*, 130; Carson, *Showing*, 42.
57. Although it is impossible to convey well in English, "except" and "whether" both translate the Greek term εἴτε.
58. Carson, *Showing*, 42.
59. R. Martin, *Congregation*, 14.

Unit C, 12:14–30: God Fashions the Body as a Symbiotic Symphony of Diverse Gifts

a: 14/ For the body does not consist of one part, but of many. 15/ If ever a foot says, "I am not a hand, so I am not a part of (ἐκ) this body," does it not remain a part of (ἐκ) the body? 16/ And if an ear says, "I am not an eye, so I am not a part of (ἐκ) this body," does it not remain a part of (ἐκ) the body? 17/ If the whole body were an eye, how would it hear? And if the whole body were an ear, how would it smell? 18/ But now God has fastened (θεὸς ἔθετο) each of these parts in the body, according to his will. 19/ And if all (πάντα) were one (ἕν) body part, how could it be a body? 20/ But now there are many parts, and one (ἐκ) body.

b: 21/ So the eye cannot say to the hand, "I have no need for you," and in the same way, the head cannot say to the feet, "I have no need for you." 22/ Instead (ἀλλά), the parts of the body that seem feeble are in fact necessary, 23/ the parts of the body that seem shameful are in fact shown to us to be abounding (περσσοτέραν) in honor (ἀτιμότερα), and the un-presentable parts of the body abound (περισσοτέραν) in importance. 24/ But our most prominent parts do not have a need for this honor.

b′: Instead (ἀλλά), God organized the body by giving abounding honor (περισσοτέραν τιμήν) to the inferior parts, 25/ in order that there might not be division in the body, and that the parts might instead (ἀλλά) care for one another in an equal manner.

a′: 26/ So if one (ἕν) part of the body suffers, every part of the body suffers. If one (ἕν) part is glorified, every part shares in that joy. 27/ Now you are the body of Christ, and each is a part of (ἐκ) the whole, 28/ whom God has fastened (ἔθετο ὁ θεός) in the Church—first are apostles; second, prophets; third, teachers; then wonder workers, then healers, helpers, administrators, and tongues-speakers. 29/ Is everyone (πάντες) an apostle? Is everyone (πάντες) a prophet? Is everyone (πάντες) a teacher? Is everyone (πάντες) a wonder worker? 30/ Does everyone (πάντες) have the gift of healing? Does everyone (πάντες) speak in tongues? Does everyone (πάντες) interpret? 31/ Continue to pursue spiritual gifts all the more.

Order in Worship and the Church, 11:2—14:40

All Parts of a Body Benefit the Whole (a), 12:14-20

Building from the image of the church community as one body incorporated by the Spirit in the previous unit (B, 12:1-13), Paul now moves to explain the analogy of the body and how it relates to the diversity and unity of the audience in Corinth. The initial element of this C unit contains a micro-ring structure.[60] The central lines present a hypothetical situation in which a foot (*pous*) and ear (*ous*) debate their own contribution to a body. Even if each says, "I am not a hand/eye, and so I am not really a part of this body," are they not still part of the body? The obvious answer is, yes, they are still connected and they are still contributing, even if they are not a hand or an eye. The *y'* line (12:16-17) develops these examples further by pointing out that if every part were a hand or an eye, the body could not hear or walk. Aesthetically this image is also persuasive: a body comprised of a hundred or so eyes would look rather nightmarish.[61]

The bracket lines affirm this analogy. This singular body is composed of many parts (*x*, 12:14), and God has fastened each diverse part together so that the diversity of the parts' functions might benefit the entire body (*x'*, 12:18). If all were the same body part, then you would not have a body. But now, by God's wisdom, each member is a body part fastened together into one ordered, well-functioning body.

The body analogy was commonly used by ancient philosophers and leaders to describe the interrelation of groups within society. One of the more famous examples was by Agrippa who used the analogy successfully to dissuade a rising tide of peasant unrest into accepting the diverse spectrum of work/reward relationships in their region.[62] The Corinthians would be familiar with this analogy, but Paul takes it in a different direction than his contemporaries. Rather than using the analogy in a purely functionalist manner, Paul instead exhorts the audience to a new level of self-awareness

---

60. a: (*x*)14/ For the body does not consist of *one* part, but of *many*.
(*y*) 15/ If ever a foot says, "*I am* not a hand, so *I am* not a part of this body," *does it not remain* a part of the body?
(*y'*) 16/ And if an ear says, "*I am* not an eye, so *I am* not a part of this body," *does it not remain* a part of the body? 17/ If the whole body were an eye, how would it hear? And if the whole body were an ear, how would it smell?
(*x'*) 18/ But now God has fastened each of these parts in the body, according to his will. 19/ And if all were *one* body part, how could it be a body? 20/ But now there are *many* parts and *one* body.

61. Witherington, *Conflict*, 259.

62. See Margaret Mitchell, *Rhetoric*, 155; Keener, *1-2 Corinthians*, 103.

and responsibility for the whole community.⁶³ This point will be developed further in this unit and the next.

A Paradoxical Relationship of Function and Honor in the Body (b, b′), 12:21–25

In the central elements Paul builds on the question of particular body parts' importance and contribution to the whole. The central lines of the microring *b* element (12:21–23) emphasize the superficial paradox of the body.⁶⁴ The parts that "seem" feeble are necessary (*y*, 12:22), and the parts that "seem" shameful and un-presentable are shown to be the most important by how they are covered or protected (*y′*, 12:23). The bracket lines affirm that, in the same manner, one cannot deduce a member's contribution at face-value. The eye and the head cannot say that they "have no need" for the hands and feet (*x*, 12:21) because, while one may cover or protect seemingly un-presentable parts (i.e., genitals), the most prominent parts (i.e., eyes, face) do not have a need for such honor or protection (*x′*, 12:23b–24a).⁶⁵

The lexical connections direct the audience to recognize God's activity as the cause for the particular order of both human bodies in general (*b′*, 12:24b–25), and the church's body in Christ in particular (*b*, 12:21–24a). In both elements the superficial gives way to the reality that lies beneath. The presumably feeble and shameful parts are in fact "abounding in honor" because God has given "abounding honor" (*b′*, 12:24) not to prominent parts, but "instead" (12:22, 24, 25), to the so-called feeble (*b*, 2:22) and inferior parts (*b′*, 2:25), in order to discourage division and encourage charity and empathy among the members for one another. The point is that God has bound the community together in a type of natural balance so that no part is expendable.⁶⁶ Here Paul points to an existing order in nature to both demonstrate God's plan in creation and conclude in an analogous way for the audience to view their own communal body in Christ.

---

63. For an illuminating study that stresses responsibility rather than blind obedience in interpreting this text, see Kim, *Christ's Body*.

64. b: (*x*) 21/ So the eye cannot say to the hand, "I *have no need* for you," and in the same way, the head cannot say to the feet, "I *have no need* for you."

(*y*) 22/ Instead, the parts of the body that *seem* shameful are in fact necessary,

(*y′*) 23/ the parts of the body that *seem* shameful are in fact shown to us to be abounding in honor, and the un-presentable parts of the body abound in importance.

(*x′*) 24/ But our most prominent parts *do not have a need* for this honor.

65. Fee, *First Epistle*, 613.

66. Orr and Walther, *I Corinthians*, 286.

You Are the Body of Christ, Fashioned by God (a´), 12:26-31

In the a´ element Paul ties God's fashioning of the church to his body analogy in the a element above (12:14-20) and rounds out the unit as a whole. "God has fastened" together every member of the church in a symbiotic and ordered body in which each is "a part of" the whole (a, 12:18), just as "God has fastened" each member of a human body to coordinate perfectly as a unit (a´, 12:28). Each member is equally a part of the body, regardless of their function. Their salvation and their present gift of the Spirit are a shared experience that molds them into an entirely interrelated and symbiotic construct so that the joy or sorrow of one is felt by all.[67] Unity and empathy become two interlocking aspects by which the Spirit edifies the church into a mature, corporate body.

The types of church offices and services Paul mentions are not so important as how he parallels these functions to the body parts within the body analogy. The Corinthians are to recognize that, regardless of the different spiritual gifts and ways people serve, no member of the church can say they are more important than another. Whether an apostle, teacher, leader, or interpreter, all are fashioned together into "one body," such that what happens to one member, whether good or bad, happens to the whole body. And this "one body" (12:20, 26-27) is Christ, to whom God has fastened the Corinthian members (6:17-20).[68]

So their salvation is not individual. It is corporate and arrives to them only because of their connection to Christ and one another. They are dead to sin because Christ died for them (6:19-20), and they receive glory because Christ was raised (15:17-24). So the "I's" seen in the a element (as well as 1:17; 3:3) can no longer be tolerated among them. Their true identity is that of gifted members who contribute to the whole united, holy, corporate body of Christ.

Unit D, 12:31b—13:13: Love as a Means of Cohesion

a: 31/ Yet, I will show you an even more extraordinary path. 13:1/ If I speak (λαλῶ) in human and angelic tongues (γλώσσαις), but do not have love, I have become (γέγονα) a clanging, incomprehensible, and cacophonous cymbal. 2/ And if I have prophecies (προφετείαν) and all knowledge, know

---

67. Keener, *1-2 Corinthians*, 104: "Ancients emphasized that true friends shared each other's joys and sorrows. Rejoicing with any honored member of the body was the opposite of envy."

68. Garland, *1 Corinthians*, 597; Matera, *Theology*, 130.

every mystery, and have faith that removes mountains, but I do not have love—I am nothing. 3/ And if I give away all of my (μου) possessions and hand over my (μου) body so that I might boast,[69] but I do not have love, I achieve nothing.

b: 4/ Love is patient. Love is merciful—not zealous. It does not boast. It does not grow arrogant. 5/ It is not shameful. It does not seek its own benefit. It does not become enraged. It does not discern evil. 6/ It does not rejoice in wickedness, but rejoices with truth. 7/ Love outlasts all things, believes all things, hopes in all things, and endures all things.

a′: 8/ Love never fails. If prophecies (προφητεῖαι), they are abolished. If tongues (γλῶσσαι), they are stopped. If knowledge (γνῶσις), it becomes irrelevant. 9/ For we know (γινώσκομεν) from parts and we prophesy (προφητεύομεν) from parts, 10/ but when completion arrives the partiality will fade away. 11/ When I was a child, I spoke (ἐλάλουν) like a child. But when I became (γέγονα) an adult, the child faded away. 12/ Up to now we see as though through a dusty mirror into a riddle. But at that time [we will see] face to face. Up to now I know (γινώσκω) things in parts, but then I will know (ἐπιγνώσομαι) in the same way that I am known (ἐπεγνώσθην). 13/ So now, faith, hope, and love endure—these three. But the greatest of these is love.

Spiritual Talents without Love Are Worthless (a), 12:31b—13:3

In the *a* element Paul presents himself in contrasting situations of acting with and without love. The examples used are taken from the letter to this point and underscore that whatever the Corinthians do, or Paul himself says, their actions are worthless if they act without love. Speaking in angelic tongues, prophesying to reveal mysteries, possessing all knowledge, and performing powerful miracles with great faith are all hyperbolic echoes of traits the Corinthians have claimed or boast in that Paul has addressed in his argument already.[70] The use of Paul's own model of self-sacrifice reminds the audience that even giving of yourself is worthless if it is not done for the right reasons or given in the right manner.

---

69. Several witnesses in the Western tradition read "so that I might burn," but the text above is to be preferred based on its early and multi-type attestation (P46 a A B 33 copsa Clement Origen Jerome).

70. Gooch, *Partial*, 144.

Comparing the Characteristics of Love with the Corinthian Community (b), 13:4–7

The *b* element turns away from Paul and outlines in grand, rhythmic Greek prose the characteristics that make love so imperative.[71] As such, this element develops the hypotheses in the *a* element that actions without love are worthless (13:1–3). The terms are, again, purposely chosen. The positive characteristics—patience, mercy, and rejoicing in truth—are far from the community, while the negative examples summarize their present dysfunctional state: jealousy, boasting, shameful, selfishness, anger, and discernment of evil. The list implies that the audience has little love among them. If they do not have love, their "spiritual talents" are worthless, their faith is a joke, their hope is in vain, and their worship services are nothing but chaotic noise.

Love as Key to Maturing and Understanding God's Unfolding Revelation (a´), 13:8–13

The theme of this micro-ring element is found in its central line (z, 13:11), in which Paul outlines how the believers need to grow to understand the fullness of God's revelation.[72] For example, when Paul was a child he acted like one. But when he grew older, it was necessary that the child fade away. If the child had remained, his adult understanding always would be limited. Similarly, the Corinthians must put aside their immature quarrels and become spiritually mature and harmonious members in the body of Christ if they hope to one day experience the fullness of God's rich knowledge and mystery. And their key to living in Christ in harmony is to live with love.[73]

---

71. Witherington, *Conflict*, 264.

72. a´: (x) 8/ *Love* never fails. If prophecies, they are abolished. If tongues, they are stopped. If knowledge, it is rendered irrelevant.

(y) 9/ For we know from *parts* and we prophesy from parts, 10/ but when completion arrives, the *partiality* will fade away.

(z) 11/ When I was a child, I spoke like a child. But when I became an adult, the child faded away.

(y´) 12/ Up to now we see as though through a dusty mirror into a riddle. But at that time [we will see] face to face. Up to now I know things in *parts*, but then I will know in the same way that I am known.

(x´) 13/ So now, faith, hope, and *love* endure—these three. But the greatest of these is *love*.

73. The maturity Paul mentions is both eschatological (so Conzelmann, *1 Corinthians*, 226) and ethical. For Paul, one's actions in the present cannot be separated from the future judgment.

The *y* and *y′* lines confirm this process of revelation. Now we know "partially" and prophesy only "partially," such that we see God's mystery as though looking through a dirty mirror into a riddle, and understand it only "partially" (*y*, 13:9). Poor spiritual vision creates a state of puzzlement like that found in children.[74] But when completion arrives, partiality will fade away (13:9), and they will see God face to face (*y′*, 13:12a) and know him and his plan in the same complete way that they are known by him. The term "partially" is not chosen arbitrarily. It is the same term used earlier to describe the members as individual "parts" of one body (12:12, 14–31). So the Corinthians can only see things "partially" while they remain focused on being individual "parts" rather than a united body. They will not see completely until they mature—and that will require them to recognize that they, together, are one.

The bracket lines show love to be the imperative means for progressing towards this completion. "Love" never fails. Prophecies, tongues, and knowledge are all limited and cannot of themselves bring about maturity. Faith (which brings about the Spirit and incorporation with Christ) and hope (which looks forward to the glorious resurrection)[75] endure, along with love, beyond human traits. But, Paul's point to the audience is, "love" is the greatest of these because, while the others are the start of the believers' belonging to one another in Christ, love maintains them in this fellowship and enables them to reflect the image of Christ that Paul models. Furthermore, Paul's example of Christ is not modeled in his charismatic powers but in the weakness of his ministry, in which he sacrifices himself in order to save others. Love is powerful because love *is* Christ.

The *a′* element also connects back to the *a* element (13:1–3) and pulls together the unit's message. It explains that "tongues-speaking," "prophecy," and "knowledge" without love are irrelevant (*a*, 13:1–2) because "prophecies," "tongues," and "knowledge" at this time are only partial.[76] These traits will fade away when full maturity arrives (13:10). When that time comes, we will "know" God in the same way that he "knows" us (13:12).

The idea of transformation and maturity are also underscored in the development of the unit. In the *a* element Paul states that if he speaks in tongues without love, he "has become" a clanging noise rather than a revelation of God's love. If he performs miracles without love, his actions and his very being are not only limited; rather, their substance is transformed into

---

74. Gooch, *Partial*, 151.

75. Barrett, *First Epistle*, 309: Hope is "the perseverance of faith . . . with the main stress lying on its future aspect."

76. Conzelmann, *1 Corinthians*, 230.

nothingness (13:1–3). But with love one can be transformed into a mature member of the unified body of Christ. When Paul "was" a child he acted as such. But when he "became" an adult the child faded away so that he could act and think like an adult. In the same way, the Corinthians should seek to be transformed into spiritually mature Christians through the selfless love of one another.

Unit C′, 14:1–13: Prophecy is Preferred because It Edifies the Faith of All

a: 1/ Pursue love, and seek (ζηλοῦτε) spiritual things, so that you prophesy all the more. 2/ For those who speak in tongues do not speak with people but with God—and nobody listens because they are speaking mysteries in the Spirit. 3/ But those who prophesy speak edification (οἰκοδομήν), comfort, and encouragement. 4/ Those who speak in tongues edify (οἰκοδομεῖ) themselves, but those who prophesy edify (οἰκοδομεῖ) the church (ἐκκλεσίαν). 5/ So I want all of you to speak in tongues, but even more that you prophesy. It is better that one prophesy than speak in tongues—unless there is an interpreter—in order that the church (ἐκκλεσία) might receive edification (οἰκοδομεῖ).

b: 6/ Now, brothers and sisters, if someone should join you while one of you is speaking in tongues, how is it better for you than if someone were speaking a revelation, or knowledge, or prophecy, or teaching? 7/ In the same way, if someone is giving (διδόντα) a lifeless noise (φωνήν), whether a flute, a harp—or if one does not make a distinction to the tones—how will (πῶς) the flute player or the harpist be understood (γνωσθήσεται)? 8/ Furthermore, if the blare of the trumpet is not given (δῷ) clearly, who will muster for war?

b′: 9/ In the same way, if you are not able to give (δῶτε) the word clearly through tongues, how will it be understood (πῶς γνωσθήσεται) by the one hearing? For you are talking to the clouds! 10/ Of course, there are different types of sounds, and they all have meaning. 11/ So, if I do not make my meaning clear from my voice (φωνῆς), I am speaking gibberish, and the one speaking to me is speaking gibberish!

a′: 12/ Even so with you: since you are pursuing (ζηλωταί) spiritual things, seek the edification (οἰκοδομήν) of the church (ἐκκλησίας), in order that you should grow abundantly. 13/ Therefore, the one who speaks in tongues must pray that it can be interpreted.

Beyond What Is Written

Prophecy Is Preferred over Tongues (a), 14:1–5

Having established in the central units a theological excursus on the identity of the community as Christ's unified body (C, 12:14–31), and love as the means for maintaining and growing that unified body (D, 12:31b—13:13), in the C′ unit Paul returns to more concrete examples of issues in the church worship services. Love remains the focus in this unit. The structure of Paul's command implores that the audience pursue prophecy as a spiritual talent because, when compared to tongues, it edifies the community, and thus requires love to develop successfully.[77] Tongues were limited in their effect for the community because they were a conversation between the ecstatic and God, but the rest of the community was left out of the equation.[78] The tongues-speaker is benefited, but not the church. In fact, although Paul does not abolish tongues-speaking, he does limit it to happen only when an interpreter is available. All of this is for the sole purpose of edifying the church. And one must be intelligible to edify others.[79]

Practical Examples of Clarity and Function for a Larger Purpose (b), 14:6–8

In the *b* element Paul gives practical examples to demonstrate his preference. If a stranger walks in to join the community, tongues-speaking does not benefit that person as much as prophecy might. More general examples of musical instruments are then offered. A flutist or harpist who plays disordered chords does no service for his audience, and an unclear war trumpet musters no army. In both cases, the functioning of the sound is tied directly to the purpose and goal of the instruments. If the worshippers are not clear to their fellow participants, they have failed their only purpose.

---

77. It is important to keep in mind that Paul's comments on prophecy can in no way be considered an exhaustive instruction on how prophecy should be reflected in Christian assemblies, but rather responds to a particular set of circumstances in Corinth at that time. Aune, *Prophecy*, 13: "Paul's discussion in 1 Corinthians is oriented toward persuading Christians to accept his view of prophecy and *glossalalia*, i.e, what their view and practice *ought* to be. Paul, therefore, is articulating an ideology of Christian prophecy. We cannot be sure that what he recommends was actually practiced anywhere in the Christian world," emphasis original.

78. According to Fitzmyer, *First Corinthians*, 509, abuses of tongues within worship at Corinth may have been the main impetus behind much of this section.

79. Blomberg, *1 Corinthians*, 272.

Order in Worship and the Church, 11:2—14:40

Spiritual Gifts Are to Be Given to the Whole Community (b´), 14:9-11

This next element emphasizes the need for clarity in worship, and thus develops the *b* element (14:6-8). Just as the harpist, flutist, and bugler fail in purpose if they "cannot be understood" or they cannot "give" a comprehensible "sound" to their audiences, so too does the church fail their purpose if, by speaking in tongues they "give" an unclear message ("sound") and "cannot be understood," by anyone in attendance. The result is cacophony and gibberish rather than purposeful worship that glorifies God and, through love, edifies the community into a solid, unified body of Christ.[80]

The cumbersome repetition of the term "give" underscores an important theme here for Paul. Earlier he referred to worship charisms as spiritual "gifts" (rather than the Corinthian term "talent") to emphasize that these qualities in the liturgy are given by God and animated by the Spirit for the edification of the church, not for the individual's boasting (12:14-31a). So too, here, Paul reminds the audience that their communication in worship, whether tongues or prophecy, are gifts of the Spirit and thus intended to edify the whole church body.

Edification of the Church through Gifts of the Spirit Is Imperative in Worship (a´), 14:12-13

Since they aim to "pursue spiritual things" (*a´*, 14:1, 12), the audience should recognize that only with love can they do so properly. Spiritual maturity is achieved not through boasting in the self, but in "edifying" one another in the "church" with the gifts of the Spirit (*a*, 14:4). So to be "spiritual" one must use the gifts of the Spirit wisely. Tongues are only permissible if there is an "interpreter" (14:5, 13). When the community learns to habitually use the Spirit's gifts properly, the Spirit will all the more edify the church's worship with abundance. Like a parent telling his children not to play with their food, Paul admonishes the Corinthians for misusing the nourishment that the Spirit provides to them. Wasting such divine gifts in trite competitions only further demonstrates their lack of maturity and understanding (see 3:3, 21).

---

80. According to Blomberg, *1 Corinthians*, 269, and Garland, *1 Corinthians*, 637, the pejorative meaning of barbarian is likely intended to sting the Apollos faction that emphasizes tongues.

Unit B´, 14:14–25: Prophecy Transforms Believers and Converts Non-Believers

a: 14/ If I pray in tongues, my spirit prays (προσεύχωμαι), but my heart is fruitless. 15/ So what then? I will pray (προσεύξεμαι) with my spirit, and I will also pray (προσεύξομαι) with my mind. I will sing with my spirit, but I will also sing with my mind. 16/ If not, when you bless with the spirit, how will the novice believer say "Amen" to your thanksgiving? —He does not know what you are saying! 17/ I'm sure you give thanks well enough—but the other person is not edified. 18/ I give thanks to God (θεῷ) that I speak in tongues more than all of you.

b: 19/ But in the church (ἐκκλησίᾳ) I'd rather say five words with my mind, in order that I might instruct others, than say myriads of words in tongues.

c: 20/ Brothers and sisters, do not be childish in thinking—sure, be like infants towards evil—but be mature in your reasoning. 21/ It is written in the Law, "In other languages—even in thousands of others—I will speak to this people, yet none of them will obey me, says the Lord."

b´: 22/ So tongues are a sign not to those who believe but for non-believers, and prophecy is not meant for non-believers but for those who believe. 23/ So if the whole church (ἐκκλησία) gathers with everyone speaking in tongues, and a novice or non-believer arrive, what will they say that you are teaching?

a´: 24/ But if all of you prophesy, and a non-believer or novice should enter, he will be convinced by everyone, judged by everyone— 25/ the hidden things of his heart will be made manifest. Then he will fall on his face and he will pray (προσκυνήσει) to God (θεῷ), proclaiming that God (θεός) is truly among you!

Tongues Do Not Edify the Whole Body, Individual or Corporate (a), 14:14–18

The penultimate unit in this large ring set continues the discussion of tongues-speaking with a larger oration on weekly practice and Scripture. The initial element contains a micro-ring in which Paul again presents himself as an expert on tongues-speaking who is qualified to caution against its misuse.[81] Following the earlier unit's concern about clarity in worship, the

---

81. a: (x) 14/ If I pray in *tongues*, my spirit prays, but my heart is fruitless. 15/ So what then? I will pray with my spirit, and I will also pray with my mind. I will sing with my spirit, but I will also sing with my mind.

central lines of this element engage the practical problem of how novice believers will be able to participate within an indiscernible liturgy. The *y* line (14:16a) asks a rhetorical question of how novices can "say 'Amen'" to tongues, and the *y'* line (14:16b) answers that they cannot because they do not know what the tongues speaker is "saying!"

In the bracket lines Paul engages his own gift of tongues to explain that it does not edify even his own body. With "tongues" his spirit prays and sings, but his heart is left empty.[82] Just as he will pray and sing with both his spirit and his mind in order that his whole body benefits (*x*, 14:15), so too does he caution that tongues do not edify others in a complete manner (*x'* 14:18). Paul underscores his credentials for offering such advice by reminding the audience that he speaks in "tongues" far more than any of them.

Five Clear Words Are Greater than Myriads of Tongues (b, c, b'), 14:19–24

Paul continues in the *b* element (14:19) by focusing on context. The preference of prophecy over tongues is heightened when it involves the church. In such a case, Paul prefers five words of instruction to myriads (10,000 or infinity) of words in tongues because those five words would do more to instruct the faithful who have gathered than any number of alleged words uttered in tongues. The key remains the edification of the church as a whole.

To underscore this point, in the central *c* element (14:20–21) Paul calls for the Corinthians to reasonably assess his citation of Scripture that supports his position of prophecy over tongues. In the text cited, Isaiah (28:11) proclaims that God will speak in thousands of other languages, yet the people of Israel will not obey him.[83] The only respect in which Paul requests the Corinthians to remain childish is evil, or, within the context here, disobedience to God.[84] But they should stop being puzzled like a child and think like adults about the Scripture on which he is teaching and how it involves their salvation.

(*y'*) 16/ If not, when you bless with the spirit, how will the novice believer *say* "Amen" to your thanksgiving?

(*y'*) He does not know what you are *saying!* 17/ I'm sure you give thanks well enough—but the other person is not edified.

(*x'*) 18/ I give thanks to God that I speak in *tongues* more than all of you.

82. Garland, *1 Corinthians*, 639: "'My spirit'... refers... to Paul's innermost deepest depths (see 1 Cor 16:18; 2 Cor 2:13; Rom 1:9). It parallels 'my mind,' which indicates that he is thinking in anthropological terms." Cf. Jewett, *Anthropological*, 190.

83. Heil, *Role*, 197.

84. Williams, *Metaphors*, 60.

The *b'* element (14:22-23) both comments on the citation in the central element and links back to the context of worship in the *b* element (14:19). Tongues are a "sign" to non-believers, but they are meant to be a confounding sign.[85] And the worship in the "church" is meant to be a place for clarity and revelation, not the re-veiling of God's mystery. Worship is where God is to be revealed and recognized as present. So anything that might confuse others and lead to disobedience is unacceptable. Tongues, according to the Scripture passage in Isaiah, are intended to confound understanding and create rebellion.[86] So Paul demands that they prophesy in order that the novice and non-believer are not led to disobedience by their tongues.[87] Just as he claims that in the "church" he would rather say five words clearly than myriads of tongues in order to instruct others in the "church" (*b*, 14:19), so too does he prefer prophesying so that non-believers who arrive at the "church" will know what is being taught (*b'*, 14:22).

Prophecy Converts the Non-Believer and Grows the Body of Christ (a'), 14:24-25

This final element ties together the unit by unpacking the transformational experience that a non-believer in Corinth might undergo upon hearing prophecy rather than tongues alone. Paul presumes that, upon hearing a clear message of Christ's death and the imminent return, the new observer will have an emotional "dark night of the soul" moment in which all the secrets of his heart are made apparent to him. Overwhelmed by this internal experience, he will then fall on his face to pray to God.[88] This conversion serves as a prerequisite for the individual to become a new member of Christ's body. Prophecy edifies the body not only by transforming the parts that are already present, but also in adding new members to the congregation.

---

85. That a prophetic spirit can unveil God's hidden plan to confound humans' understanding has precedent in the story of Micaiah and Ahab (1 Kings 22).

86. Aune, *Prophecy*, 202: "Paul claims that 'prophecy is not for unbelievers but for believers,' yet the context makes it clear that it also has an effect on unbelievers (vv. 23-25)."

87. Blomberg, *1 Corinthians*, 274.

88. Heil, *Role*, 195, notes that the phrasing in 14:25 echoes several OT conversion stories (e.g., Gen 17:3; Ezek 11:13; 1 Kgs 18:39; Dan 2:46) in which the character receives a powerful revelation from God, and also alludes to the prominent apocalyptic idea of God's immanent presence with his people (Isa 45:14; Zech 8:23). Thus, in Paul's line of argument, the presence of the Spirit in the community's prophesying truly reveals God and makes him present to the world as a fulfillment of prophecy.

Paul's hope is that the non-believer will develop from only "praying" to "God" and acknowledging his presence (14:25), to "praying" and giving thanks to "God" with those who have faith and know they are saved by Christ (14:15), so as to be filled by the Spirit and prophesy for the continued edification of the church. And this organic, symbiotic, and cyclical process, with a growing and transforming body of Christ, can repeat until the prophecies are fulfilled at Christ's return. But in order to give thanks and begin this process, the non-believer must first hear a comprehensible message of the gospel when they arrive. For the news of the gospel to be "good," it must first be understood. And it is the existing members of the church body who are responsible for the clear and intelligible proclamation of this good news.

Unit A´, 14:26–33, 36–40: Proper Order in the Worship

a: 26/ So what of this, brothers and sisters (ἀδελφοί)? When you come together, each has a psalm, a teaching, a revelation, speaking in tongues, and an interpretation—All of these must be (γινέσθω) done for your edification!

b: 27/ If some speak in tongues, let it be two or three at most—but one at a time—and one person must interpret. 28/ But if there is no interpreter, then the tongues-speaker must remain silent in the church. He can speak to himself and to God (θεῷ). 29/ Two or three prophets (προφῆται) may speak, but they must not contradict each other. 30/ And if someone seated has a revelation, he must first remain silent. 31/ You can all prophesy, but one at a time, so that you may all learn and all be comforted. 32/ The spirits (πνεύματα) of prophets (προφητῶν) are to remain subordinate to the prophets (προφήταις). 33/ For God (θεός) is not disorder but peace, as in all the churches of the sanctified.[89]

b´: 36/ Does the word of God (θεοῦ) come from you alone, or does it dwell only in you? 37/ If anyone thinks he is a spiritual prophet (προφήτης εἶναι ἢ πνευματικός), he must know what I wrote to you, which is the Lord's command: 38/ if anyone rejects this, he is rejected.

a´: 39/ So, brothers and sisters (ἀδελφοί), seek prophecy and do not restrain those who speak in tongues. 40/ But everything must be (γινέσθω) appropriate and properly ordered.

---

89. On the omission of 14:34–35, see the initial section of this chapter.

Proper Procedure in Worship (a), 14:26

Having addressed the issue of tongues convincingly in the last two units, Paul now closes this large ring set with an oration on proper order in the proceedings of church worship. In the initial *a* element, Paul outlines an appropriate worship service: a song, a teaching (Scripture reading and sermon), a revelation (prophecy), tongues-speaking, and an interpretation thereof. But all things are in proper order and to fulfill a primary purpose—*the edification of the whole community*.[90] Recall from the C′ unit that an instrument can only fulfill its purpose if it communicates clearly (14:6–11).

Proper Order in Worship for Tongues and Prophets (b), 14:27–33

The rich *b* element continues this oration on tongues and prophecy in worship with a complex micro-ring.[91] The central lines demand that "everyone" be able to prophesy, but one at a time (*z*, 14:31a), in order that "everyone" may learn and "everyone" may be consoled (*z′*, 14:31b). This three-fold repetition serves as the emphatic pivot point that underscores the main concern of the micro-ring.[92] Proper order in worship facilitates edification through learning and consolation of each participant. The adjacent lines offer procedure for the central message. Two or three "prophets" may speak, but must do so one at a time. In addition, the others in worship must discern the veracity of any revelation. Those seated must remain silent while they wait their turn (*y*, 14:30). This discipline requires that the spirits of the "prophets" be subordinate to the "prophets"—that is, the prophets must be responsible for their actions in worship and must not become so frazzled by inspiration that they disrupt the edification of those assembled (*y′*, 14:32).

The bracket lines open and close the element by reminding these visible participants of the true foci of worship—God and the church. Paul

---

90. Margaret Mitchell, *Rhetoric*, 280: "As in ch. 12, Paul admits the inevitable differentiation and distribution of spiritual gifts among the members of the church (14:26), but gives advice for their orderly expression."

91. b: (*x*) 27/ If some speak in tongues, let it be two or three at most—but one at a time—and one person must interpret. 28/ But if there is no interpreter, then the tongues-speaker must remain silent in the *church*. He can speak to himself and to *God*.

(*y*) 29/ Two or three *prophets* may speak, but they must not contradict each other. 30/ And if someone seated has a revelation, he must first remain silent.

(*z*) 31/ You can *all* prophesy, but one at a time,

(*z′*) so that you may *all* learn and *all* be comforted.

(*y′*) 32/ The spirits of prophets are to remain subordinate to the *prophets*.

(*x′*) 33/ For *God* is not disorder but peace, as *in* all the *churches* of the sanctified.

92. Margaret Mitchell, *Rhetoric*, 281.

outlines this ordered process by which tongues-speakers act one-at-a-time, and for which interpretation is mandatory. If there is no interpreter, the tongues-speaker must remain silent before the "church" and speak only to "God" (*x*, 14:27–28). All of the instructions given here serve to glorify "God," who is peace and not chaos, and to homogenize this community's worship so that they join in and glorify God in the same manner as all of his other sanctified "churches" (*x'*, 14:33).

In short, a cacophony of prophets or tongues-speakers comforts no one. Since God is peace and not disorder his Spirit brings order and peace in the animation of worship. So prophets should not blame the Spirit if they get out of hand. They are still responsible for how they act while inspired since the spirit of the person is the part that both receives God's Spirit and enables the believers to prophesy accordingly.[93]

One can only imagine what worship in Corinth looked like to warrant such instructions. Given that three separate units cover the issue, it appears that speaking in tongues had become a problem among the community in worship. It is possible that these spiritual "talents" were being played against one another, like a sort of grand, spiritual competition on Sundays. It also appears that the community did not intend for Paul to find out about these problems. Perhaps this was one more portion of information that Chloe's people had given Paul while he was in Macedonia.

Rebuttal to Anticipated Tension (*b'*), 14:36–38

The *b'* element shifts to a combative tone, but develops the need for order in the *b* element. Are the alleged prophets and spiritual persons in Corinth the only ones through whom "God" speaks (*b'*, 14:36)? Surely not! For "God's" Spirit animates all of his churches (*b*, 14:33). So, since "prophets" and tongues-speakers must worship in an orderly manner so as to edify the community and glorify "God" (*b'*, 14:36), and since the "spirits" of the "prophets" must be subordinate to the "prophets" (*b*, 14:32) who communicate the message of "God," who is peace (*b*, 14:33), Paul demands those who consider themselves to be "prophets" or "spiritual" to acquiesce to his instructions (*b'*, 14:38). Peace cannot animate disorder. To disagree with Paul's communication of Christ's decree disqualifies one as not inspired by God. Disorder in the church comes not from God but from human arrogance (11:22).

---

93. The order that Paul presents conforms to that found in contemporary synagogues of Paul's and the Corinthians' time. So Moore, *Judaism*, 1:289–95.

Beyond What Is Written

Since Paul is filled with God's Spirit and an apostle of Christ who is qualified to bear his commands, no prophet claiming to be inspired can reject his instruction on worship. Those who are truly inspired can only affirm the truth that Paul preaches regarding how to worship the God of peace in a manner that glorifies their Lord Christ, with whom they are one body (12:29).

A Defensive Tone and Warning (a'), 14:39–40

The a' element ties back to the a element (14:26) to wrap up this final unit, and the ring set as a whole. The repetition of "brothers and sisters" (14:26, 38) was a common tool in ancient rhetoric where a speaker wishes to emphasize a personal relationship within the logic of their argument. The filial address elevates the Corinthians from the previous "children" and "infants" and treats them more like equals. But this leveling is two-edged: since they are treated as equals they are also more culpable if they reject Paul's message.

At the close of this lengthy ring set that argues for unity and order in the worship service, Paul offers an ultimatum to possible dissenters (a common form in ancient rhetoric). Anyone who rejects his words will himself or herself be rejected by every church that Paul leads (14:33, 37). And those who claim to be "spiritual prophets" must recognize that the word of God does not animate them alone or allow them to contradict Paul. He too has the Spirit (11:1) and the spirits of prophets must be subordinate so as not to contradict one another or bring disorder to the community. To do so would cause the church to fail in its sole purpose of preaching a unified and coherent message. To fulfill that mission, "everything" in the worship "must be" harmonious and within a well-ordered (a', 14:40) procedure—with songs, teachings, prophecies, tongues, and interpretation—because "everything" that occurs in worship "must be" for the edification of the faithful elect, who are Christ's body (a, 14:26).[94]

---

94. Although he does not go so far as to deduce a larger ring pattern, Furnish, *Theology*, 88, also denotes the connection of 14:26 and 14:40 as bracketing a section on church order.

Order in Worship and the Church, 11:2—14:40

INTERRELATION OF UNITS

Outline

Disorder in the Lord's Supper (A, 11:2-3a, 16-34)

Since the Corinthians eat the Lord's Supper in a divided manner, Paul admonishes their activity by demanding that they eat equal portions as a group and examine the Body *of which* they *partake* and *in which* they *participate*. "If anyone thinks" (εἰ τις δοκεῖ) to cause an uproar over this, Paul informs the Corinthians, there is no custom like theirs found anywhere among the "churches of God" (ἐκκλησίαι τοῦ θεοῦ) (11:16–17).

Many Gifts, but One Spirit (B, 12:1–13)

God empowers his elect in worship by distributing his Spirit to each member. But God distributes his one Spirit to each person in such a manner that the unity of its power is "manifest" (φανέρωσις) in a diversity of external gifts (12:7). To one is given wise speech, to "another" (ἄλλῳ) knowledge according to the same Spirit (12:8); to "a different one" (ἑτέρῳ) faith, to "another" (ἄλλῳ) the gift of healing (12:9), to "another" (ἄλλῳ) powerful works, to "another" (ἄλλῳ) prophecy, to "another" (ἄλλῳ) spiritual discernment, to "another" (ἄλλῳ) prophecy, to a "different one" (ἑτέρῳ) tongues-speaking, and to "another" (ἄλλῳ) the interpretation of tongues (12:10).

Many Parts, but One Body (C, 12:14–31a)

The human body is not made of just one part, but a variety of parts. God has fashioned each member in an orderly manner, so that they work in a symbiotic unity in which every part has a necessary contribution. So also with the church, God has fashioned the members together in an orderly manner: "apostles" (ἀποστόλους) first, "prophets" (προφήτας) second, "teachers" (διδασκάλους) third (12:28); and then there are a variety of other spiritual gifts. Not all are "apostles" (ἀπόστολοι), or "prophets" (προφῆται), or "teachers" (διδάσκαλοι), but all contribute in a necessary manner to the one body of Christ (12:29), such that God's order enables every part of this body to "abound" (περισσοτέραν) together with honor (12:23). Having this gift of an orderly and symbiotic interrelatedness with one another, the Corinthians should "zealously pursue" (ζηλοῦτε) spiritual gifts all the more (12:31a).

Beyond What Is Written

Love Is the Key to Cohesion in Christ (D, 12:31b—13:13)

Love is the key to every activity of every member who exists within a symbiotic body. Love is patient and merciful; it stands in stark contrast to the ways in which the Corinthians, have been arrogant, self-interested, harsh, and cold toward one another (13:4-6). In order to be truly mature they must become imitators of Paul and Christ by manifesting God's gift of love through the Spirit consistently with one another (13:9-13). Only with love can the Corinthians complete their transformation to receive full knowledge of God.

Prophecy Edifies Christ's Existing Body (C´, 14:1-13)

In order to edify the whole body the Corinthians are encouraged to pursue love but all the more to "zealously pursue" (ζηλοῦτε) the spiritual gifts, which include the aspects of the Spirit that were freely given by God to them (14:1, 12). These gifts are most clearly seen when the Corinthians worship in proper order: first a "revelation" (ἀποκαλύψει), then a "prophecy" (προφητείᾳ), then a "teaching" (διδαχῇ) (14:6). And they should maintain this order so that all 1) are edified, 2) are able to properly and "zealously pursue" (ζηλοῦτε) God's spiritual gifts offered to them, and 3) they might "abound all the more" (περισσεύητε) in spiritual edification (14:12).

Prophecy Grows Christ's Body through Converts (B´, 14:14-25)

Paul instructs the Corinthians to prophesy more than they speak in tongues because the latter edifies the speaker but not the "other" (ἕτερος) who is listening (14:17). He even prefers that they speak in five human words rather than myriads of tongues so that those who are "different" (ἄλλους) from the speaker are also benefited (14:19). Also, tongues are a sign for the "non-believer" (ἀπίστοις), not for those who "believe" (πιστεύουσιν); rather, prophecy is for those who "believe" (πιστεύουσιν). Scripture affirms this with the prophetic exclamation that God will speak in "other languages" (ἑτερογλώσσοις), and hundreds of "others" (ἑτέρων) to his people, yet they will still disobey him (14:21). So the Corinthians should prophesy so that a "non-believer" (ἄπιστοι) who joins their worship will be convicted and experience a powerful "manifestation" (φανερά) of God's power through the revelation of his inner-self (14:24-25).

Order in Worship and the Church, 11:2—14:40

Order Is Required when Worshipping the God of Peace (A´, 14:26-33, 36-40)

Paul outlines for the Corinthians the proper procedure for an ordered worship so that the community may be edified. The manner of worship reflects the object of worship—the one God, who is peace, and who animates and fashions "all the churches of the sanctified" (πάσαις ταῖς ἐκκλησίαις τῶν ἁγίων) (14:33). "If anyone considers" (εἴ τις δοκεῖ) to disagree with Paul (14:37), they must recognize that such dissension immediately disqualifies their message as uninspired.

Conclusion

The central D unit (12:31b—13:13) concerning love and eschatological transformation serves as the pivotal passage for the entire oration on the unity and order of the church in worship. The unit builds on the symbiotic relationship presented in the B and C units (12:1-13, 14-31a) and anticipates the appropriate treatment of one another through orderly worship in the C´ and B´ units (14:1-13, 14-25). That the Corinthians' should focus on the edification of the whole church, rather than on their individual powers, is a theme that is prominently shared in the bracket A and A´ units (11:2-3a, 16-34; 14:26-33, 36-40).

To this point, the Corinthians' focus has incorrectly been placed on the external demonstration of the Spirit in themselves rather than the unifying love by which the Spirit binds them to one another in one body. Only when they realize that the true source of their power is in fact in their unity, will they be able to mature and become spiritual adults. Now they see one another and God's presence as through a dusty mirror; but, when they mature, they will see clearly how they are connected to one another and to God in a truly spiritual and substantive manner (13:9-13).

Following the interest in love, the C´ unit (14:1-13) develops the C unit (12:14-31a). In as much as the Corinthians are urged to "zealously pursue" spiritual gifts in the assembly (C´, 14:6), the proper order of worship of a "revelation," a "prophecy," and a "teaching" enables them to "abound" all the more in spiritual gifts through their "zealous pursuit" (C´, 14:1, 12), just as God has fashioned them together into the body of Christ in which there are "apostles," "prophets," "teachers," and many others (C, 12:29). Not all are "apostles," or "prophets," or "teachers." However, it is through the diversity of gifts that God demonstrates his one Spirit so that honor might "abound" through every part of the body in a symbiotic manner. Their spiritual identity and gifts being at the same time individual and corporate; and this paradoxical relationship reflects both how they are interrelated with one another (C, 12:23) and why they are called to pursue these diverse gifts all the more (C′, 12:31a).

In a similar manner, the B′ unit (14:14–25) develops the message of the B unit (12:1–13) by demonstrating that the "others" who have "other" gifts in the church are "others" whom each Christian should focus their worship to edify. That is, the worship is not for one's own edification alone, but for the purpose of edifying the "others" in your community, just as the "others" seek to build you. So that, as all seek to build "others," the diverse group of "others" is transformed into a united entity of Christ, in whom there is no "other" but the sanctified. So all of those who are baptized, regardless of background or status, drink of the same Spirit; but the one Spirit is manifest in a variety of ways through the diversity of the parts of Christ's body.

Finally, the A′ unit (14:25–33, 36–40) brings the entire ring set to a close with a focus on proper procedure and mutual respect with all members of the worshipping body of Christ. Just as "all of God's churches" have rules that eliminate division or harmful status concerns in the A unit (11:2–3a, 15–34), so too in the A′ unit do "all the churches of the sanctified" have rules that maintain order in worship, afford equal respect to each speaker, and aim to edify the whole congregation as a unified body of Christ that glorifies the God of peace in an orderly manner. "If anyone considers" to disagree with Paul in the matter of the Lord's Supper (A, 11:16), or if "anyone considers" to disagree with him with regard to proper order of worship (A′, 14:36), they must recognize that God is peace and so disorder in the assembly cannot be animated by his Spirit. Their continued objections only affirm Paul's assertions that they misunderstood God's gifts and remain attached to the corrupt world that is fading away.

In sum, the church members must begin to recognize that all of their diverse gifts are from the same Spirit and appreciate how God has fashioned their diverse parts into a single body so that they might love one another with the gifts God gave them in mutual respect. Only when they recognize this truth—that they are not spiritually powerful in and of themselves, but rather God, through their unity and the Spirit, manifests his love through each member to every other member of the body—can they fully mature and clearly see God, themselves, and one another. Now they see everything drearily. But when they love properly they will see clearly that, because of God's binding power of the Spirit, there will be no clear way to see where they end and the other members begin. And, likewise, there will be no clear way to see where they end and Christ and God's glory begins. They are truly one body, conformed through the Spirit, in Christ, to become God's righteousness, redemption, and sanctification as a manifestation of God's true wisdom to teach the corrupt world to distinguish between what is true and what is a fading illusion.

The Corinthians can only be a part of this manifestation of the gospel if they themselves can distinguish between truth and illusion, between God's wisdom and human power, between their own talents and the gifts of the Spirit that God has offered them to share. The distinction will be made clear to them only when they recognize that their edification comes not from themselves but from the unity and the love they share through God's Spirit.

10

Resurrection and Hope of the Community, 15:1–58

Section A′, Ring Set β

ANALYSIS OF UNITS

Having just addressed the identity of the community as the body of Christ and the proper protocol for how to worship in proper order and love so as to give glory appropriately to the God of peace, Paul now moves to engage the issue of the resurrection. The placement of this topic is deliberate. Although his letters are thoroughly eschatological, Paul normally engages matters of the parousia towards the end of a correspondence (e.g., 1 Thess 4:15—5:10).[1] Such a strategy gears the hearers to view the author's eschatological message as the summation and summit of their faith and activity in Christ.

The exact nature and nuance of the argument that certain Corinthians put forward to question the resurrection of the body (or whether they were influenced by outsiders) is unclear. Numerous ideas of the afterlife proliferated in Hellenistic Rome, including a sense that the soul lived on without the body, or that there was no conscious existence at all.[2] Even Jews at this

---

1. Margaret Mitchell, *Rhetoric*, 176: "Even this appeal to future life to urge concord in the present is not unparalleled in deliberative discourses for unity from antiquity. In *Or.* 23, also near the end of the argument, Aristides uses the same appeal."

2. See Keener, *1-2 Corinthians*, 122–23; Murphy-O'Connor, *1 Corinthians*, 137; Fitzmyer, *First Corinthians*, 559–61; D. Martin, *Body*, 108–17. Witherington, *Conflict*,

Resurrection and Hope of the Community, 15:1-58

time differed on their exact feelings. Those who were influenced by the more apocalyptic texts of Daniel and the Enochic literature, such as the Pharisees and many Galileans, viewed the resurrection of the dead as imperative to God's saving plan.[3] Paul would certainly side with this group, as would a majority of the early church. But groups that did not fully accept the prophets or Daniel as Scripture, such as the Sadducees, were not as inclined to accept the concept of a bodily resurrection (as seen in, e.g., Mark 12:18–23; Acts 23:6–8).

For the purposes of our study, it seems appropriate and sufficient to consider the Corinthian dissenters' opposition along both anthropological and temporal lines.[4] They may have considered the resurrection to be something they presently experienced and so did not need to accept the overtly apocalyptic tradition of the bodily resurrection of the dead. What is clear about their position is that they likely ridiculed Paul about this topic, to the extent that he responds with a mockingly hostile tone (rivaled only within this correspondence by his later tirade on his weakness in 2 Cor 10:1—13:10).

Although it is difficult to discern the opponents' position from the limited *vituperatio*-based attack that Paul provides, it is possible that some high-status members of the community were heavily influenced by Roman imperial eschatology. This particular tradition was a part of Roman propaganda which purported that Roman emperors fulfilled the will of the gods and previous prophecies by being a climactic leader who offers the blessings of safety, health, and material gain to his "friends," i.e., the most socially- and

---

293–94, expounds on the Romans' concern for the afterlife. Many tombs had tables where mourners could dine with the departed, and sacrifices were often offered on behalf of the dead. At times, tombs even contained a spout by which wine could be poured down from the surface.

3. Moore, *Judaism*, 2:379–82; Sanders, *Judaism*, 151–52; Gowan, *Eschatology*, 59–62; Collins, "Prophecy," 147; Wright, *Resurrection*, 420–29; Conzelmann, *1 Corinthians*, 261.

4. According to Tuckett, "Resurrection," 247–50, and Thiselton, "Realized," 108–18, the opposition viewed "resurrection" as something of a realized or present state and denied its future or bodily potential. So the opponents' protest was based both on anthropological and temporal concerns. Grosheide, *First Epistle*, 356, posits another, albeit more difficult, option in which the Corinthians accept that Christ was raised but deny that anyone else can be. Margaret Mitchell, *Rhetoric*, 176–77, considers the possibility that various factions have somewhat nuanced and different views on the nature of the resurrection. D. Martin, *Body*, 105–107, sees the focus of the dissenters as mainly anthropological. To be sure, the focus of Paul's rhetoric and choice of terminology all center around the idea of "type" or "manner" of resurrection. The time is never really an issue.

politically-connected families of the empire.[5] This would be a material, limited, and status-oriented eschatology in which only the wealthiest members of the community would receive the greatest rewards, while the lesser parties received little. If this were the case, then Paul's harsh reply that focuses on the spiritual and universal itinerary in which all worldly powers (including Rome's benefactors) are defeated makes considerable sense.

Unit A, 15:1–11: The Tradition of Christ's Resurrection as the Basis for Faith

a: 1/ I want to make known to you, brothers and sisters, the gospel that we proclaimed to you, and that you received—in which you now stand, 2/ and through which you are saved—this message we proclaimed to you so that you might hold it. Otherwise, you have believed (πιστεύετε) in vain.

b: 3/ For I gave to you in the beginning what I received: Christ died for our sins, according to the Scriptures; 4/ and he was buried and raised on the third day, according to the Scriptures—5/ and he appeared (ὤφθη) to Cephas and to the rest of the Twelve.

c: 6/ Then he appeared (ἔπειτα ὤφθη) to five hundred brothers at once—many of whom remain even now, while others have already fallen asleep.

c′: 7/ Then he appeared (ἔπειτα ὤφθη) to James and to all of the apostles.

b′: 8/ And last of all, like one born premature, he appeared (ὤφθη) even to me. 9/ For I am the least of the apostles—one who is not worthy of being called an apostle—because I persecuted God's church.

a′: 10/ But by God's grace I am what I am, and his grace for me did not arrive in vain. Rather, it overflows all the more in everything that I suffer—not me, but the grace of God that is with me. 11/ So whether from me or from one of the others, that is what we proclaimed, and that is what you believed (πιστεύετε).

Recalling the Initial Proclamation of the Gospel (a), 15:1–3

In this opening element, Paul engages common ground with the Corinthians by pointing back to the gospel message as the starting point of their sanctification to God, in Christ, through the Spirit. All of Paul's language is meant to ground the audience in recalling their initial experiences of conversion

---

5. See Witherington, *Conflict*, 295–98, 310–14, for an excellent excursus on the topic of Roman imperial eschatology. See also D. Martin, *Body*, 106.

Resurrection and Hope of the Community, 15:1–58

and the power of the Spirit at hearing the "good news" of his message. What was so good about this news was that, so long as the Corinthians believed and held fast to what Paul passed on to them, they would be saved. Paul here usurps Roman imperial language to express Christ's prominence in terms the Corinthians can understand.

Paul brings a gospel of Christ's victory, from which the audience can look to the future parousia when he will destroy the other powers (1:18—2:5) and glorify his faithful elect. The resurrection initiated the last days and marked the new era as climactic and final.[6] Salvation for the audience means that they will not have their sins counted against them, and so will be rescued from God's judgment against those who are perishing and who cling to the wisdom of the world (1:18, 25). Here in this element Paul reminds the Corinthians that the resurrection was always a necessary aspect of the gospel they received, held fast to, and believed. His implied question to them is then, "What caused you to lose it?" And his underlying warning weighs heavily at the end of the element: if the Corinthians reject the tradition by which they will be saved, then their initial faith will have been in vain.

It is unclear whether, when he focuses on their faith activity, Paul is addressing just those whom he converted. If this were the case, then the dissenters would fall mainly within the ranks of Apollos' group, and Paul is (in the *a* element) attempting to win back members of his original core who have been led astray by this more libertine/power-oriented contingent (see "do not be deceived," 15:34; also 5:9). If this group is the same as those who dissented against the cross (and perhaps also used the slogan "everything is lawful" with regard to sex and idolatry), then they represent a significant problem to the spiritual development of the community that Paul had founded.[7]

According to the Scriptures (b), 15:4–6

The brief *b* element contains a micro-ring structure.[8] The central lines testify that Jesus Christ died for our sins "according to the Scriptures" (*y*, 15:3b) and that he was subsequently buried and raised on the third day "according

---

6. Dunn, *Theology*, 240.

7. The exact identity of the dissenters/opponents and their relationship with the community is not entirely clear. See Fitzmyer, *First Corinthians*, 558.

8. b: (*x*) 3/ For *I gave* to you in the beginning what I received:
(*y*) Christ died for our sins, *according to the Scriptures*—
(*y'*) 4/ and that he was buried, and he was raised on the third day, *according to the Scriptures.*—
(*x'*) 5/ And that he appeared to Cephas and to the rest of *the Twelve.*

to the Scriptures" (y', 15:4).[9] They should recognize that Christ's resurrection, of which they are dubious, is attested to by the same Scriptures that testify that he died for their sins and their sanctification, as their initial faith and the presence of the Spirit affirm.[10] Although some particular Scripture passages may be in view here, it is very likely that Paul seeks to present the whole narrative that concerns humanity's salvation in Scripture as testimony to the resurrection's necessity and veracity.[11] Just as they cannot have the Spirit without the cross (1:18—3:3), they also cannot have new life without Christ's resurrection and the hope for the same to happen for all of the dead. Paul's point is that any faith in Christ, as is held to by all the churches of God and his Scriptures, requires them to accept the resurrection as central to their faith narrative.[12]

The bracket lines of the element emphasize the stewardship of the tradition of Christ's resurrection.[13] Just as Christ appeared to Cephas, and then the rest of the Twelve (*dodeka*), to commission them to proclaim the gospel to others (x', 15:5), so too did Paul pass on (*paredoka*) at their community's beginning the message of this gospel to serve as the foundation of their identity and their salvation in Christ (x, 15:3a).[14] The Corinthians serve as the fulfillment of Christ's post-resurrection commission to the apostle, and this reception of the message—especially Paul's—serves as testimony to Christ's resurrection. The community's very existence is dependent on the message that began with the risen Christ.

---

9. According to Murphy-O'Connor, *1 Corinthians*, 138, this brief formula likely comes from an early Aramaic creed.

10. The rich phrase "died for us/our sins" likely has both sacrificial and substitutionary meanings within it. See Hooker, "Interchange," 121; Matera, *II Corinthians*, 149; Milinovich, *Now*, 123.

11. Wright, *Resurrection*, 320.

12. The phrase "according to the Scriptures" is deliberately vague so as to encompass the whole of God's plan to save humanity that is found throughout Scripture (so Conzelmann, *1 Corinthians*, 255; Wright, *Resurrection*, 249).

13. Conzelmann, *1 Corinthians*, 249: "The creed is vastly more than a formal proof. Rather, it is grounded in the fact that the resurrection itself is posited 'in Christ.' Christ is not merely the first to be raised, but is constitutive for our being raised: the dead will be made alive 'in him.'"

14. Although there is no strong lexical connection between the bracket lines, there is a significant oral echo in the Greek between "gave to you" (*paredoka*) and "the Twelve" (*dodeka*). This alignment is solidified by the unmistakable parallels of "according to Scripture" in the y and y' lines.

Resurrection and Hope of the Community, 15:1–58

Additional Appearances (c, c′), 15:6–7

After demanding the Corinthians to recall the apostolic message that he first preached to them, Paul goes on to report in the central elements of significant additional appearances to further support their faith in the risen Lord. If the apostolic missions of Peter and the Twelve were not convincing to them, in the *c* element (15:6) Paul relays how Christ "then appeared" to five hundred brothers and sisters at once. These specific details emphasize the veracity of his claim. It is very difficult for five hundred people to spontaneously and simultaneously experience the same vision and message.[15] Paul adds that, although some have fallen asleep, many are still alive who can continue to attest to the veracity of Christ's resurrection.

In the parallel *c′* element (15:7) Paul adds how Christ "then appeared" to James and the rest of the apostles. The order of Christ's appearances follows a pattern of primary to secondary actors: Peter and the Twelve, to a massive exposition, to James (a previous doubter), and then the rest of the apostles (those who received the commission after the church had already begun to form). This pattern, underscored by the repetition of "and then he appeared," shows Christ's apparitions to be orderly. They are not haphazard but demonstrate the same sense of order and clarity that God demands in his church (14:26–33).

Last of All, to Paul (b′), 15:8–9

To round out his recitation of witnesses to the apparitions of the risen Lord, Paul himself takes the stand to testify to the veracity of Christ's resurrection. In proper order, Christ appeared to Paul last of all because he had persecuted the church. Again, the details serve to support the testimony. Paul was a persecutor of the faith: he has no benefit to preach the resurrection. To do so convicts him as having been a persecutor of God's people and a self-righteous murderer. Yet, to his indictment, this is exactly what Paul does.

And, as in the *b* element above, Paul ties this testimony of the resurrection to the audience's existence and hope for salvation. Just as Christ "appeared" to the apostles to proclaim the gospel (*b*, 15:4–6), so too did he "appear" to and commission Paul to preach the gospel (*b′*, 15:8). The manifestation of the Spirit in their worship affirms that the Corinthians themselves are recipients of the gospel.[16] So there cannot be any separa-

---

15. Keener, *1–2 Corinthians*, 125.
16. Murphy-O'Connor, *1 Corinthians*, 139: "It is noteworthy that Paul makes no distinction between the appearance to himself and the appearances to the other

tion for the Corinthians between the resurrection and the Spirit. The Spirit comes to them because of the resurrection.[17]

Implied in Paul's self-abasing biographical material is a marker of his clear significance.[18] Although a persecutor of the church, Christ appeared to him not for retribution but to recruit him to build up the church (see Gal 2:1–10; Acts 9:1–22; 22:1–20). And while he claims to be the least, he also denotes (perhaps incorrectly) that he is the last one to have received a commission from Christ.[19] Paul makes himself a punctuation mark on the summary of Christ's commission to the apostles, and he fully intends to be an exclamation point to God's plan. His own story, along with the witnesses presented in the corresponding central elements, serves to commend the resurrection to the Corinthians as a verifiable event for which the apostolic missions and the network of sanctified churches remain as evidence. Any continued refusal of the resurrection from them, in Paul's view, stands in contradiction to this clearly presented evidence.

---

witnesses. He takes it for granted that the Jesus who appeared was a real person and not some sort of Spirit (Luke 24:36–43)."

17. Witherington (*Conflict*, 300) notes that the ring-like progression "of *eita, epeita, epeita, eita* ('then, afterward, afterward, then')" in 15:5–7 does in fact underscore a chronological order to Paul's report.

18. The interpretation of Paul's self-description is complicated by a multivalent term ἔκτρωμα, which can mean an aborted fetus, a child who is miscarried, or a child who is born severely premature. Each of these has been offered at times to explain the verse (see Conzelmann, *1 Corinthians*, 259; Hollander, "Abortion," 224–36; Witherington, *Conflict*, 300). Given the temporal nature of the surrounding context, Paul likely has in mind that he is like a child who is born severely premature, but with a particular nuance (e.g., Wright, *Resurrection*, 433). A child who is born premature often cannot survive, particularly in ancient times. Some children who are born premature within a close proximity to their development can survive, but with significant ailments that last throughout their life. Just as there is a particular window in which a child can be born and survive, so too did Paul see that there was a certain window of time in the early life of the church in which Jesus appeared to commission his select apostles. Paul, being the last of these, made it just within the window. As one who was a persecutor and now graced with a commission from the risen Lord as the last of his apostles, Paul likely placed an emphatic sense on his own calling as a gift. It is common for parents of children who are born premature and survive to emphasize the "gift" aspect of the child even more than usual, often reflecting on how, but by the grace of God, the child would not be here. This seems to be the most coherent way to understand Paul's use of ἔκτρωμα to describe himself, especially with his emphasis on God's grace in his call. In his view, he barely made it. As a result, he had many more obstacles than the other apostles. But it is the "gift" aspect of his apostleship that he would later say "compelled" him to proclaim the gospel to the Gentiles (2 Cor 5:14).

19. Conzelmann, *1 Corinthians*, 258: "This sounds as if the circle of apostles was a closed one, and not identical with the circle of the Twelve."

By the Grace of God (a´), 15:10–11

In the final element of the unit, Paul returns to the issue of the Corinthians' faith via his own experience. God's grace turned Paul from persecutor to proclaimer—from one who was willing to kill the church to one who was willing to die for it—and it is this same sense of *gift* that Paul points to in order to emphasize the magnitude of what they received in the gospel.

That the Corinthians first accepted and "believed" his and the apostles' message of the resurrection (a´, 15:11) reminds them that rejecting the concept of a bodily resurrection could cause their whole pursuit and "belief" to have been in vain. Connecting the Corinthians' initial faith to the grace of God that he himself experienced is an organic development. After all, the gospel was originally preached to them by God's grace acting through Paul in order to facilitate Christ's commission to build up the church among the Gentiles. Paul is not the ultimate recipient of God's grace; he is an agent to communicate God's grace in the gospel from Christ to the elect in Corinth. This was a major portent of the faith that united them together in the Spirit to Christ. It is this sense of unity, and the pure and uncorrupted nature of their initial reception of the gospel, that Paul calls this fractured community to remember.[20]

The unit as a whole closes as it began, by addressing common ground with the audience. Paul wants to persuade the Corinthians to hold fast to the message of the resurrection that they first received from him. Both Paul's testimony to, and the Corinthians' reception of, the resurrection came about by God's grace, and both are affirmed by the Spirit that they received in baptism and continues in their worship and daily life.

This common experience serves as the nexus for their future glory: judging angels, growing in the power of the Spirit, attaining God's glory, and inheriting his kingdom through fellowship with his Son. But none of these are possible without the first step. Without the resurrection, there is no risen Lord with whom the Corinthians can have fellowship or an inheritance. They cannot be established spiritually for future glorification into a man who is still dead and buried. The resurrection must have happened for their faith to mean anything. It meant something once, when he first preached to them. And now Paul calls on the Corinthians to remember that initial faith and the experience of the Spirit to recognize the veracity of the risen Lord. Otherwise, their faith, and his entire mission to them, will have been in vain.

---

20. Margaret Mitchell, *Rhetoric*, 288–89.

Beyond What Is Written

Unit B, 15:12–34: The Second Adam's Final Campaign against the Cosmic Powers

a: 12/ But if Christ is proclaimed as raised from the dead, how can there be some (τινες) among you who say, "There is no resurrection of the dead"? 13/ If there is "no resurrection of the dead," then Christ was not raised! 14/ And if Christ was not raised then our message is worthless and your faith is worthless! 15/ And we would be indicted for testifying falsely against God, since we testified that God raised Christ, who cannot be raised unless the dead can be raised! 16/ For if the dead cannot be raised, then Christ cannot be raised. 17/ And if Christ was not raised, then your faith is garbage and you are still consumed by your sins (ἁμαρτίαις)!

b: 18/ So already those who have fallen asleep in Christ (ἐν Χριστῷ) have perished. 19/ If we have set our hope in Christ (ἐν Χριστῷ) for this life, then we are the most pitiable of all (πάντων) humanity. 20/ But now Christ is raised from the dead as the first fruits of those who have fallen asleep. 21/ For, since death came because of a human, the resurrection of the dead comes because of a human as well. 22/ For just as all (πάντες) those who are in Adam die, so too all (πάντες) those who are in Christ (ἐν Χριστῷ) are brought to life! 23/ And each has its own place: Christ is the first fruits, then those who are in Christ (ἐν Χριστῷ) when he returns. 24/ It is at this final point when he has abolished (καταργήσῃ) every (πᾶσαν) ruler, every (πᾶσαν) authority, and every (πᾶσαν) cosmic power, that he will hand over the kingdom (βασιλείαν) to God the Father.

b′: 25/ For it is necessary for him to rule (βασιλεύειν) over and set all (πάντας) of his enemies under his feet, 26/ and the last of these to be abolished (καταργεῖται) is Death. 27/ For all things (πάντα) must be made subordinate under his feet. But when it says, "He has made all things subordinate," it cannot include the one who has made all things subordinate to him. 28/ So when everything (πάντα) has been made subordinate to him, then the Son himself will make himself subordinate to God, in order that God might be all in all (πάντα ἐν πᾶσιν). 29/ Otherwise, what of those who are baptized on the dead's behalf? If the dead are not raised, why does anyone get baptized for them? 30/ And why do we put ourselves in danger all of the time? 31/ Brothers and sisters—so help me, God—I swear to you, by the boast I have in you to our Lord Jesus Christ (ἐν Χριστῷ): I die every day!

a′: 32/ If I am just battling beasts in Ephesus for people, what good would this do me? If the dead are not raised, "let's eat and drink—for tomorrow we die!" 33/ Do not be fooled! Good people can be lead astray by bad company.

34/ Sober up the right way and sin (ἁμαρτάνετε) no more! Some of those (τινες) among you know nothing of God—I say this to your shame!

The Corinthians' Faith Cannot Afford to Lose the Resurrection (a), 15:12–17

In the initial words of the B unit, we are confronted with the impetus for Paul's present oration. Some among the Corinthians are questioning the veracity of the bodily resurrection. Rather than attacking them directly, Paul has set forward in the A unit significant proofs, both from within the community and without, for the bodily resurrection of Christ. Standing firm on this foundation, he now moves forward to sweep out the legs of his dissenters. If in fact they have faith in the gospel, the manifestation of the Spirit in their worship, and hope to judge at Christ's return, how then can any of them deny a bodily resurrection?

The *a* element (15:12–17) contains a micro-ring structure.[21] The center lines focus on Paul, his fellow apostles, and their potential indictment for blasphemy for offering false "testimony" against God (*y*, 15:15a) since they "testified" that God raised his Son Jesus from the dead as the first fruits of the resurrection (*y′*, 15:15b–16). The bracket lines look to the Corinthians' own problems if their position is proved correct. First, since the gospel proclaims the risen Lord has conquered death on their behalf, their denial of the resurrection would nullify "[their] faith" (*x*, 15:12–14). The final line develops this point by explaining to the audience that if "[their] faith," which brings salvation, is nullified, then they are still in their sins before God's judgment (*x′*, 15:17).

So the Corinthians' denial of the resurrection would have considerable consequences. If they were correct, then the faith in which they stand is worthless, the apostles would be perjurers against God, and they would all still be accountable for their sins.[22] In light of Scripture (such as Isa 40:1–11;

---

21. a: (*x*) 12/ But if Christ is proclaimed as raised from the dead, how can there be some among you who say, "There is no resurrection of the dead"? 13/ If there is "no resurrection of the dead," then Christ was not raised! 14/ And if Christ was not raised then our message is worthless and *your faith* is worthless!
(*y*) 15/ And we would be indicted for *testifying* falsely against God,
(*y′*) since we *testified* that God raised Christ, who cannot be raised unless the dead can be raised! 16/ For if the dead cannot be raised, then Christ cannot be raised.
(*x′*) 17/ And if Christ was not raised, then *your faith* is garbage and you are still consumed by your sins!

22. Gaffin, *Resurrection*, 40. Gowan, *Eschatology*, 59, notes that the forgiveness of sins was necessary for the eschatological era since sin caused corruption and made one feel unworthy before God. Sins must then be expunged before one can attain God's

Jer 31:31–34; Ezek 36:22–34), however, the absolution of sins was imperative for those who wished to have life in the new age.²³ So, once again, the Corinthians' attempt to pick and choose the concepts they find acceptable is presented as illogical and detrimental to their salvation.

Die in Adam or Live in Christ (b), 15:18–24

The *b* element continues in a micro-ring format to build support for the resurrection with proofs that concern the whole of humanity.²⁴ The central lines contend that if Christ was not raised then there can be no first fruits "of the dead" (15:20). But, pointing to the idea that God's world works in an orderly fashion that offers a corrective to injustice or corruption, the *y'* line (15:21) counters that, since death came through a person (Adam), so too must the resurrection "of the dead" (through Christ). Hence, Paul intones, Christ must be the first fruits of the resurrection. As the "first fruits," a significant cultic term, Jesus represents the totality of the bodily resurrection that will take place at his parousia for the judgment.²⁵ As the new Adam, his resurrection opens the door to a new type of existence for the elect.²⁶

The bracket lines of the element take this idea even further. In the initial *x* line (15:25–26) Paul reminds the Corinthians that some of their own members have died "in" Christ, and that if this present "life" is all that they have to hope for "in" Christ as a fulfillment of their faith, then they are indeed a pitiable people. But in the *x'* line (15:28) Paul explains that, in God's ordered plan for the salvation of his elect and the renewal of his creation,

---

glory or inheritance.

23. Wright, *Resurrection*, 320.

24. b: (*x*) 18/ So already those who have fallen asleep *in* Christ have perished. 19/ If we have set our hope *in* Christ for this life, then we are the most pitiable of *all* humanity.

(*y*) 20/ But now Christ is raised from the *dead* as the first fruits of those who have fallen asleep.

(*y'*) 21/ For since death came because of a human, the resurrection of the *dead* comes because of a human as well.

(*x'*) 22/ For just as all those who are in Adam die, so too *all* those who are *in* Christ are brought to life! 23/ And each has its own place: Christ is the first fruits; then those who are *in* Christ, when he returns. 24/ It is at this final point when he will hand over the kingdom to God the Father and abolish *every* ruler, *every* authority, and *every* cosmic power.

25. Gaffin, *Resurrection*, 34: "[First fruits refers to] the offerings of grain, wine, cattle, and the like, appointed by Moses. The point to these sacrifices is that they are not offered up for their own sake . . . but as representative of the total harvest. . . . Thus 'first fruits' does not simply have a temporal force. [It] expresses the notion of organic connection and unity, the inseparability of the initial from the whole."

26. Dunn, *Theology*, 242.

just as those who are "in" Adam die, so too do those who are "in" Christ have the opportunity to escape corruption and death and "be made alive."[27] But this itinerary of salvation happens "in" a particular order: Christ is raised as the first fruits, and then those of Christ will be raised "in" his return for judgment. At this final point Christ will hand over the bundle of all worldly powers to be subsumed under God's authority. These worldly powers are those that have corrupted and attained domination over the cosmos.[28]

Christ's Orderly Campaign against the Worldly Powers (b´), 15:25–32

The b´ element expands on the process of Christ's campaign against the worldly powers in a micro-ring structure.[29] The central lines outline the itinerary by which Christ will subdue and submit the totality of the universe to God the Father. God saw fit within his plan to overthrow the powers of the world to "subordinate all things (i.e., all worldly authorities) to him (Christ)." This fulfills the Scripture that "all things must be subordinate to him" (Ps 110:1), but Paul clarifies that "all things" pertain to the world and cannot include the Almighty himself. Rather, the y´ line (15:28) explains, when "all things are subordinate to him," Christ, the obedient Son, will then subordinate himself to the One who made all things "subordinate to him." Through his submission to God, Christ, acting as humanity's representative, restores the dominion humanity was intended to have over the cosmos as a messianic ruler over a renewed creation.[30] This process fulfills the main goal of God's plan that he, as creator, might be all in all. All things would be in him, and his righteousness would proliferate an entirely renewed "every-

---

27. There is no conclusive evidence whether Paul understood non-believers to be included in the resurrection. For differing views, see Barrett, *First Epistle*, 296; Turner, "Interim," 338.

28. Barrett, *First Epistle*, 357.

29. b´: (x) 25/ For it is necessary for him to rule over and set all of his enemies under his feet, 26/ and the last of these to be abolished is *death*.
(y) 27/ For he has made all things *subordinate* under his feet. But when it says, "He has made all things *subordinate*," it cannot include the one who has made *all things subordinate to him*.
(y´) 28/ So when everything has been made *subordinate to him*, then the Son himself will make himself subordinate to the one who made *all things subordinate to him*, in order that God might be all in all.
(x´) 29/ So why are we baptizing the dead, if there is no resurrection of the dead anyway? And if the dead are not raised, why do we have them baptized? 30/ Why do we put ourselves in danger all of the time? 31/ Brothers and sisters—so help me God—I swear to you, by the boast I have in you to our Lord Jesus Christ: I *die* every day!

30. Barrett, *First Epistle*, 361; Wright, *Resurrection*, 334.

thing" (15:28). For an audience who presently live in a Roman colony, the parousia account has unmistakable royal and political overtones that God's kingdom will invade and overthrow the present rulers.[31]

The bracket lines underscore the main enemy that Christ must subdue in his campaign against the worldly powers. The certainty of Christ's victory over Death in the x line (15:25–26) affects how Paul proclaims Christ in the x' line (15:29–32). Paul does not fear "Death," and is willing to nearly "die" every day in the perpetuation of the gospel, because he is the apostle of the risen Lord who will defeat "Death" once and for all at the universal resurrection (see Dan 12:12–14). The last line in particular emphasizes the actions of the community and Paul in light of this new relationship with Death. They baptize the dead because they look forward to the time when Death's power over humanity is eliminated.[32] Paul even profoundly swears that he battles accusations of treason against Rome regularly in courtrooms like figurative beasts, and that he also nearly dies daily for the Corinthians, who stand as proof to their risen Lord of Paul's success as a minister of the gospel (15:28–39).

How then can they give up the idea of the resurrection? If they choose to do so, Paul mockingly offers, they should all change their self-sacrificing life-styles and engage debauchery instead. After all, if they could "die" tomorrow, then they might as well eat and drink it up while they can (15:32). The echo of Isa 22:13 recalls the Judeans of the South who were fully aware of their sinful activities but decided to face God's wrath through frivolity rather than get serious and repent from their sins. Paul's citation of this quote then adds a prophetic indictment against the dissenters who are repeating the mistakes of their spiritual ancestors.[33]

But the terms "eat" and "drink," while echoing Isaiah's satire, may also recall the concerns about eating and drinking before idols (1 Cor 10:1–19), and eating and drinking unworthily the Eucharist at worship (11:2–3, 17–34). The latter actions specifically anticipate the return and judgment of the risen Lord (11:33–34).[34] So the echo to these previous texts may color Paul's incorporation with more than just mocking the Corinthians' position as a slippery slope to hedonism. He may in fact be arguing that if Christ is not raised, as some of the Corinthians propose, then they nullify the center of

---

31. Wright, *Resurrection*, 337.

32. This mysterious line likely refers to some sort of vicarious baptism for friends or relatives. There is some precedent for this procedure in the mystery religions. However, the exact nature of the ritual and Paul's approval of its practice are debated points. See Barrett, *First Epistle*, 363.

33. Wright, *Resurrection*, 339.

34. Stambaugh and Balch, *Environment*, 59.

the worship in which they experience the Spirit. They may as well then eat and drink before demons since Christ has no meaning for their present or future if he has not been raised from the dead.

But Paul's main point in these lines is that Death's hold on humanity has already begun to weaken and will soon completely vanish. The Corinthians should embrace the faith in the resurrection that gives them hope in the face of Death so that they can give meaning to those whom they lost, and to Paul, who is willing to lose himself for their faith.

The *b´* element (15:25–32) connects to and completes the *b* element's itinerary of Christ's cosmic takeover (15:12–24). "Death" entered the world through Adam's sin, and all who are in Adam "die" (*b*, 5:21–22). But God saves humanity through the resurrection of the dead that comes through Jesus Christ, who will defeat "Death" and all the other cosmic powers that afflict the world when he returns in glory (*b´*, 5:25).[35]

Just as Christ will "abolish" all cosmic powers to establish and hand over a renewed kingdom to God the Father at his parousia (*b*, 5:23), so too will he in the general resurrection "abolish" Death forever (*b´*, 5:25). That Christ will "rule" over all cosmic powers and Death (*b´*, 15:25) clarifies the totality of the "kingdom" that Christ will hand over to God the Father (*b*, 15:23–24).

For Paul and the elect in Corinth, their identity, hope, and destiny all take place "in Christ." Those who have fallen asleep "in Christ" have not yet truly perished, just as those who have hoped "in Christ" do not act in vain, since those who are "in Christ" are as sure to follow him in glory as the remaining harvest follows the first fruits (B, 15:23). And since all those who are "in Christ" have the promise of new life (B, 15:22), Paul can challenge danger and death knowing that his churches, in whom he boasts, will receive new life because they are "in Christ" (B´, 15:34). This certainty of Christ's victory over the cosmic powers, and the orderly fashion in which he dispatches God's opponents, fits a primary aspect of Jewish Apocalypticism that views the end times as holding a fixed pattern of events and predetermined ending.[36]

In order to save his elect and renew creation, the "everything" that the Father has subordinated to Christ includes "all" people, "all" rulers, and "all"

---

35. Fitzmyer, *First Corinthians*, 566: "These verses may seem like a digression . . . yet their importance to what Paul has been arguing for in the preceding vv. 12–19 is especially great: the role of the risen Christ over death, which afflicts all human beings. Those who deny the resurrection of the dead (v. 12b) are denying, in effect, the power of God over death and God's role in all things."

36. See Conzelmann, *1 Corinthians*, 269. Determinism is ubiquitous throughout Jewish apocalyptic literature, e.g., *1 Enoch* 1–36; Dan 12:1–14.

authorities and powers, who are "all" enemies of God and his plan.[37] But these authorities and powers are not obliterated in Christ's conquest. After he rules over all of them, and sets them "all" under his feet, he will then hand them and himself over to the Father in order that God might be "all in all." God does not destroy the powers but subjugates them within a renewed cosmos that subsists fully within his presence and authority.[38]

Indictment against the Dissenters and the Community (a′), 15:33-34

The brief but final *a′* element brings the unit to a close with a harsh rebuke of the community's dependence on Paul's dissenters, whom he claims know little of God. Paul speaks pointedly to "some among you" who say there is no resurrection of the dead (*a*, 15:12) when he retorts that there are "some among you" who have no knowledge of God and points out, to the Corinthians' shame, that they have acquiesced to the dissenters for too long already (*a′*, 15:34).[39]

The "sins" of the community, for which Christ died (15:5) and in which the community remains if he was not raised from the dead (15:16), are still effective if they continue to be deceived by the dissenters' rejection of the resurrection. Within this context, Paul's command to "sin" no longer means they should embrace the faith in the resurrection that they had when they first received the gospel and rejected the dissenters' arguments against Paul's proclamation that serves as the hope for the salvation of the community and the cosmos.[40]

---

37. According to Turner, "Interim," 337, the itinerary of 1 Cor 15:22–26 strongly matches that found in Rev 20:4–14. If 1 Cor 15:26 and 15:50–55 are not the same event, then Paul has in view here a terrestrial messianic reign between the resurrection and the final defeat of Death. However, Turner's view that 15:20–28 forms an "apocalyptic digression" misses the coordinated argument of the unit. Further, Paul's concern is the resurrection and its import for humanity, and it is difficult to draw conclusions about the special natures of the kingdom or the fate of non-believers from this passage. As Luedemann, "Hope," 199, points out, the differences between 1 Thes 4–5 and 1 Cor 15 make it difficult to form any theological conclusion from their comparison.

38. Barrett, *First Epistle*, 361; Wright, *Resurrection*, 335.

39. *Pace* Bultmann, *Theology*, 1:295, the arguments within this unit in particular demonstrate the resurrection as more than just a theoretical proposition. Paul certainly recognizes this as a historical event in that it took place at a particular point in his own life and in the history of the Church, as did his conversion. And faith in this event is imperative for one's overall faith in Christ to be of any worth.

40. His work on 11:3–16 notwithstanding, Walker's argument that 15:29–34 is an interpolation ("1 Cor 15:29–34," 84–100) does not stand in light of the present analysis.

Unit B′, 15:35–49: Christians Brought to Life by the Second, Spiritual Adam

a: 35/ But one of those people will say, "How are the dead raised?" or, "With what type of body does this thing happen?" 36/ You idiot! Don't you know that a seed cannot be made alive (ζωποιεῖται) unless it first dies? 37/ And what you sow is not the body that will come, but a naked kernel—a type of wheat, or barley, or something else. 38/ Now God will give a body to each as he chooses—each seed gets its own body.

b: 39/ Not everything has the same flesh—humans have one type, and animals have another, and birds have another, and fish have another. 40/ It's the same way with heavenly bodies and earthly bodies—one has a heavenly glory (δόξα), and the other an earthly. 41/ The sun has another type of glory (δόξα), and the moon has another type of glory (δόξα), and the stars have another type of glory (δόξα). For stars differ from one another in glory (δόξῃ)

b′: 42/ It is the same way with the resurrection of the dead. It is sown in corruption, but raised in incorruption. 43/ It is sown in disrepute, but raised in glory (δόξῃ). It is sown in weakness—it is raised in power! 44/ It is sown with an ordinary body, but it is raised with a spiritual body.—If there is an ordinary body there is also a spiritual body!

a′: 45/ It is the same way in what is written: "Adam, the first human, came about as a living (ζῶσαν) being, but the last Adam as a life-giving (ζῳοποιοῦν) Spirit." 46/ The spiritual was not first, the ordinary was—then came the spiritual. 47/ The first person came from dust, but the second came from heaven. 48/ Those of the earthly one belong to the dust, but those of the heavenly one belong to heaven. 49/ And just as we have worn the mark of the dust, so too do we now wear the mark of the heavenly one.

The Resurrection and Seeds in New Life (a), 15:35–38

Having in the last unit presented the soteriological narrative of Christ's orderly campaign against all worldly powers and Death in order to undo the harm of Adam's fall, in the B′ unit Paul discusses more details about the resurrection and the soteriological contrast between Adam and Christ. His strategy to this point has been to aggressively drive a wedge between the dissenters and the community through shame and dissociation. Now that he has separated the offending party from the rest of the community,

---

And his concern for v. 33 is well addressed by Wright, *Resurrection*, 337.

Paul directs his harshest words at the dissenters who "have no knowledge of God."

Paul begins this foray by engaging a fictive "straw man" dissenter in verbal combat. The context presumes that even after the arguments Paul has set forward, someone will still ask how exactly the dead are raised and with what type of body. The response is harsh: "Idiot!"[41] From there Paul gives everyday examples that even the least educated would understand. Paul's choice of using agriculture rather than Plato to support his position would serve his invective against dissenters who likely claimed some education in philosophy and other Hellenistic traditions. Paul points out that, in reality, a plant cannot grow unless the seed first dies, and the plant that arises from the process looks nothing like the kernel at the beginning. But Paul is not interested in agriculture or the exact correspondence between the resurrection and seeds. His goal is primarily to demonstrate how his argument is evident in even the most basic natural processes. So the dissenters' questions are as idiotic as their position and betray that they have "no knowledge of God" (15:34).

A Different Type of Glory (b, b'), 15:39–44

The patronizing, mocking tone and agricultural examples continue in the *b* element (15:39–41). Not all flesh/bodies are the same. He explains that humans, fish, birds, and animals all have different types of bodies, just as the heavenly bodies of stars, the sun, and moon also differ in glory from one another. This element serves to undermine the dissenters' foundational objections, but the distinction between heavenly and earthly bodies also anticipates his argument for the rest of the unit.

The *b'* element (15:42–44) builds on the rhetorical context of the *b* element (15:39–41) by moving from the physical realm to the theological. What is true for seeds and bodies in the physical realm of agriculture and astronomy is also true for bodies in the resurrection of the dead. The human body, like a seed, is sown in corruption, but raised in perfection; sown in the dishonor of death, but raised in glory; sown in the weakness of small size, but raised by God's power in Christ. In short, the human body is sown as an earthly, ordinary body, but it is raised as a glorious, spiritual body.[42] Here the σῶμα πνευματικόν ("spiritual body") likely refers not to the bodies'

---

41. Paul's harsh response may mischaracterize the dissenters' concerns. Based on the various Greco-Roman views of the body after death, the Corinthians' objections to the resurrection were relatively understandable; see Witherington, *Conflict*, 307.

42. Gaffin, *Resurrection*, 79.

composition, but rather, what animates it: hence, the "spiritual body" is one that is enlivened and fueled solely by the Spirit,[43] or that acts in a spiritual manner.[44] Such terminology is dependent on traditions of God animating his elect for a new age that are found in Jer 31:31–34 and Ezek 36–37.

The logic of Paul's argument to this point is that the spiritual body is necessarily different from the regular body in such a way as to be incomparable. So, once again, Paul's response to the straw man dissenter's position is that their questions questions lack even lack even the most basic knowledge of the physical world, not to mention God. The development of the *b′* element (15:42–44) from the *b* element (15:39–41) serves to punctuate this rhetorical onslaught. The "glory" in which the human body is raised is different from any type of ordinary body because it is a spiritual body; and the difference between the "glory" of a spiritual body and an ordinary body is as vast as the difference between the "glory" of the earthly bodies of fish, birds, and animals and the heavenly bodies of the sun, moon, and stars.

Between Adam and Christ (*a′*), 15:45–49

Having supported his rebuke against the dissenters with agriculture and astronomy, Paul now utilizes Scripture and the Adam/Christ comparison to further his rhetorical counterattack. With the formulary "as it is written," Paul points to the creation stories of Genesis to deduce the difference between humanity's past in Adam and their future in Christ. The first man, Adam, came as a living being, but the last man, Christ, came as a life-giving Spirit. Paul here appears to draw on Philo's interpretation of a spiritual human and an earthly human in the two creation accounts of Genesis.[45] The difference is profound: a living being can only survive, but a life-giving Spirit subsists by God's own power and gives life to others. The vast difference between the earthly body and spiritual body parallels that between Adam and Christ. The two distinctions serve to underscore the heightened level of the mystery of the resurrection. A third pair, dust and heavens, parallels the Adam/Christ contrast. Those who are with Adam will inherit the dust in their future. But those who are with Christ, the heavenly man, have the heavens as their promised inheritance. This inheritance is marked by putting on the image of Christ or of Adam (dust). There is little doubt that one group is dramatically more attractive than the other. A way of knowing

---

43. Wright, *Resurrection*, 352.
44. Witherington, *Conflict*, 309.
45. Barrett, *First Epistle*, 373–75; Wright, *Resurrection*, 356.

(human and spiritual) in 2:1–13 now becomes one's manner of being (human and spiritual) and eternal identity (the dust, or the heavens).[46]

The development from the *a* element (15:35–38) explains how this heavenly inheritance comes about for those who are in Christ. The power by which the seed is "brought to life" only after it dies belongs to Christ, who is not a "living" being alone like Adam but a "life-giving" Spirit. This imagery coheres with Paul's earlier declaration that God will raise believers by Christ's power and verifies for the audience the faithfulness of the resurrection (6:15–20). If the audience believes that God would send his Son to redeem them and sanctify them with his Spirit to preserve them for their heavenly inheritance, how then can they say that he would not complete his plan for them? If the gospel in which they believed and the manifestation of the Spirit in them are anything worth their salt, then God has already begun to fulfill his promises for their salvation.

Unit A´, 15:50–58: The Resurrection and Christ's Parousia as the Basis for Hope

a: 50/ This is what I'm saying, brothers and sisters (ἀδελφοί): flesh and blood are not empowered (οὐ δύναται) to inherit God's kingdom, just as corruption is not able to inherit perfection. 51/ Behold, I tell you a mystery: We will not all (πάντες) sleep, but we will all (πάντες) be changed. 52/ In a split second, in the blink of an eye, at the last trumpet—for it will blare and the dead will be raised as perfect and we will be changed.

b: 53/ For it is necessary that the corruption put on incorruption, and for mortality to put on immortality (τὸ φθαρτὸν τοῦτο ἐνδύσασθαι ἀφθαρσίαν καὶ τὸ θνητὸν τοῦτο ἐνδύσασθαι ἀθανασίαν).

b´: 54/ And when corruption has put on incorruption and mortality has put on immortality (τὸ φθαρτὸν τοῦτο ἐνδύσηται ἀφθαρσίαν καὶ τὸ θνητὸν τοῦτο ἐνδύσηται ἀθανασίαν) then the message that was written will come to pass: "Death is swallowed in victory! 55/ O, Death, where is your victory? O, Death, where is your sting?"

a´: 56/ Now sin is death's sting, and the Law is sin's power (δύναμις). 57/ But thanks be to God, who brings us victory through Jesus Christ. 58/ So, my beloved brothers and sisters (ἀδελφοί), become firm pillars, abounding in every (πάντοτε) work of the Lord, knowing that your labor is not in vain when it is in the Lord.

---

46. Johnson, "Upside Down," 302.

Resurrection and Hope of the Community, 15:1–58

Itinerary for the Parousia (a), 15:49–52

Having again proved the necessity of the resurrection of the dead in the B′ unit, Paul now returns to address how the particular events will take place. While he spoke of how Christ would complete his campaign against the cosmic powers in the B unit, now he outlines how this campaign begins so that the Corinthians can recognize it when it arrives. Again, the certainty that pervades Paul's rhetorical argument serves to persuade the audience to see the veracity of his claims. It is not a matter of "if" but "when" Christ will arrive to complete God's plan and bring them all to glory.

As in many of his closing units to this point, Paul opens with a vocative to appeal to the familial relationship that he and the audience share in Christ by addressing them as his brothers and sisters. This rhetorical move also serves to show how Paul distinguishes between the dissenters who are idiots and have no knowledge of God and the (majority of his?) audience who have received the Spirit and fellowship with him as children of God and co-heirs of Christ.

Paul then explains the root cause of the elect's future glorification: they will not all sleep, but they will all be changed. The rapid succession of events from heaven and earth cohere with Paul's emphasis on the immediacy of the parousia. The universality of the transformation may well serve to squelch any synchronism with Roman imperial eschatology that benefits only a few.[47]

The exact process of the transformation takes place off stage from the apocalyptic drama that unfolds here. Instead, the content of that transformation is expressed in the line that proceeds: the dead will be raised as uncorrupted (15:45–47). That is, they will have taken on the glory that is uniquely heavenly, spiritual, made alive by Christ, and vastly different from the ordinary bodies that are earthly and made terminal by Adam (15:48). The difference between the pre-transformation body and the post-transformation body is as vast as that between fish and stars (15:39–45).

Putting on Incorruption and Immortality (b, b′), 15:53–54

The brief but theologically dense central elements attempt to unpack the nature, though not the details, of the transformation process described briefly in the *a* element (15:51–52). The *b* element (15:53) opens up as one that is both explanatory and causal: it is necessary that the corruptible body put on incorruption and that the mortal body put on immortality, since corruption

---

47. Witherington, *Conflict*, 310.

cannot inherit incorruption and mortal flesh and blood cannot inherit God's kingdom (15:50).[48] God requires that the regular, earthly bodies that otherwise would inherit dust be utterly transformed into the likeness of his Heir in order that they can also be heirs of his heavenly inheritance, the Kingdom.[49]

The b′ element (15:54) completes the rich explanation by appealing to Scripture. When God has completed his work for the elect that began through the Spirit at their reception of the gospel in hope for inheriting God's Kingdom in the future, then the Scripture will be fulfilled that says, "Death is swallowed in victory!" (Isa 25:8). Paul adds further Scripture support that serves to mock Death by asking where is his victory or his sting (Hos 13:4). The force of these two elements makes the nature of the transformation and its divinely-instituted necessity the center of the unit overall.[50]

The Grace of Victory in Christ (a′), 15:55–58

The final unit and this ring set on the resurrection come to a close with an appeal for the audience's understanding. The element opens with a shorthand explanation of previous forms of salvation that anticipate a distinction with the new path in grace through Christ. The reason why Christ is necessary is because Death had become far too powerful for humanity to handle. Death's "sting" is found in humanity's sin; that is, humanity falls into Death's clutches by consistently drinking the poisonous venom of sin.

Paul then states too briefly that "the law is the power of sin," which can easily be misunderstood on face value.[51] Unpacked, the statement likely means that the Law makes clear what is sinful and what is not, and therefore can be used against humanity to show exactly in what manner, and how many times, humanity has sinned against God. In a sense, a law when followed is a good guide; but when it is broken any law subsequently becomes an indictment. And because of its inability to follow God's will on their own through the Law, humanity was in danger of God's impending wrath.

---

48. Grosheide, *First Epistle*, 393.

49. Johnson, "Trump Card," 190: "In its rhetorical context, the phrase ['flesh and blood'] functions as a part of Paul's overall argument that even the fleshly material of the human body will be transformed and incorporated into the reign of God / new creation."

50. Wright (*Resurrection*, 357) notes how the repetition of the phrasing in 15:53–54 stresses the central role of these verses to the unit's overall message.

51. See Milinovich, *Now*, 84.

But, by his grace—through Christ's death, resurrection, and future successful campaign against the cosmos—God has given his elect victory over Death in order that they can inherit his Kingdom as uncorrupted, completely renewed, and transformed co-heirs with Christ. Having presented these powerful points to the audience, Paul exhorts them as his beloved brothers and sisters in the Lord to pursue every work in a manner that reflects positively on their future hope and inheritance.

The a' element connects back to the a element (15:50–52) on significant points to draw the unit, and the ring set, to a close. Flesh and blood are "not able" to inherit the kingdom of God (a, 15:50) because the Law became an insurmountably "powerful" agent of Sin and Death by indicting humans for their infractions against God (a', 15:55). Just as "all" will not sleep, but "all" will be changed as a totality for the resurrection because God requires that corruption take on perfection and mortality take on immortality, so too must the Corinthians live in hope that their "every" action in the present life will cohere and keep them bound in Christ in order to receive their inheritance.

But they must keep in mind that while they are required to live within certain perimeters to maintain the inheritance, the victory that they receive in Christ is a total gift from God: they are not able to attain salvation on their own because of their weaknesses to sin. Their potential for corruption led to sin and then to Death. But in Christ God has empowered them to receive the inheritance that he had prepared for them. So, while he calls them his "brothers and sisters" who cannot inherit God's kingdom as flesh and blood, except through additional help in the a element, in his closing element Paul exhorts his "beloved brothers and sisters"—those who are loved by Paul and also by God their Father and their shared Lord Jesus Christ—to live and believe with steadfast hope that everything they do in this life is not at all in vain.[52] Their future life in God's Kingdom is a gift and, so long as they remain in Christ, remains guaranteed.

---

52. Margaret Mitchell (*Rhetoric*, 177) notes that the term "steadfast" recalls the building metaphor used to exhort the Corinthians to unity and similar rhetoric throughout the letter. Such terminology at the close of a letter is strategic and intended to persuade the audience away from their factionalism.

Beyond What Is Written

INTERRELATION OF UNITS

The Tradition of Christ's Resurrection as the Basis for the Community's Faith (A, 15:1–11)

Paul reminds his sanctified "brothers and sisters" (ἀδελφοῖ) in Corinth that the resurrection of Jesus Christ was the good news that he first reported to them, and from which they received their faith and sanctification (15:1–3; see also 1:4–9). The report is validated by the numerous witnesses who can attest to seeing the risen Lord, the last of these being Paul himself (15:8). Since he views his last-minute recruitment to be an apostle as a full extension of "God's grace" (χάρις θεοῦ), he works in his ministry to assure that this "grace from God" (χάρις θεοῦ) did not arrive to him in vain. Rather, he endeavors so that "God's grace" (χάρις θεοῦ) abounds in how he preaches Christ's resurrection and salvation for the Corinthians.

The Second Adam's Final Campaign against the Cosmic Powers (B, 15:12–34)

Paul contends with those who dissent against the resurrection of the dead that, if they are correct, then Christ was not raised either, and their faith for salvation is in vain because they are still in their sins (15:17). Paul counters that since Death entered the world because of the first man, so too must the resurrection of the dead come from the last. So, just as all those who are in "Adam" (Αδαμ) die, all those who are in Christ are "brought to life" (ζωοποίεται) in his resurrection (15:21–22).

The Elect Are Brought to Life by the Second, Spiritual Adam (B´, 15:35–49)

Paul continues his campaign against the dissenters by explaining that there are different types of bodies, and the resurrected bodies of the dead are transformed to a new type of glory that is different than their corruptible, earthly bodies (15:35–39). These different bodies and destinations are represented in two men. The first man, "Adam" (Αδαμ), was brought to life as a living being, but the last "Adam" (Αδαμ), Christ, is a "life-giving" (ζωοποίεται) Spirit, through whom God animates and glorifies earthly human bodies (15:45–46). Those who attach themselves to Christ attach themselves also to a heavenly future inheritance (15:49).

Resurrection and Hope of the Community, 15:1–58

The Resurrection and Christ's Parousia as the Basis for Hope (A´, 15:50–58)

Paul clarifies for his "brothers and sisters" (ἀδελφοι) in Corinth that flesh and blood are not able to enter God's kingdom; rather, all must be transformed from corruptible to incorruptible, and from mortal to immortal (15:50). Humanity on its own cannot achieve this transformation, nor can the Law; but, by God's grace (χάρις θεοῦ), the elect can share in Christ's victory over Death to receive immortality (15:57). Following from this hope, Paul exhorts his beloved "brothers and sisters" (ἀδελφοι) to stand firm and labor all the more for Christ, knowing that their labor cannot be in vain when it is for the Lord who brings them eternal life (15:58).

Conclusion

The central B and B´ units summarize humanity's creation, sin, and salvation in a tale of two men. The first man, "Adam," who was a living being, brought Death into the world through his transgression, and all humans die as a result (B, 15:21–22). But the last "Adam," Christ, is a "life-giving" Spirit in whom all those who would be of dust and die in the first Adam can now be "brought to life" through faith in the gospel and hope for salvation (B´, 15:45–46). The two Adams' origins prefigure two different destinies for humanity: for one group there is burial in the dust, but for the other there is new life in heaven (B´, 15:49). As a result, the Corinthians are exhorted to put on Christ's identity so as to prefigure their clothing in a transformed resurrection body (see 15:53–54) as co-heirs of God's Kingdom.

The bracket units center on the relationship that Paul and the Corinthians share in Christ and future hope in the resurrection that come about because of God's grace. Paul is convinced that "God's grace," by which Christ appeared to Paul and recruited him to edify the church by preaching the gospel to the Gentiles, did not arrive to him in vain because "God's grace" has made Paul the apostle that he is. Furthermore, "God's grace" overflowed through Paul's initial ministry to the Corinthians (A, 15:1–3, 9–11) when they believed his proclamation of the gospel of Christ's resurrection and their own future glory with him (see 6:14). This victory over Death, which God gives to the elect through Christ, serves as a demonstration of "God's grace" in its totality, and thus calls them to a new way of life in a new family that finds their identity in Christ apart from their imperial contexts (A´, 15:56–58).

Beyond What Is Written

The Corinthian Christians are Paul's siblings because of the gift that they have received from God in the gospel. And, while Paul admonishes his "brothers and sisters" in the audience to remember the root of their relationship that is the hope of the resurrection and the good news of a new Lord in the risen Christ (A, 15:1–3), he also reminds these "brothers and sisters" that flesh and blood cannot enter God's Kingdom but must undergo an incredible transformation that is animated by the risen Lord (A´, 15:51–52). Likewise, he calls on his "beloved brothers and sisters" to transform their own lives now to conform to the standards of their risen Lord without fear of Death since they can know that victory has already been given to them in Christ over humanity's most inescapable opponent (A´, 15:58).

So, for Paul, there is no separation between his apostolic commission and God's grace. And there is no separation between God's grace and his relationship with the Corinthians. For him, all three of these ideas are tied together as one massive gift from God so that they might all share in Christ's victory over Death and attain to God's glory in a transformed reality as incorruptible and immortal heirs of God's Kingdom.

11

Closing and Preparations for the Next Visit, 16:1–24

Section A′, Ring Set α′

ANALYSIS OF UNITS

CONFORMING TO HIS CONTEMPORARY literary genre, Paul's opening and closing ring sets serve to introduce and conclude, respectively, the major concerns that will be found in the letter. The closing in ring set α′ continues the important theme of unity in the church at Corinth, but also underscores the inevitability of Paul's return to greet and evaluate the community's formation in the Spirit. As his rhetoric makes clear, it is not a matter of "if," but "when" he returns to this broken community. The repeated warnings in this farewell impress all the more how seriously the Corinthians must consider the directives in the body of the letter.

Unit A, 16:1–4: The Collection and Paul's Arrival

a: 1/ Now concerning the collection for the intentions of (εἰς) the sanctified: just as I instructed the churches of Galatia, so too do I instruct you (ὑμεῖς) to do. 2/ On the first day of the week, each of you (ὑμῶν) should take of his wages and set aside what he considers appropriate, b: so that I do not need to take a collection when I arrive (ὅταν γίνοται).

b′: 3/ But when I do arrive (ὅταν παραγένωμαι),

a′: if you should select certain individuals, I will send these with commendation letters to bear your (ὑμῶν) gift for the intentions of (εἰς) Jerusalem. 4/ And if you think it's better for me to go too, then they would accompany me.

The Collection for the Sanctified (a) 16:1–2a

The opening to his final section of the letter addresses Paul's arrival and the collection that he hopes to take from his Gentile churches to Jerusalem. That 16:1 opens with περὶ δέ (meaning "with regard to/ concerning"), which is used elsewhere in this letter to address the Corinthians' concerns (7:1; 8:1; 15:1), leads us to believe that the Corinthians had asked Paul for further instructions on his collection in their letter to him.[1] His response is direct, clear, and based on precedent. He wants to demonstrate that he is not asking them to do anything that he has not asked other communities to do. On the first day of the week (i.e., the day that they meet as a community) they should set aside funds from their surplus to offer for the sanctified.

The collection was part of Paul's promise to Peter and James in their acceptance of his mission to the Gentiles (Gal 2:9–13). The collection represented several things. First, it showed that Paul had kept his word to the pillars of the Church in Jerusalem (something that perhaps they had not done when they did not apply more political pressure on his Judaizing opponents to relent in their mission against Paul). Second, it fulfilled several OT passages that spoke of Gentiles sending wealth to Jerusalem as a sign of God's imminent judgment (Hag 2:6–8; Zech 8:18–23; see also Joel 3:1–5). Early Christian preaching and interpretation of Scripture was rich in eschatological anticipation, and in the collection Paul presented his own churches as those Gentiles who fulfill God's plan for Israel's reconstitution and the renewal of the cosmos. Third, it demonstrated the unity of the Christian movement—both Jews and Gentiles—as entering a new stage in their relationship and existence. If Gentiles could invest monetarily in this movement and provide for the Temple and the community in Jerusalem, then they rightfully had a place among the sanctified and the renewed understanding of God's elect. So it makes sense that Paul was willing to put his life on the line for the collection since it demonstrated and summarized the scope and purpose of his entire ministry.

---

1. Witherington, *Conflict*, 313; cf. Conzelmann, *1 Corinthians*, 295.

Closing and Preparations for the Next Visit, 16:1–24

Paul's Arrival (b, b´) 16:2b–3a

The central elements concern Paul's main interest in this ring set: his next visit to this fractured community. The sense of his imminent return helps to galvanize all of his instructions and creates a sense of urgency for the Corinthians to become again a unified and ethically sound entity—a group that can effectively live up to its title as "God's church in Corinth" (1:2).

The *b* element (16:2b) completes the idea that began in the previous element. The Corinthians should do as Paul instructed the Galatians and collect small portions weekly so that he does not need to take up a large collection all at once "when he arrives" (16:2b). The *b´* element repeats the phrase "when I arrive," using the particle that denotes Paul's certainty of his return. It is not a question of "if," but "when" he will arrive to evaluate the progress of his church in Corinth and their formation in Christ (16:3a; see also 4:18–21; 14:40).

On many levels the entire rhetorical demonstration of the letter prepares for this statement and this upcoming event. Paul knows that an absent pastor is often an ineffective pastor. The letter serves to show some of his presence and power upfront and guarantees that he will be arriving in the near future.

The Collection for Jerusalem (a´), 16:3b–4

The *a´* element repeats the concerns of the *a* element (16:1–2a) and clarifies that the "sanctified" for whom the collection is "intended" are those who are in Jerusalem. Paul reminds the Corinthians of their imperative role in this collection with the repetition of the pronoun "you." It is "your" gift (16:4) that Paul is directing "you" in Corinth to make on a weekly basis as each of "you" (16:2a) set aside a portion from personal financial resources. The use of both singular and plural pronouns shows that the collection is something that the Corinthians should understand as both an individual and corporate responsibility. They each need to contribute so that the church as a whole can take part in a demonstration of the fulfillment of Paul's mission to the Gentiles by successfully investing in the Christian movement's base location. It also shows the Corinthians' solidarity with other Christian churches.[2]

While Paul's return is certain, that imperative is contrast with contingent particle "if," that the Corinthians may execute by their choosing. In this way Paul is able to soften his directives on the collection. Paul will acquiesce to any request "if" they would choose to collect the portions every

---

2. Fitzmyer, *First Corinthians*, 612.

week (16:2a). Or, "if" they decide to select some members to accompany him to Jerusalem, and "if" they consider it necessary to assure its safe arrival (16:4) they may do so. The rhetorical strategy of these verses is quite diplomatic. Paul is instructing the Corinthians to give their money to him, but in a manner in which it is their own decision to take part, along with his other churches. By fulfilling the collection and aiding those who are suffering in Jerusalem, they assure their place among God's sanctified and convince Paul's opponents that his gospel to the Gentiles is effective and within God's will. To this point, considering the stark political nature of this topic in the early church, Paul is challenging the Corinthians to argue for their own legitimacy among the sanctified. As we have seen throughout the letter, arguing for their rightful place in anything is something of a specialty of this community.

Unit B, 16:5–12: Travelogues for Paul, Timothy, and Apollos

a: 5/ And I will come (ἐλεύσομαι) to you on my journey through Macedonia, for I will be journeying through Macedonia. 6/ And when I arrive to you I hope to stay with you through the winter, so that you can send me on to wherever I might go. 7/ For I do not want (θέλω) to see you for just a short time; rather, I hope to remain with you for a while, if the Lord allows.

b: 8/ For now, I am staying in Ephesus until Pentecost. 9/ For a great door has been opened to me for work (ἐνεργής), but there are many obstacles.

b': 10/ Now when Timothy arrives, see that he has nothing to fear while he is with you, because his work (ἔργον) is the work (ἐργάζεται) of the Lord, as is mine. 11/ No one must harass him. Since he is traveling with the brothers, send him on peacefully so that he can come back to me.

a': 12/ Now concerning Apollos our brother: I have encouraged him many times to come to you with the brothers, but he did not want (θέλημα) to come at this time. He will come (ἐλεύσεται) when he sees fit.

Paul's Travel Plan Details (a, b) 16:5–9

Paul now moves to explain his travel plan in more detail to give the Corinthians a clearer idea of how soon he will be arriving. He explains that his return will not occur immediately, but he will come by and see them following his inspections of other communities in Macedonia (which likely include Philippi and Thessalonica). He makes sure to point out that he is arriving to Corinth last not because they are least important, but because he

Closing and Preparations for the Next Visit, 16:1–24

hopes to spend an extended amount of time with them throughout the winter. This extended amount of time may very well be necessary to repair what has become one of his most problematic communities. But there is also the practical reason for wanting to winter in Corinth: of the three Macedonian cities, Corinth is one of the few Greek cities where the secular leaders did not seek Paul's life. If he is to survive this trip and the winter to carry forward his collection, it serves him best to do so with the Corinthians.

The *b* element (16:8–9) expresses why he has not come already. He intends to stay in Ephesus until Pentecost because he has had much success in his mission work there. This comment puts his absence from the community in a positive light. He is not avoiding them out of fear of defeat but rather is working hard and succeeding elsewhere.

Travels of Paul's Co-Workers (b´, a´) 16:10–12

Next Paul addresses ministers whom he has already claimed as his co-workers. Timothy, who has already embarked and will arrive to Corinth soon (unless dispatched elsewhere following a change in news), is to be received and welcomed by the community (16:10–11). Given how Paul introduced Timothy at the beginning, and his stern warning of any mistreatment against the young missionary, we can assume that there was bad blood of some sort between Timothy and some members of the Corinthian church (likely the libertines or Apollos group). Instead, the Corinthians are to welcome him and send him on "in peace" back to Paul (16:11). Following this itinerary, Timothy is able to measure the community's reception of the present letter. Their treatment of him will demonstrate how well they have accepted Paul's instructions in this letter.[3]

Finally, Paul addresses his co-worker Apollos and whether he will be returning to the community as well. As above, Paul's comments are worded so that they can either be benign and informative or accusatory and critical. For instance, that Paul has spoken to Apollos about the community and their future plans to visit bespeaks an amicable relationship and may simply inform the church that Apollos is not able to return now. However, the specific words that Paul uses—θέλω and εὐχαίρω, rather than δύναμει—may underscore Apollos' absence is more of an issue of "desire" than "ability." For instance, a primary candidate for the presidency who is speaking to a crowd in Iowa about an opponent's lack of desire to leave New Hampshire and return to the Hawkeye state "when she/he chooses" would be a shot

---

3. Witherington, *Conflict*, 316; Keener, *1–2 Corinthians*, 137.

across the bough of the other candidate's campaign, and a question of that candidate's genuine interest in winning over the caucus state.

This distinction in pastoral investment is emphasized by the repetition of key terms that are used in contrasting manners between Paul in the *a* element (16:5–7) and Apollos in the *a´* element (16:12). Paul is certain that he "will come" to Corinth in the course of his Macedonian journey because he "wants" to spend the winter with them (*a*, 16:5), but Apollos does not "want" to come now and "will come" when he pleases (*a´*, 16:12). The implication of Apollos' diminished interest in the community serves at least as a partial victory for the pro-Pauline faction. Although he demurred to some of their extreme interpretations of his teachings, this unit makes clear to both factions that only one apostle is clearly invested in this community enough to send an interim supervisor (Stephanus), a lieutenant (Timothy), and then arrive himself in haste.

Unit A´, 16:13–24: Formal Closing

a: 13/ Be watchful, stand firm in the faith, be heroic and courageous. 14/ All of you must act lovingly (ἀγάπη) toward one another. 15/ I exhort you, brothers and sisters—you know the household (οἰκίαν) of Stephanus, who are the first fruits of Achaia, and they commend themselves for the ministry of the sanctified (ἁγίοις).

b: 16/ So be subordinate to these certain individuals (τοιούτοις) and to all those who work and labor with them.

c: 17/ I rejoice at the arrival of Stephanus, Fortunatus, and Achaius, for they carried over your gifts.

b´: 18/ They refreshed my spirit and yours. So recognize these certain individuals (τοιούτοις).

a´: 19/ The churches of Asia greet you. Aquila and Prisca greet you in the Lord with their house (οἶκον) church. 20/ All the brothers and sisters greet you. Greet one another with sanctified (ἁγίῳ) devotion. 21/ I, Paul, write this greeting with my own hand. 22/ If anyone does not show devotion to the Lord, he must be cursed. Our Lord, come! 23/ The grace of the Lord Jesus be with you always. 24/ And my love (ἀγάπη) in Christ Jesus be with all of you.

Closing and Preparations for the Next Visit, 16:1-24

Final Exhortation (a, b, c, b´) 16:13-18

The final unit of this letter begins with an exhortation to be disciplined and subordinate to those commended to be their pastoral leaders. The first, third, and fourth imperatives echo commands from apocalyptic (Matt 24:13; 25:16) and pre-battle (Josh 10:25; 2 Chr 32:7) speeches, respectively. These, along with the Pauline order to "stand in the faith" (1 Cor 15:2, 12; also), create a single internal narrative for the audience. The sum of what Paul has taught in this letter is part of an intense eschatological battle, for which the Corinthians must continue to prepare.

The four-fold directive sets up what appears to be a primary concern in Paul's mind—the pastoral oversight of the community, and the community's proper treatment of their overseers. Stephanas and his household, whom Paul himself baptized (1 Cor 1:12), have placed themselves in the service of the sanctified churches, and Paul wishes for the Corinthians to treat them with due respect. Although it is normally inappropriate to commend oneself to ministry (e.g., 2 Cor 4:1), in this case it appears more that it is the work that Stephanas and his household have already done in Achaia that commends them for service to the Corinthians in particular. The *b* element (16:16) affirms that the Corinthians appropriate reaction to Stephanas' ministry should be subordination and/or appreciation, since he and those with him are laboring on Christ's behalf.

The central element (*c*, 16:17) of the unit focuses on Stephanas, along with Fortunatus and Achaichus, who are serving as intermediaries in the present correspondence. It appears that these three brought with them the letter that the Corinthians had written to Paul (e.g., 7:1; 15:1; 16:1), and perhaps now have returned with 1 Corinthians in hand. It is unclear who may be performing the letter to the community—perhaps Stephanas, or a member of the household. If such is the case, then Stephanas, his compatriots, and his family, have a great challenge ahead of them in overseeing the execution of the letter's demands among the community.

This idea is carried forward in the *b´* element (16:18), which, for its part, caps off Paul's wishes in the central elements. Those "certain individuals"—Stephanus and his household—whom Paul commends to the Corinthians, and to whom he requests they be subordinate (*b*, 16:16), are clarified further as "those certain individuals" whom the community are to recognize because they served Paul during their stay with him (*b´*, 16:18). Thus the central elements of this closing unit serve to solidify the authority of certain members who are also loyal to Paul, who may oversee the proper implementation of the letter's exhortations, and prepare for Timothy's and Paul's own upcoming visits to the city.

Beyond What Is Written

Farewell and Blessing (a'), 16:19–24

The final element of the letter contains a micro-ring structure.[4] The central line (z, 16:21) denotes that Paul has taken up the pen himself, and likely applies to the entire element 16:19–24 (not just vv. 21–24). In doing so, he is attempting to demonstrate a personal connection that is indicative of his fatherly relationship with the community (see 4:18–21).

The next layer of lines concerns affection within the church community. As he commonly does, Paul calls on his audience to greet one another with sanctified "devotion" (i.e., "a holy kiss," 1 Thes 5:26; 2 Cor 13:12; Rom 16:16). In the parallel y' line (16:22), he pronounces that anyone who is not "devoted" to the Lord must be accursed. He then immediately heralds the Lord's arrival with an Aramaic formula that must be very early in the church. The term "anathema," in the LXX, and Rom 9:3, refers to separation from God or, in this case, the dissolution of one's relationship and inheritance in Christ. Here "loving" the Lord would mean declaring him and loving him as your Lord in place of Caesar or Greco-Roman conventions. To love the Lord would also mean to accept his commands and the apostles whom he sends to direct his churches. Those who do not "adore" the Lord in such a manner effectively abdicate the spiritual blessings that were attained through Christ and the Spirit for their future glory and salvation (1:4–9).

The bracket lines focus on the whole of the community and personalize the greeting by repeating the second-person pronouns. In the x line (16:19) Paul expresses the well wishes of those who are with him to "you," the Corinthians. The total adjectives, "all of the brothers and sisters" (16:19) greet "all of you" (16:24), express the unity the Corinthians should attain, not only with themselves, but also with the rest of the churches under Paul and throughout the empire (see 1:1–3; 11:16; 14:33). The interrelation of the lines also underscores the relationship between the community, Paul's friends, and Paul himself. "You," the audience, are tied through Christ to the churches of Asia, to Aquila and Prisca (their former teachers, Acts 18:1–4), and all the brothers and sisters; and evenmoreso, "you" are tied to Paul, Christ's apostle, who was sent as a father to preach the gospel and plant a

---

4. a': (x) 19/ The churches of Asia greet *you*. Aquila and Prisca greet *you* in the Lord with their house church. *All* the brothers and sisters greet *you*.

(y) 20/ Greet one another with sanctified *devotion*.

(z) 21/ I, Paul, write this greeting with my own hand.

(y') 22/ If anyone does not show *devotion* to the Lord, he must be anathema. Our Lord, come!

(x') 23/ The grace of the Lord Jesus be with *you* always. 24/ And my love in Christ Jesus be with *all of you*.

Closing and Preparations for the Next Visit, 16:1-24

church of God's elect in Corinth, and now sends his own love demonstrated in this letter, until he may see "you" again.

INTERRELATION OF UNITS

Outline

The Collection and Paul's Arrival (A, 16:1-4)

Paul informs the Corinthians to collect funds on behalf of the "sanctified" (ἁγίους) in Jerusalem, just as he directed the "churches" (ἐκκλησίαις) of Galatia (1:1). This offering is a "gift" (χάριν) that affirms the relationship of the Gentile Christians with their base in Jerusalem and gives theological and political support to the mission that Paul has been struggling to maintain (1:3).

Paul and Timothy Will Return, but Apollos Is Uncertain (B, 16:5-12)

In this unit, Paul gives clearer details about his imminent return to Corinth, which serves as both a promise and a warning to the problematic community. In addressing his return, he must also mention Timothy and Apollos. The former serves as a preliminary barometer to the community's reception of this letter and their relationship with Paul (16:10-11). The mention of the latter underscores that, while Apollos does not want to come now but will when he wishes, Paul assures the community that he does want to arrive to them soon and will (16:12).

Commendation of Stephanus and Final Greetings (A´, 16:13-24)

Paul commends Stephanus to oversee the community until he or Timothy return because of his previous successful work with the "sanctified" (ἁγίοις) in Achaia. He informs the Corinthians that all of the "churches" (ἐκκλησίαι) in Asia and the house "church" (ἐκκλησίᾳ) of Prisca and Aquila that are aligned with him send their greetings (16:19), and encourages them to greet one another with "sanctified" (ἁγίῳ) affection (16:20). Finally, he wishes that the "grace" (χάρις) of the Lord Jesus be with them in Corinth (16:23).

Conclusion

The B unit carries the central points of Paul's farewell in this letter. The dramatis personae of this triangular and complex pastoral relationship—Paul, Timothy, and Apollos—are set before the community. Paul's main point is that he and Timothy will be arriving, and soon. Apollos' plans and desires to return, however, remain painfully unclear. This ambiguous information stands in contrast to Paul's definitive tone and plans. Rhetorically speaking, these two lines might serve, at the very least, as a semi-victory for the pro-Pauline faction. Although he demurred to some of their extreme interpretations of his teachings, this unit makes clear to both factions that only one apostle is clearly invested in this community enough to send a supervisor (Stephanus), a lieutenant (Timothy), and then arrive himself.

While many in the community have used their sanctification by the Spirit to overemphasize knowledge, freedom, or asceticism, Paul here uses the adjective to re-contour the Corinthians' perspective away from their myriad misunderstandings. The "sanctified" include those who are far away, and whom the Corinthians are called to help (A, 16:1); but they are also those nearby (in Achaia) who commend their new supervisor, Stephanus (A´, 16:20).

Throughout this ring set Paul strategically asserts that he is not alone. There are many "churches" that align with him and support his mission: those in Galatia (A, 16:1), in Asia (a massive and prominent Roman province), and with Prisca and Aquila's local group (A´, 16:19). This greeting also serves to remind the Corinthians that they are not the only members of God's elect (see 1:1–3; 14:39).

Finally, Paul recalls that what the Corinthians have gained in Christ are "gifts" from God and are not their own talents or power. Although "gift" (A, 16:3) is monetary in nature, and "grace" (A´, 16:23) is more theological, the lexical echo communicates to the audience that since Christ has given them many "gifts" through the Spirit for them to edify their community (see 12:14–31), they should freely "give" to the sanctified in Jerusalem to fulfill the complete and cyclical purpose of spiritual gifts in Christ. Lastly, and most importantly, "sanctified" defines the manner in which they are to treat and interact with one another. For a divided community that has been bickering for months regarding the impact and meaning of their own sanctification, Paul ironically turns this against them to underscore that they can only truly demonstrate to be in a sanctified state when they act with love toward one another. Knowledge, freedom, and asceticism are nothing, and cannot commend them as God's chosen people, if they cannot first learn to love one another.

Closing and Preparations for the Next Visit, 16:1–24

INTERRELATION OF RING SETS

Outline

Worshipping God Properly Requires Order, Peace, and Love (α, 11:2—14:40)

Given that the entire letter anticipates Paul's upcoming visit and is read aloud in a liturgical setting (at the community's gathering), it is appropriate that the lexical connections in the outer units of the ring set underscore the future meeting and order in a worship context.

First, Paul claims that "when he arrives" (11:34) he will instruct the community further on conduct and procedures in worship, aside from his discussion on the Eucharist abuse. Second, he explains that, since the spirits of the prophets must be subordinate to the prophets, no one can say "cursed be Jesus" by the animation of the holy Spirit (12:3). Rather, the Spirit animates worshippers to proclaim clearly that Jesus is Lord and to edify the body of Christ so that a new member who is participating can understand, faithfully agree, and respond "Amen" to their proclamations (14:16).

Third, "love" is the key that should orient their thought and action toward another and lead to their maturation as God's spiritual people. Finally, the goal of all actions in the community is "peace," the sense of completion and internal stability. This state reflects the God of peace, not disorder (14:33). And all of the churches that are sanctified to him are called to live and worship in peace in like manner.

Christ's Resurrection Is the Basis for the Community's Present Faith and Future Glory (β, 15:1–58)

In the central ring set, Paul engages those in the community who reject the resurrection of the dead, as well as those who have been led astray by these dissenters. He reminds them that the grace and Spirit that they received come about because the risen Lord Jesus commissioned his apostles to proclaim the gospel. Furthermore, there must be a resurrection of the dead in order that Christ, the last Adam, can bring life and correct the actions of the first Adam that brought death (15:21–22). At his parousia, Christ will complete his campaign against the worldly powers and vanquish Death. After he subordinates all worldly authorities he will conclude by submitting himself to God so that God might be all in all (15:25–29).

The resurrection is also necessary because flesh and blood cannot inherit God's kingdom. The earthly, ordinary bodies of the Corinthians must be transformed into uncorrupted, immortal spiritual bodies, just as seeds die to become new plants. For this reason, the Corinthians should reject these dissenters and accept the message that they first received with faith in the Spirit. Otherwise, they will be left in their sins and their faith (and Paul's work with them) will be in vain (15:1–3, 9–14, 56–58).

Paul's Final Exhortations to Unity and Love (α', 16:1–24)

Paul instructs the Corinthians on how to take up their collection for those in Jerusalem in the time before his arrival. When (not "if") he arrives he will come (ἐλεύσομαι) to them through Macedonia after Pentecost. As for Apollos, he will come (ἐλεύσεται) when he sees fit (16:12). Anyone who does not adore the Lord must be anathema (16:22). In addition, everyone should act with "love" (ἀγάπη) toward one another (16:14), just as Paul offers his "love" in Christ to all in the audience (16:24). And they should send Timothy along in "peace" (εἰρηνή) when he arrives (16:13).

Conclusion to Section A'

The pivotal β set (15:1–58) reorients the Corinthians' focus on identity and power in the Spirit to the origins of the gospel and their present spiritual state. Just as Paul utilized the community's rejection of the cross (1:18—3:3) to act as the pivot in his oration on church identity and unity in Section A (1:1—4:21), he now sets their rejection of the resurrection as the pivotal set in his oration on the audience's present identity and future in Christ in Section A' (11:2—16:24). Both pivotal ring sets are immersed in eschatological expectation. Without the resurrection, there would be no present in the Spirit, and no hope for the future heavenly inheritance. In the same way, without the resurrection of the dead, they cannot hope to attain that which has been promised to them in Christ, in whom they have been washed, sanctified, redeemed, and justified. Since flesh and blood cannot enter the kingdom, the audience needs this internal, spiritual transformation of the body, as well as the future transformation in the resurrection, in order to attain their heavenly inheritance. The dissenters who consider the resurrection foolish prove themselves to have no knowledge of God. God's plan is to save his elect through his Son, whose death and resurrection makes possible that the elect can be bought back and raised to new life in him (6:20). Their identity is found in God's wisdom and power of life in the second Adam, not the conventional "wisdom" of those who follow in the steps of the first Adam to share his same fate.

Closing and Preparations for the Next Visit, 16:1–24

The α (11:2—14:40) and α′ (16:1–24) sets address how the identity and internal activity of the church body center around peace and love of one another. In particular, these sets focus on the necessary presence of love and unity within a community that claims to be God's sanctified church. The β set fills well its pivotal role because it addresses the resurrection as the basis of faith around which all in the community must rally. Only once they agree on the resurrection—a past event that makes possible their present sanctified state, bound together by the Spirit as the body of Christ, and enables them to look forward to future glory. But to make their past reception of the gospel credible, and to make their accession of glory in the future possible, they must first learn to live and love in peace to preserve their sanctified state, worship God properly, and find complete, spiritual knowledge.

In order to see themselves and one another properly, they must acknowledge the import each member has to the whole body and treat one another with love. All other gifts they have (freedom, powers, knowledge) can fade away, but love's impact, in how it builds the body of Christ and solidifies their relationship to one another and Christ, remains beyond the fading of this world. Love enables them to see beyond their present circumstances and status battles to see God face-to-face, because, when they experience love, they experience Christ. Love should be their focus because love endures beyond all things. And love endures beyond all things because love is Christ.

OVERALL STRUCTURE OF 1 CORINTHIANS

The overall structure of 1 Corinthians is as concentric as its sectional ring sets, and the lexical repetitions that denote this pattern also help to underscore several useful points for interpreting Paul's overall message in the letter.

Overview of Sections

Disunity and Identity (A, 1:1—4:21)

The first section addresses the community's most external symptoms of spiritual illness: they have developed factions around two of their apostles, "Paul" and "Apollos." However, the extent of the illness goes deeper: the audience's attachment to worldly power and wisdom has skewed their understanding of spiritual gifts and increased their arrogance and in-fighting. Paul counters by convicting their spiritual immaturity and worldly focus as like that of "ordinary" people who are perishing and who do not have the Spirit or any knowledge (2:14—3:3). He also argues that he and Apollos are both stewards of God's "mysteries" whose different gifts are given by God to benefit the community to not become arrogant against one another or their apostles (4:6).

To aid their recovery, he is sending "Timothy" and "Stephanus" to remind the audience that they are no different than "all the other churches of God" who are sanctified by the Spirit, and so have no place for arrogance. And they must also recall their true identity as the body of Christ and the holy temple for God's Spirit. Their sanctity and destiny are directly tied to their integrity. Without unity they cannot fully become the house that God has begun to build with them.

Life in Christ, outside the Community (B, 5:1—11:1)

The central B section explains how the Corinthians, who are God's sanctified temple, can live as individuals in the daily events of the world outside of the house churches. First, Paul condemns sexual immorality as a toxin that will infect the whole body of the church, just as leaven affects bread. So, while members are able to act freely, they must understand that all moral actions of any member affect the entirety of the body, which is Christ (5:1-13; 6:9-20). Second, he demands that they bring trials between members before the church to be decided since they are to judge angels in the new age, and so that the unjust wisdom of the courts does not corrupt the rest of the church (6:1-8). Third, he commands marriage as an acceptable lifestyle for the sanctified, though he prefers all to be celibate like himself (7:1-40). The key guidelines for the elect are to live peacefully and, if possible, to remain in the same state as when they were called (7:24-40). Lastly, Paul condemns those who eat idol meat at temples to the detriment of their brothers' faith. As with moral actions before, although the Corinthians can eat this meat, they should still refrain when it scandalizes and harms another member's conscience. For to offend one member of Christ is to sin against Christ himself (8:1-13; 10:1-31).

Order, Harmony, and Love (A´, 11:2—16:24)

Having addressed the thorny problems that the audience encounters daily (which likely abetted the factions in the church), Paul returns to the identity and internal activities of the audience as a community. First of all, they are to worship and act with one another as they are to live with those outside, namely, peacefully and harmoniously. Such is deemed appropriate among "all the churches of God" (11:16; 14:33). Better worship and spiritual maturity can be attained only when the church acts with love. This edifying emotion aids believers to see God face-to-face and transforms them to better understanding of their unity as the body of Christ (12:31b—13:13). They must also reclaim their faith in the mystery of the resurrection, which is the source of their ultimate salvation and key to attaining their future inheritance. But they cannot inherit this heavenly promise with "ordinary" bodies of flesh and blood; rather, since their ordinary bodies are corrupt and mortal because of the First Adam and destined for the dust, they must put on the mark of the Second Adam so that they can put on spiritual bodies of incorruption and immortality and be made alive with Christ. And this mark of Christ can only be seen through their faith and love—both to Christ and to one another (15:12-49).

To aid their recovery, "Paul," their founding apostle who greets them with Christ's love, is sending "Stephanus," a worthy minister and early convert, to act as interim overseer to the church, and Timothy, his lieutenant. How the audience treats Stephanus and Timothy will reflect their response to this letter and their assessment of Paul's qualifications to remain their pastoral leader. "Apollos," although of great concern to several in the community, is not yet planning to return. In the meantime, then, the church will need to accept their founding apostle, Paul, as the revealer of God's "mysteries," and his teachings as inspired by the Spirit and Christ who sent him with binding authority. As such, they should prepare to receive and execute Paul's teachings in this letter in anticipation of when he arrives with the same ardor and respect that they would continue to do for Christ himself.

Conclusion: Overall Performative Structure and Rhetorical Effect, 1:1—16:24

Role of Section B in the Structure of the Letter

The B section has significant rhetorical effect on the letter's argument with its strategic placement. First, it allows Paul to address several issues that increased divisions in the community after he has already accused the Corinthians of worldly attachment and spiritual immaturity. Since he has already diminished the Corinthians' credibility in discerning spiritual issues in Section A, the central Section uses the community's own failings as leverage when he corrects their present behavior—particularly with the so-called "strong" faction.

Second, given that the Corinthians had written to Paul regarding several issues found in 7:1—11:1, the placement of these topics in Section B forces the audience to listen intently to the very critical material found in 1:1—6:20 before they even begin to receive a response to their questions.

Third, its placement denotes the central or core teaching of this letter, namely, how those who are sanctified in Christ and life in Corinth can lead effective lives with outsiders while still maintaining the sanctified state that is held by all of God's churches. To this point, the factions had theorized their own guidelines in Paul's absence. Now, in this pivotal section, he makes known to both factions his commands as one entrusted by Christ: 1) imitate him (Paul), as he does Christ; 2) live in peace with those within and without the church; 3) remain in the state in which God called you; 4) defer always to the common good, that is, to the benefit of the whole of Christ's body.

The Interrelatedness of Sections A and A'

Overview

The bracket A and A' Sections treat the Corinthians' worrisome state by pointing to where they have failed, then to their ideal identity, and then explaining the distance between. They are sanctified to God by the Spirit for fellowship with Christ and the fullness of all spiritual gifts (1:1-9). And yet they are fractured (1:10-17), overly consumed by Rome's cultural standards of power (1:18—3:3), and spiritually immature to the point of being like ordinary people who do not have any spiritual gifts (3:4—4:21). They should instead recognize their true identity as the unified body of Christ who are also the temple of God's Spirit.

And, in the same way, they presently worship God passionately and await future glory with Christ; yet they worship the God of peace in a chaotic and cacophonous manner, and dissent against the resurrection. They should instead worship in a way that edifies and nourishes Christ's body, live in love with one another, and recognize the imperative nature of their transformation to put on a spiritual body that is uncorrupted and immortal over their ordinary bodies, so that they can attain the glory and inheritance they can receive through fellowship with Christ.

Essentially, then, all of the exhortations to fully realize their identity as God's sanctified church in 1:10—4:21 and 11:2—16:24 are founded on, and meant to complete, what they have and might yet still receive from God through the Spirit for fellowship with Christ and all the spiritual blessings in 1:4-9. These points are underscored by the development found through

Closing and Preparations for the Next Visit, 16:1-24

the progression of repeated terms in the parallel A and A´ Sections, which present a *dramatis personae* for the unfolding tension among diverse leaders, their multifarious followers, and all of their complex interrelationships.

"Stephanus" (A, 1:14-16; A´, 16:15-17)

Paul's opaque mention that he baptized "Stephanus" in the opening ring set is clarified when he commends "Stephanus" as the minister whom he has appointed to oversee the audience's reception, interpretation, and execution of his present instructions in this letter. The previous mention in 1:14, combined with this announcement of his appointment, inform both factions that the overseer who is now with them is explicitly loyal to Paul.

"Timothy" (A, 4:18-21; A´ 16:10-11)

Paul's senior lieutenant is well-known to the community, such that the apostle has no need to commend him. His reminder to them that Timothy is his own loyal child who will instruct the other children how better to imitate their father in Christ is developed with his additional request that the Corinthians not harass or mistreat "Timothy" when he arrives to correct them. The combination of the two mentions of Timothy demonstrate how contentious the issue has become; even that Paul anticipates the possibility of some Corinthians abusing, either verbally or physically (?), one of his top assistants.

"Paul and Apollos" (A, 1:10-17; 3:4-23; 4:6-21; A´, 16:12)

Paul and Apollos are both stewards of God's mysteries who have each contributed diverse gifts to the edification of the church in Corinth. Yet Paul is at pains to balance their relationship since their diverse styles (whether intended or not) are also part of the reason for the community's dilapidated condition. To assert his authority and primary place among the church, but also aid their re-unification, he explains their roles as qualitatively equal but temporally separate. Apollos is gifted and converted many, but his work was to water the church that Paul had founded; Paul thus remains their father in Christ. The audience should not judge either now because they will be judged by the Lord, who commissioned them to proclaim the gospel based on how their communities have received their respective messages. The true evaluation of these apostles, then, will be based on how well this church that they nurtured in Christ unites and stands firmly in the faith.

This tensely balanced interrelationship is then developed, albeit vaguely, in the A´ Section when Paul echoes his initial apostolic greeting and mediation of the Lord Jesus Christ's love, grace and peace to the audience, and also commissions two subordinates to precede his already planned trip to return and evaluate them as their father (16:5–12). Yet, while he mentions very briefly that he (Paul) is certainly returning and desires greatly to do so, Apollos has not considered such a trip to be a priority, and will return (if he ever does) when/if he sees fit. The A´ Section, then, gives a fitting cap to Paul's own account of the "Apollos–Paul–Corinth" drama: whether or not Apollos is concerned with them, Paul is still very invested in their continued formation in Christ, and this letter and his future travel plans both stand as proof of Paul's intentions to lead them and stand in contrast to Apollos' absence—both physically and by letter. Perhaps most notable is that Apollos communicates with Corinth only through Paul (16:12).

"Mystery" (A, 4:1–2; A´, 15:51)

That Paul is called by God to be a steward of his "mysteries" is affirmed throughout the letter as he teaches and commands on several matters, but in particular, when he discloses to them the ultimate goal of their faith and the culmination of God's "mysterious" and "foolish" plan to choose and save the weak and lowly of the world through the death of his Son, Jesus Christ, at whose return the world will be conquered and the elect will be transformed to receive the heavenly inheritance and rule with Christ in the new age.

This development points to two things. First, that Paul preaches a "mystery" that can only be comprehended by spiritual people who have the Spirit and can see and understand the truth of God's plan means that, for the Corinthians to understand or comprehend the "mystery" of the bodily resurrection, they must first have the Spirit and think like spiritually mature people who can see the truth, power, and wisdom behind God's "mysterious" plan. Second, this development shows that, for Paul, the "mystery" was neither just the plan or its culmination, but both. In the mystery of God's gracious act in the Christ event, the purpose, goal, and manner of their proclamation are all equally "hidden" to those who are attached to the fading world; but to those who believe, the veil of the mystery is removed so that they can see Christ as the power and wisdom of God.

Closing and Preparations for the Next Visit, 16:1–24

"When I Arrive" (A, 4:21; A´, 11:34; 16:3–5)

While Paul asks whether the community wants him "to arrive" with either a rod or "gentle spirit" in the A Section (4:21), we find in the A´ Section that he fully intends to return with both: on the one hand, he will harshly address the worship practices "when [he] arrives" (11:34); but on the other hand, he will also help to affirm the audience's solidarity with all of God's churches and extend his apostolic love "when [he] arrives" (16:3–5).

"All the Churches of God" (1:1–2; 11:16; 14:33)

A key point that Paul wishes for the Corinthians to recall is that they are not the only group of God's elect who are sanctified with spiritual gifts (4:20; 14:38). Rather, they stand along with all "the churches of God" who call on God's name. This affiliation with other churches obliges them to worship with unity and status equality (11:16), and in peace and harmony (14:33) as do "all the other churches of God." Only then will the Spirit fully animate and edify them to be Christ's body. But, as they pursue this spiritual maturity through love, they must also recognize that the Spirit animates and edifies the other sanctified churches of God to grow together as one spiritual temple of God's presence.

"Ordinary People" (A, 1:19, 30–31; 3:3; 4:6; A´, 14:33)

Finally, the proclamation of the gospel divides the world into two groups: the ordinary and the spiritual. This dichotomous anthropology is reflected in Paul's brief creation narrative and the identities of two Adams: the first was the earthly, living-being; but the second, Christ, is the life-giving Spirit who brings the elect to life. In order to properly access these spiritual gifts and the destiny to which they were called, the elect must stand in their faith and put on the mark of Christ, in order to put on their perfect and immortal spiritual bodies over their present mortal ones—lest they remain ordinary and succumb to Death and the dust.

These eschatological points develop the earlier pastoral and pneumalogical anthropology that Paul put forward when he criticized the church's divisions. Their fractures, arrogance, and connections to worldly power demonstrate the deep extent of their spiritual immaturity. They were not even close to attaining the spiritual gifts Paul hoped to be completed for them in 1:4–9. As it stood, they were acting like "ordinary" people.

The Corinthians' problems are shown to be anthropological, phenomenological (based on understanding the Spirit), and eschatological. If the Corinthians do not start to recognize (phenomenological) the truth of the Spirit (i.e., God's "foolish" plan to conquer the world through "weakness"), then they will remain spiritually immature, be no different than the rest of "ordinary" humanity who remain trapped in Adam's state who are already perishing and fading (anthropological), and will be subject to judgment when Christ conquers all of the worldly powers, including Death (eschatological).

To receive the fullness of God's blessings they must first understand the difficult truth of the gospel: namely, that God saw fit to save the lowly of the world through the death of his Son, in whom God justifies, sanctifies, and redeems them from their ordinary condition, and with whom he gives them a heavenly inheritance and future glory in the new age. And, most painfully, all of these actions are of God's grace, that is, they are primarily and ultimately gifts from God, so that no elect member can claim that they attained it on their own (A, 1:19, 30–31; 4:6), or that they can discern a level of holiness and spiritual status greater than any other member's (A′, 14:33).

12

Summary and Conclusions

SUMMARY

Purpose and Method

THIS STUDY SOUGHT TO engage the structure and message of 1 Corinthians within its most relevant context of late Western antiquity's oral culture. Using a text-centered methodology, this study demonstrated and analyzed a series of concentric patterns (or ring formations) through which Paul presented and developed his arguments to the Corinthian church. Such patterns were ubiquitous in oral cultures and their literature. These structures, which are defined by objective lexical repetitions, aided the interpretation of an overall concentric pattern of three sections (A, 1:1—4:21; B, 5:1—11:1; A´, 11:2—16:24), nine ring sets (α, 1:1-17; β, 1:18—3:3; α´, 3:4—4:21; α, 5:1—6:20; β, 7:1-40; α´, 8:1—11:1; α, 11:2—14:40; β, 15:1-58; α´, 16:1-24), thirty-five ring units (e.g., 1:1-17; 5:1-13; 10:1-17; 15:12-24), and numerous micro-rings (e.g., 4:6-8; 8:1-4; 11:2-3a, 16-22). Analyzing these lexical repetitions in each unit allowed us to engage a demonstrably coherent message as it progressed through the concentric structures of the text.

These findings represent a departure from previous treatments that analyzed the letter as if it were a linear, modern essay. As shown throughout this work, such linear treatments tend to ignore important rhetorical connections in the concentric textual units, and also miss the inherent cohesiveness of the complex, yet integral, message that Paul wished to convey to this community on the verge of collapse.

The order in Paul's letter stands in stark contrast to the chaos that was unfolding in Corinth's church.

Section A (1:1—4:21)

From a panoramic perspective, the first major section of the letter greets the Corinthians with apostolic blessings, but also quickly addresses their divisions, spiritual immaturity, and attachment to Roman imperial standards of power and wisdom. The pivotal β ring set (1:18—3:3) engages their divisions through the example of their incompatibility with the wisdom of the cross. Because they are still attached to worldly wisdom and power, they see the cross as "foolish" and "weak" when they should instead recognize it as the means of their present sanctification (1:31) and future salvation (1:18-21). Their refusal to leave the world behind leads them to compete with one another like ordinary people, judge between apostles within their competitions, divide God's holy temple and Christ's body, and remain spiritually immature (3:1-3). As a result, they cannot understand the teachings of the Spirit (2:6, 13).

Whereas the pivotal set, 1:18—3:3, deduces the cause of the divisions, the bracket sets (1:1-17; 3:4—4:21) engage the nature and consequences of the divisions and directly exhort the community to be united in one body under the authority of their apostles. Paul explains in the α set (1:1-17) that by God's will he was "sent" (1:1) to proclaim the gospel of the cross so that they might be established and fulfilled with all spiritual blessings in Christ to await as a sanctified body the "revelation" of the Lord's return (1:7-9). He was not "sent" to baptize or to proclaim the gospel in terms of human standards. And yet, the Corinthians have become divided with the slogans, "I am with Paul," and, "I am with Apollos" (1:10, 17).

The α´ set (3:4—4:21) develops these points from the initial set in that, when the Corinthians announce, "I am with Paul," or ,"I am with Apollos," they show themselves to be acting like ordinary people (3:4). While they are bound together to await the Lord's "revelation" (α, 1:4) they should not judge the apostles and become divided; they will be judged on the Lord's day when God "reveals" their hearts (α´, 3:21; 4:5). And they should not consider themselves to be fulfilled (α´, 4:20) in all things beyond the apostles, as if they achieved anything by themselves. In truth, Paul was "sent" by God's will as an "apostle" not to baptize but to proclaim the gospel of the cross (α, 1:1, 17); and yet, it is God's demonstration of his "apostles" as the least

Summary and Conclusions

of all humanity and a spectacle before all of creation that best proclaims the meaning of God's paradoxical gift in the cross, his campaign to invert the standards of human wisdom, and his election of the weak (α´, 4:9). If the Corinthians wish to attain spiritual maturity, they must begin to imitate their "weak" father and become "foolish" like him so that they can become "wise" in matters of the Spirit and finally receive the fullness of God's wisdom and power in Christ (α, 1:4–9) that their attachment to the world is presently forcing them to reject (α´, 4:1).

Section B (5:1—11:1)

Whereas the initial Section of the letter greeted the community and treated their divisions in light of their attachment to worldly wisdom, their apostles, and their spiritual immaturity, the central section moves its focus outward to address how these sanctified can live in a secular area like Corinth. The bracket α (5:1—6:20) and α´ (8:1—11:1) ring sets address living with others and fulfilling one's own will, while the pivotal β ring set (7:1–40) lays out guidelines to aid the church members in Corinth to live a moderately peaceful life among non-believers and remain in a spiritually sanctified state in Christ.

The repetition of the slogan, "Everything is lawful to me" (6:12; 10:23) addresses two different existing situations in the community that parallel one another. In the first use of the slogan, Paul decries their presumption of sexual freedom from the empowerment of the Spirit as a complete misuse and misunderstanding of the washing, sanctification, and justification that they received in the name of Christ (6:11, 17–20). In the same way, Paul rebukes their presumptive consumption of idol meat in temples as a misuse of the spiritual knowledge in the α´ set. In both cases, Paul challenges the slogans as short-sighted, selfish, and incomplete. In truth, although everything is possible for the Corinthians, not every action edifies the community. In both bracket sets, Paul denounces selfish desires and upholds the common good as a guiding principle. In this case, the common good is not the *polis*, but the body of Christ—local and universal, present and eschatological. The "strong" only endanger the sanctity and unity of Christ's body with their self-centered actions.

Section A´ (11:2—16:24)

The opening set of the final Section returns to internal community issues. But, whereas the A Section addressed the core issues of divisions, pride, and immaturity, the A′ Section will engage how they are to worship and live together in the present and what they can expect in the future.

The pivotal β set (15:1–58) addresses one of the most emotionally charged issues for the apostle. Christ's resurrection is central to Paul's calling and the Spirit that sanctifies and justifies the elect so that they can hope for victory over death and future glory when they are raised through Christ's power. To deny the latter is to deny the former; and to deny Christ's resurrection completely nullifies their faith and Paul's own work to nurture their fellowship in Christ and life in the Spirit. In short, every other instruction in the letter is worthless if they cannot reclaim and hold fast to their original faith in the resurrection (15:2, 11). This key faith component stands as the core of the gospel and links them to God's act in Christ in the past, his continuing grace through the Spirit with them in the present, and looks forward to their future glory in God's kingdom and presence.

The bracket α and α′ sets (11:2—14:40; 16:1–24) address worship in the present and the imminent return of Paul. In a sense, then, both bracket sets of the final section look to restore order and harmony to a contentious and cacophonous community. One set of lexical connections between the bracket sets focus on Paul's visit. "When he arrives" (not "if") Paul will evaluate the audience's reception and execution of this letter and their treatment of Timothy (α′, 16:3–5) and will teach further about unity and order in worship (α, 11:34). Second, the audience is to do all things in peace and harmony since God who elected them is peace and not worldly, corrupt chaos. This includes how they worship the God of "peace" in an orderly manner (α, 14:33) and how they are expected to treat his servants, such as Paul and Timothy (α′, 16:11). Lastly, the lexical connections in the bracket sets show that spiritual knowledge and power are given only through Christ. So no one can say "Christ is *anathema*" by the Spirit (α, 12:3), and those who receive these gifts become "*anathema*" if they do not love Christ as their Lord (α′, 16:22, 24). The proper use of spiritual gifts and the proper respect of Christ as Lord are significantly interconnected.

Finally, the bracket sets show that, along with respecting Christ as Lord, the elect in Corinth are also called to act out their spiritual gifts with love toward one another. "Love" is the greatest of God's spiritual gifts because it empowers the elect to mature spiritually and see God clearly as though face-to-face (13:10–13). This "love," which is extended to the audience from Christ through his apostle Paul, exhorts the community to return to their Lord Jesus through peace, unity, and order in worship (16:20–24). And they can demonstrate this conversion most by loving one another without factions or discord, and again loving their apostle, as they did when they first believed the message that he preached.

Summary and Conclusions

Listening to 1 Corinthians to recognize its inherent concentric patters and the respective lexical connections, so as to understand their impact on Paul's exhortatory message to a community consumed by corruption and infected by desire for power, aids our own interpretation of the letter's message that remains as relevant and imperative today as it was for the original audience. For this reason we must pursue evermore to reach beyond what is written in our modern translations, and even our scholarly Greek texts, in order to fully appreciate a message that was performed to this group of converts with the same passion and vibrancy as the original good news of salvation.

CONCLUSIONS

Particular Contributions

A full overview of what "listening" to the performative structure of 1 Corinthians can offer an interpreter is not warranted at this point. It is more beneficial to highlight some of the most helpful and far-reaching contributions that begin with such an engagement of 1 Corinthians as oral literature.

For example, the performative structure demonstrates the integral nature and structure of the letter. The central section (5:1—11:1) addresses the many problems and questions this church of God has encountered in living as sanctified people in an imperial Roman city that is full of corruption and sin. The bracket sections (1:1—4:21; 11:2—16:24) attend to the church's unity, internal respect and love for one another, spiritual maturation, and the community's relationships with its respective ministers.

On another level, the structure of the initial section shows that Paul's main concern for writing goes beyond the divisions that have formed in the community between himself and Apollos. The letter also involves the cause of these divisions and how to repair them. For the former, Paul consistently underscores how the divisions are not due to him and Apollos, but rather come from the internal and spiritual flaws of the Corinthian members themselves (1:10-17; 3:3—4:21; 11:2—14:40). Chief among these flaws is their attraction to corrupt Imperial standards and ways of thinking, which in turn leads them to misunderstand Paul's gospel and remain like ordinary people (3:3; 4:6-10). For the latter, Paul outlines his own plan for fixing the community. He himself will certainly return (a point that he makes explicitly no less than six times in the opening and closing sections) to personally address their problems. In the meantime, he is sending Timothy, Stephanus, and others loyal to him to steward and guide the church while he wraps up a successful ministry in Ephesus (16:10–14).

Whether as a rhetorical shot or benign comment, Paul contrasts his desire to return with Apollos' ambivalence. Also, his explicit identification of Chloe's people, Stephanus, and the churches of Achaia (twice) seem to further remind his opponents in the community that many within and around their church in Corinth (including Apollos himself) are on good terms with Paul and respect his apostleship and ministry.

As the pivot of the initial and crucial ring set, the thanksgiving in 1:4–9 underscores two key rhetorical points that will serve as Paul's baseline argument throughout the letter. First, every spiritual gift the Corinthians have are in fact gifts from God and received only through Christ upon hearing Christ's gospel. Their gifts are not their own. Second, these gifts demonstrate the end of the age to be effective and, even more pointedly, remind the church what they will lose if they remain attached to worldly standards like ordinary people who have not received these spiritual gifts.

Listening to the text, so as to show 1:1–17 and 3:4—4:21 as parallel ring sets within a larger concentric section, shows how Apollos is the major issue in the A Section and there are likely only two (not three or four) factions within the church (1:10–12). The unit structure of 1:10–17 also shows how the Christ and Peter parties are arbitrary rhetorical creations meant to point out the fractures in the church, while also softening the indictment of divisions in the audience.

In the central section, the narration on the courts (6:1–8) is rhetorically and theologically linked with its context between passages of sexual immorality (5:1–13; 6:9–20). The sum of these shows Paul's concern for corruption in the community from both sexual and financial temptations—both of which symbolize imperial, sinful corruption and further division in the church.

The self-example in 9:1–27 is also strategically placed, not as a mere digression, but as an intricate part of Paul's exhortation to the community to sacrifice one's own pleasures and rights in order to benefit and defer to a fellow believer's conscience. The Corinthians have many rights (6:16–20; 10:28–31), just as Paul has many rights (9:1–9, 21–23), but they are all obligated by the law of Christ to love one another and build up the church's corporate body.

Food does not affect their salvation (8:7), but eating food before idols at temples can and will (10:41–21). The high-status ("strong") members' desire to hob-nob with Roman elites at temples is causing the low-status ("weak") to fall back into pagan practices. Just as *porneia* (5:1–13; 6:9–20) and *adikia* (6:1–8) can bring sin back to the body of Christ, so too can idol temple worshippers infect the unleavened body of Christ with imperial corruption and harm those for whom Christ died (8:9–10).

Finally, the semi-lyrical text 13:1–13 stands as the pivotal unit of the massive and intricate ring set 11:2—14:40. It builds on the need for respecting other members—despite status differences (11:2–3a, 17–34)—as equally-sharing members of Christ's body that God has fashioned together for its edification (12:1–31), and looks forward to the need to respect one another and the God of peace by keeping order in the worship. Since they are animated by God's Spirit for the purpose of multivalent edification, they should use these gifts to edify one another toward individual spiritual maturity and to edify the body of Christ as a whole. Love and respect bring order; order brings spiritual animation; spiritual animation brings edification of the church and spiritual maturation of all its members.

Overarching Contributions

Outside of benefiting the exegesis of particular biblical texts, listening to the performative structure offers several contributions to the study of oral literature. On a smaller level, the micro-rings aid the interpreter with an internal exegetical key for problematic verses, such as 3:16–23; 4:6–8; 6:15–20; 9:19–23; and 13:8–13. For example, the micro-structure clarifies the opaque phrase "beyond what is written" in that it shows 4:6–8 to be a micro-ring that underscores the gift status of everything the Corinthians have received from God. Paul and Apollos are included as God's gifts to organize and edify the church and, as such, the Corinthians should not boast in their own talents or become puffed up against their apostles (4:8). Likewise, the micro-ring of 9:19–23 underscores the universality of Paul's message ("all things/ people"), his self-effacing means of preaching to all ("becoming" like others), and contrasting cultural customs with the self-sacrifice of Christ as a model for serving others ("Law, Law of Christ," 9:20b–21). These micro-formations underscore the ubiquity of the form in oral societies and show how careful attention to this structure aids a culturally-sensitive study of the text.

The rings also offer partial evidence to deduce the presence of interpolations in the text, as seen with 11:3b–15 and 14:34–35. Prior to this point, scholars deduced interpolations through textual comparisons with other Pauline or disputed letters but lacked significant objective evidence to support these claims. The structure of seven units in 11:2—14:40, rather than the current set of eight, demonstrates a cohesive oration on church order and unity without any mention of women. These findings cohere with the fact that problems with women are not found in the rest of the ring set or the letter as a whole. Micro-rings and unit structures also show how 11:3b–15 and 14:34–35 are not necessary to their respective contexts. In fact, in the case of the former, the focus of the entire ring set is obscured from a focus on equal treatment of believers at the Eucharistic table to a fabricated concern over women's conduct in the worship space.

Study of these forms also illuminates Paul's rhetorical strategy throughout the letter. The discussions on the cross and resurrection are strategically placed to add eschatological imperatives to his surrounding teachings. The consistent use of eschatological themes and terminology in the pivotal units and ring sets of the respective formations also raises the possibility of more complex oral connections across sets and sections. For instance, the anthropological and eschatological discussion of how the Corinthians are "ordinary" people within the scope of Paul's eschatological narrative (1:18—3:3) is dutifully picked up and completed in the discussion of the resurrection in 15:1–58. Why is Paul so concerned about their disunity? Because, the connected arguments point out, their divisions show that they have rejected the message of the cross and misuse the talents of the Spirit, and thus indict themselves as being like "ordinary people" who do not know the Spirit and remain aligned with the worldly authorities whom God is currently conquering through Christ. Since "ordinary people" remain in their sins as corrupt and moral associates of Adam and inherit the dust, they will perish at Christ's return (15:26–40). This interrupted, yet underlying argument from eschatological immanence brackets and supports the exhortations for how one of God's sanctified churches is to remain united in love and holiness while they live in the fading corruption of an imperial system (3:4—14:40).

In addition to the points offered above, it is of benefit to add that the interrelation of focus on performative structure and insights to the anti-imperial arguments within Paul's theology and rhetoric. Both bring us closer to the author's intentions and thus also to the social and historical contexts of the intended audience. This is seen in the parallel eschatological narratives (1:18—3:3; 15:1–58) that together tell of how Christ has already begun to conquer Rome to become the sole ruler of the cosmos. As such, no human can boast in his/her own power or be puffed up against one another. There is one ruler for one universe: and all of his subjects are equivocated under his singular lordship, whether Jew or Gentile, male or female, slave or free.

These numerous conclusions found with this preliminary engagement of the performative structure of 1 Corinthians demonstrate how useful listening carefully to a New Testament text can contribute fresh insights that are not based in modern academic theories but in the very culture and communicative customs of late Western antiquity of the author and intended audience. Studies of this nature have already been performed on several of Paul's letters, but there remain many more texts throughout canonical and extracanonical literature that warrant the same level of interest. As mentioned in the Introduction, studies of this sort were stifled by some of the early Christian commentators who did not want to accept human rhetorical forms or structures as relevant to studying inspired texts. The evolution of biblical studies over the last two millennia has proven the engagement of such forms to be indispensable for critical analysis and deeper understanding of the texts. As such, scholars who are befuddled by a particular text, or who are looking for a new but culturally-relevant approach for study, should consider "listening" carefully to the text to see what exegetical keys may already exist from the author's own hand to be heard by an orally-conditioned audience.

As mentioned above, we have a lot of time to make up for.

Bibliography

Achtemeier, Paul J. "*Omne Verbum Sonat*: The New Testament and the Oral Environment of Late Western Antiquity." *JBL* 109 (1993) 3–27.
Agosto, Efrain. *1 y 2 Corintios*. Minneapolis: Fortress, 2007.
Arnold, Clinton. *Powers of Darkness: Principalities and Powers in Paul's Letters*. Downers Grove, IL: InterVarsity, 1992.
Aune, David. *Prophecy in Early Christianity and the Ancient Mediterranean World*. Grand Rapids: Eerdmans, 1983.
Bailey, James, and Lyle Vander Broek. *Literary Forms in the New Testament*. Louisville: Westminster John Knox, 1992.
Barre, M. "To Marry or to Burn: *Pyrousthai* in 1 Cor 7:9." *CBQ* 36 (1974) 193–202.
Barrett, C. K. *The First Epistle of Paul to the Corinthians*. HNTC. New York: Harper & Row, 1968.
Bassler, Jouette M. "The Widow's Tale: A Fresh Look at 1 Tim 5:3–16." *JBL* 103 (1984) 23–41.
Baur, Frederick. "The Two Epistles to the Corinthians." In Adams and Horrell, 51–60.
Beale, G. K. *We Become What We Worship: A Biblical Theology of Idolatry*. Downers Grove, IL: InterVarsity, 2008.
Beavis, Mary Ann. "Christian Origins, Egalitarianism, and Utopia." *JFSR* 23 (2007) 23–49.
Blomberg, Craig. "The Structure of 2 Corinthians 1–7." *CTR* 4 (1989) 3–20.
———. *1 Corinthians*. NIVAC. Grand Rapids: Zondervan, 1995.
de Boer, Marcus. "Paul's Use of a Resurrection Tradition in 1 Cor 15:20–28." In *The Corinthian Correspondence*, edited by R. Bieringer, 639–51. BETL 125. Leuven: Leuven University Press, 1996.
Borg, Marcus, and John Crossan. *The First Paul*. New York: HarperOne, 2010.
Brannick, Vincent. "Apocalyptic Paul?" *CBQ* 47 (1985) 664–75.
Bray, Gerald. *1–2 Corinthians*. ACCS NT 7. Downers Grove, IL: InterVarsity, 2005.
Brown, Alexandra. *The Cross and Human Transformation: Paul's Apocalyptic Word in 1 Corinthians*. Minneapolis: Fortress, 1995.
Bruce, F. F. *1 and 2 Corinthians*. NCB. Grand Rapids: Eerdmans, 1981.
———. *1 and 2 Thessalonians*. WBC. Waco: Word, 1982.
———. *The Pauline Circle*. London: Oxford University Press, 1985.
Brunt, J. "Rejected, Ignored, or Misunderstood? The Fate of Paul's Approach to the Problem of Food Offered to Idols in Early Christianity." *NTS* 31 (1985) 113–24.

Bibliography

Byrne, Brendan. "Sinning against One's Own Body: Paul's Understanding of the Sexual Relationship in 1 Corinthians 6:18." *CBQ* 45 (1983) 608–16.

Caragounis, C. C. "'Fornication' and 'Concession'? Interpreting 1 Cor 7:1–7." In *The Corinthian Correspondence*, edited by R. Bieringer, 543–59. BETL 125. Leuven: Leuven University Press, 1996.

Carson, D. A. *Showing the Spirit: A Theological Exposition of 1 Coirnthians 12–14*. Grand Rapids: Baker, 1986.

Childs, Brevard S. *The Book of Exodus*. OTL. Louisville: Westminster, 1974.

Chow, John K. "The Rich Patron." In Adams and Horrell, 197–206.

Cleary, Francis. "Women in the NT: St. Paul and the Early Pauline Churches." *BTB* 10 (1980) 78–81.

Collins, John J. "From Prophecy to Apocalypticism: The Expectation of the End." In *The Encyclopedia of Apocalypticism*, edited by John J. Collins, 1:129–61. New York: Continuum, 2002.

Collins, Raymond F. *Divorce in the New Testament*. GNS. Collegeville, MN: Liturgical, 2002.

———. *First Corinthians*. SP 7. Collegeville, MN: Liturgical, 1990.

———. "The Unity of Paul's Paranesis in 1 Thess 4:3–8, 1 Cor 7:1–7: A Significant Parallel." *NTS* 29 (1983) 420–29.

Conzelmann, Hans. *1 Corinthians*. Hermeneia. Minneapolis: Fortress, 1970.

Cope, L. "1 Cor 11:2–16: One Step Further." *JBL* 97 (1978) 435–56.

D'Angelo, Mary Rose. "Women Partners in the New Testament." *JFSR* 6 (1990) 65–86.

Dawes, G. "'But if You Can Gain Your Freedom' (1 Corinthians 7:17–24)." *CBQ* 52 (1990) 681–97.

DeMaris, Richard. "Corinthian Religion and Baptism for the Dead (1Corinthians 15:29): Insights from Archaeology and Anthropology." *JBL* 114 (1995) 661–82.

Deming, W. *Paul on Marriage and Celibacy: The Hellenistic Background of 1 Corinthians 7*. Grand Rapids: Eerdmans, 2004.

Douglas, Mary. *Thinking in Circles: An Essay on Ring Composition*. Terry Lecture Series. New Haven: Yale University Press, 2007.

Dunn, James D. G. *1 Corinthians*. NTG. Sheffield: Sheffield Academic, 1995.

———. *Theology of Paul the Apostle*. Grand Rapids: Eerdmans, 1998.

Durham, John I. *Exodus*. WBC. Waco: Word Publishers, 1987.

Elliott, John K. "Paul's Teaching on Marriage in First Corinthians: Some Problems Reconsidered." *NTS* 19 (1972–73) 219–25.

Fee, Gordon. *The First Epistle to the Corinthians*. NICNT. Grand Rapids: Eerdmans, 1987.

Ferguson, Everett. *Backgrounds of Early Christianity*. Grand Rapids: Eerdmans, 1987.

Fishbane, Michael. *Biblical Interpretation in Ancient Israel*. Oxford: Clarendon, 1985.

Fisk, Bruce. "Violation." *NTS* 42 (1996) 540–58.

Fitzmyer, Joseph A. *First Corinthians*. AB 32. New Haven: Yale University Press, 2008.

Flanagan, Neal. "Did Paul Put Down Women in 1 Cor 14:34–36?" *BTB* 11 (1981) 10–12.

Francis, J. "'As Babes in Christ.' Some Proposals Regarding 1 Corinthians 3:1–3." *JSNT* 7 (1980) 41–60.

Fotopoulos, J. "Arguments Concerning Food Offered to Idols: Corinthian Quotations and Pauline Refutations in a Rhetorical Partitio (1 Corinthians 8:1–9)." *CBQ* 67 (2005) 611–31.

Bibliography

Furnish, Victor Paul. *Theology of the First Letter to the Corinthians.* NTT. Cambridge: Cambridge University Press, 1999.

Gaffin, Richard. *Resurrection and Redemption: A Study in Paul's Soteriology.* Philipsburg, NJ: Presbyterian and Reformed, 1987.

Garland, David E. *1 Corinthians.* BECNT. Grand Rapids: Baker, 2003.

Giblin, C. "Three Monotheistic Texts in Paul." *CBQ* 37 (1975) 525-47.

Glancy, Jennifer. "Obstacles to Slaves' Participation in the Corinthian Church." *JBL* 117 (1998) 481-501.

Gooch, Paul. "'Conscience' in 1 Corinthians 8 and 10." *NTS* 33 (1987) 244-54.

———. *Partial Knowledge: Philosophical Studies in Paul.* Notre Dame: University of Notre Dame Press, 1987.

Gorman, Michael. *Apostle of the Crucified Lord: A Theological Introduction to Paul and His Letters.* Grand Rapids: Eerdmans, 2004.

Goulder, Michael. "Σοφια in 1 Corinthians." In *Christianity at Corinth: The Quest for the Pauline Church,* edited by E. Adams and D. Horrell, 173-82. Louisville: Westminster John Knox, 2004.

Gowan, Donald E. *Eschatology in the Old Testament.* Edinburgh: T. & T. Clark, 2000.

Grosheide, F. W. *First Epistle to the Corinthians.* NICNT. Grand Rapids: Eerdmans, 1953.

Gundry-Volf, Judith. "Controlling the Bodies: A Theological Profile of the Corinthian Sexual Ascetics (1 Cor 7)." In *CCor,* 519-41.

Hanges, James C. "1 Corinthians 4:6 and the Possibility of Written Bylaws in the Corinthian Church." *JBL* 117 (1998) 275-98.

Harris, Gerald. "Church Discipline: 1 Corinthians 5." *NTS* 37 (1991) 2-21.

Harvey, John D. *Listening to the Text: Oral Patterning in Paul's Letters.* ETS Studies 1. Grand Rapids: Baker, 1998.

Hays, Richard B. *Echoes of Scripture in the Letters of Paul.* New Haven: Yale University Press, 1989.

———. *First Corinthians.* Interpretation. Louisville: Westminster, 2011.

Heil, John Paul. "The Chiastic Structure and Meaning to Paul's Letter to Philemon." *Bib* 82 (2001) 179-206.

———. *Colossians: Encouragement to Walk in All Wisdom as Holy Ones in Christ.* SBLECL 4. Atlanta: SBL, 2010.

———. *Ephesians: Empowerment to Walk in Love for the Unity of All in Christ.* SBLSBS 13. Atlanta: SBL, 2007.

———. *Hebrews: Chiastic Structures and Audience Response.* CBQMS 46. Washington, DC: Catholic Biblical Association, 2010.

———. *The Rhetorical Role of Scripture in 1 Corinthians.* SBLSBS 15. Atlanta: SBL, 2005.

Hill, Craig. "Paul's Understanding of Christ's Kingdom in 1 Corinthians 15:20-28." *NovT* 30 (1988) 297-320.

Hollander, Harm. "The Testing by Fire of the Builders' Works: 1 Corinthians 3:10-15." *NTS* 40 (1994) 89-104.

Hollander, Harm, and J. Holleman. "The Relationship of Death, Sin, and Law in 1 Cor 15:56." *NovT* 35 (1993) 270-93.

Hollander, Harm, and Gijsbert van der Hout. "The Apostle Paul Calling Himself 'an Abortion:' 1 Cor 15:8 within the Context of 1 Cor 15:8-10." *NovT* 38 (1996) 224-36.

Bibliography

Holleman, J. "Jesus' Resurrection as the Beginning of the Eschatological Resurrection (1 Cor 15, 20)." In *The Corinthian Correspondence*, edited by R. Bieringer, 653–60. BETL 125. Leuven: Leuven University Press, 1996.
Hooker, Morna D. "Interchange and Atonement." In *From Adam to Christ: Essays on Paul*, 26–41. Cambridge: Cambridge University Press, 1990.
Horsley, Richard. *1 Corinthians*. ANTC. Nashville: Abingdon, 1998.
———. "Gnosis in Corinth: 1 Corinthians 8:1–6." *NTS* 27 (1980–81) 32–51.
Hultgren, Stephen. "The Origin of Paul's Doctrine of the Two Adams in 1 Corinthians 15:45–49." *JSNT* 25 (2003) 343–70.
Jewett, Robert. *Paul's Anthropological Terms: A Study of Their Use in Conflict Settings*. AGSU 10. Leiden: Brill, 1971.
Johnson, Andrew. "On Removing a Trump Card: Flesh and Blood and the Reign of God." *BBR* 13 (2003) 173–92.
———. "Turning the World Upside Down in 1 Corinthians 15: Apocalyptic Epistemology, the Resurrected Body, and the New Creation." *EvQ* 75 (2003) 291–309.
Keener, Craig. *1–2 Corinthians*. CNTC. Cambridge: Cambridge University Press, 2005.
———. *Paul, Women, and Wives: Marriage and Women's Ministry in the Letters of Paul*. Peabody, MA: Hendrickson, 1992.
Kim, Yung-Suk. *Christ's Body in Corinth: The Politics of a Metaphor*. PCC. Minneapolis: Fortress, 2008.
Klaus, Nathan. *Pivot Patterns in the Former Prophets*. JSOTSup 247. Sheffield: Sheffield Academic, 2007.
Koet, Bart. "As Close to the Synagogue as Can Be: Paul in Corinth (Acts 18:1–18)." In *The Corinthian Correspondence*, edited by R. Bieringer, 397–415. BETL 125. Leuven: Leuven University Press, 1996.
Kroeger, C. C. "Women in the Greco-Roman World and Judaism." In *DNTB*, 1276–82.
Kurek-Chomycz, Dominika A. "Is There an 'Anti-Priscan' Tendency in the Manuscripts? Some Textual Problems with Prisca and Aquila." *JBL* 125 (2006) 107–28.
Lambrecht, Jan. "Structure and Line of Thought in 2 Cor 2:14—4:6." *Bib* 64 (1983) 344–80.
Lopez, Davina. *Apostle to the Conquered*. PCC. Minneapolis: Fortress, 2009.
Lowery, David K. "The Head Covering and Lord's Supper in 1 Cor 11:2–34." *BibSac* 143 (1986) 155–63.
Luedemann, Gerd. "The Hope of the Early Paul: From the Foundation-preaching at Thessalonika to 1 Cor 15:51–57." *Perspectives in Religious Studies* 7 (1980) 195–201.
Lund, Nils Wilhelm. *Chiasmus in the New Testament: A Study in the Form and Function of Chiastic Structures*. Peabody, MA: Hendrickson, 1992.
———. "The Presence of Chiasmus in the New Testament." *Journal of Religion* 10 (1930) 74–93.
MacDonald, Margaret. "Women Holy in Body and Spirit: The Social Setting of 1 Corinthians 7." In *Christianity at Corinth: The Quest for the Pauline Church*, edited by E. Adams and D. Horrell, 161–72. Louisville: Westminster John Knox, 2004.
MacDonald, Margaret, and Leif Vaage. "Unclean but Holy Children: Paul's Everyday Quandary in 1 Corinthians 7:14c." *CBQ* 73 (2011) 526–46.
Malina, Bruce. *Social Science Commentary on the Synoptic Gospels*. Minneapolis: Fortress, 2000.

Bibliography

Martin, Dale B. *The Corinthian Body*. New Haven: Yale University Press, 1999.

———. *Slavery as Salvation: The Metaphor of Slavery in Pauline Christianity*. New Haven: Yale University Press, 1990.

———. "Tongues of Angels and Other Status Indicators." *JAAR* 59 (1991) 547–89.

Martin, Ralph. *1, 2 Corinthians*. WBT. Waco: Word, 1988.

———. *The Spirit and the Congregation: Studies in 1 Corinthians 12—15*. Grand Rapids, Eerdmans, 1984.

Matera, Frank. *New Testament Theology: Unity and Diversity*. Louisville: Westminster John Knox, 2007.

———. *II Corinthians*. Louisville: Westminster John Knox, 2004.

Meeks, Wayne. *The First Urban Christians: The Social World of the Apostle Paul*. New Haven: Yale University Press, 1983.

Metzger, Bruce. *A Textual Commentary on the Greek New Testament*. New York: Hendrickson, 2005.

Milinovich, Timothy. "Form Criticism and the *Rib* in Isaiah 41:21—42:4." *Biblische Notizen* 136 (2008) 45–62.

———. *Now Is the Day of Salvation: An Audience-Oriented Study of 2 Corinthians 5:16—6:2*. Eugene, OR: Pickwick, 2011.

———. *Revelation and Sacred Scripture: A Reader in Interpretation*. Winona, MI: St. Mary's, 2011.

Mitchell, Alan C. "Rich and Poor in the Courts of Corinth: Litigiousness and Status in 1 Corinthians 6:1–11." *NTS* 39 (1993) 562–86.

Mitchell, Margaret. *Paul and the Rhetoric of Reconciliation: An Exegetical Investigation of the Language and Composition of 1 Corinthians*. Louisville: Westminster John Knox, 1992.

Mitchell, Matthew. "Reexamining the 'Aborted Apostle': An Exploration of Paul's Self-Description in 1 Corinthians 15:8." *JSNT* 25 (2003) 469–85.

Moore, George Foot. *Judaism in the First Centuries of the Christian Era*. 2 vols. New York: Schocken, 1971.

Morris, Leon. *1 Corinthians*. TNTC. Grand Rapids: Eerdmans, 1987.

Mount, Christopher. "1 Corinthians 11:3–16: Spirit Possession and Authority in a Non-Pauline Interpolation." *JBL* 124 (2005) 313–40.

Munro, Winsome. "Women, Text, and Canon: The Strange Case of 1 Corinthians 14:33–35." *BTB* 18 (1988) 26–31.

Murphy-O'Connor, Jerome. *1 Corinthians*. New Testament Message 10. Collegeville, MN: Liturgical, 1991.

———. "Interpolations in 1 Corinthians." *CBQ* 48 (1986) 81–94.

———. "The Non-Pauline Character of 1 Cor 11:2–16?" *JBL* 95 (1976) 615–21.

Nasuti, H. "The Woes of the Prophets and the Rights of the Apostle: The Internal Dynamics of 1 Corinthians 9." *CBQ* 50 (1988) 246–64.

Neirynck, Frans. "The Sayings of Jesus in 1 Corinthians." In *The Corinthian Correspondence*, edited by R. Bieringer, 141–76. BETL 125. Leuven: Leuven University Press, 1996.

O'Brien, P. T. *Gospel and Mission in the Writings of Paul*. Grand Rapids: Baker, 1993.

O'Day, Gail. "Jeremiah 9:22–23 and 1 Corinthians 1:26–31: A Study in Intertextuality." *JBL* 109 (1990) 259–67.

Orr, William, and James A. Walther. *I Corinthians*. AB 33. New Haven: Yale University Press, 1995.

Bibliography

Pascuzzi, Maria. "Baptism-based Allegiance and the Divisions in Corinth: A Reexamination of 1 Corinthians 1:13–17." *CBQ* 71 (2009) 813–29.

Paton, Lewis. "The Hebrew Idea of the Future Life: I. Earliest Conceptions of the Soul." *The Biblical World* 35 (1910) 8–10.

Perriman, Andrew C. "What Eve Did, What Women Shouldn't Do: The Meaning of *authenteo* in 1 Timothy 2:12." *TynBul* 44 (1993) 129–42.

Perry, Greg. "Phoebe of Cenchrae and 'Women' of Ephesus: 'Deacons' in the Earliest Churches." *Presbyterion* 36 (2010) 9–36.

Phipps, W. "Is Paul's Attitude toward Sexual Relations Contained in 1 Cor 7:1?" *NTS* 28 (1982) 125–31.

Rosner, Brian S. "Corporate Responsibility in 1 Corinthians 5." *NTS* 38 (1992) 470–73.

Sanders, E. P. *Paul and Palestinian Judaism: A Comparison of Patterns of Religion*. Minneapolis: Fortress, 1977.

Schnelle, Udo. *Apostle Paul: His Life and Theology*. Translated by M. E. Boring. Grand Rapids: Baker Academic, 2005.

———. *The History and Theology of the New Testament Writings*. Translated by M. E. Boring. Minneapolis: Fortress, 1998.

Schüssler Fiorenza, Elizabeth. *In Memory of Her*. New York: Crossroad, 1984.

Scroggs, Robin. *The New Testament and Homosexuality*. Minneapolis: Fortress, 1984.

Sellin, Gerhard. "1 Kor 5—6 und der 'Vorbrief' nach Korinth." *NTS* 37 (1991) 535–58.

Shoemaker, Thomas. "Unveiling of Equality: 1 Corinthians 11:2–16." *BTB* 17 (1987) 60–63.

Soards, Marion. *1 Corinthians*. NIBC. Peabody, MA: Hendrickson, 1999.

Stambaugh, John, and David Balch. *The New Testament in Its Social Environment*. LEC. Philadelphia: Westminster, 1986.

Sterling, Gregory. "'Wisdom among the Perfect:' Creation Traditions in Alexandrian Judaism and Corinthian Christianity." *NovT* 37 (1995) 355–84.

Stock, Augustine. "Chiastic Awareness and Antiquity." *BTB* 14 (1984) 22–28.

Stowers, Stanley K. *Letter Writing in Greco-Roman Antiquity*. LEC. Philadelphia: Westminster, 1989.

Theissen, Gerd. "Social Stratification in the Corinthian Community: A Contribution to the Sociology of Early Hellenistic Christianity." In *Christianity at Corinth: The Quest for the Pauline Church*, edited by E. Adams and D. Horrell, 97–106. Louisville: Westminster John Knox, 2004.

Thielman, F. "The Coherence of Paul's View of the Law: The Evidence of First Corinthians." *NTS* 38 (1992) 235–53.

Thiselton, Anthony C. *The First Epistle to the Corinthians: A Commentary on the Greek Text*. NIGTC. Grand Rapids: Eerdmans, 2000.

———. "Realized Eschatology at Corinth." In Adams and Horrell, 107–118.

Trompf, G. W. "On Attitudes toward Women in Paul and Paulinist Literature: 1 Corinthians 11:3–16 and Its Context." *CBQ* 42 (1980) 196–215.

Tuckett, C. M. "The Corinthians Who Say 'There is no resurrection of the dead' (1 Cor 15, 12)." In *The Corinthian Correspondence*, edited by R. Bieringer, 247–75. BETL 125. Leuven: Leuven University Press, 1996.

Turner, Seth. "The Interim, Earthly Messianic Kingdom in Paul." *JSNT* 25 (2003) 323–42.

Tyler, R. L. "First Corinthians 4:6 and Hellenistic Pedagogy." *CBQ* 60 (1998) 97–103.

Vawter, B. "Divorce and the New Testament." *CBQ* 39 (1977) 528–42.

Verhoef, E. "The Senders of the Letters to the Corinthians and the Use of 'I' and 'We.'" In *The Corinthian Correspondence*, edited by R. Bieringer, 427–32. BETL 125. Leuven: Leuven University Press, 1996.

Vos, Craig S. "Stepmothers, Concubines, and the Case of πορνεια in 1 Corinthians 5." *NTS* 44 (1988) 104–14.

Walker, William. "1 Corinthians 11:2–16 and Paul's Views Regarding Women." *JBL* (1976) 84–111.

———. "1 Corinthians 15:29–34 as a Non-Pauline Interpolation." *CBQ* (2007) 84–110.

———. "The Vocabulary of 1 Corinthians 11:3–15: Pauline or Non-Pauline?" *JSNT* 35 (1989) 75–88.

Ward, Roy. "Musonius and Paul on Marriage." *NTS* 36 (1990) 281–89.

Watson, Francis. "The Authority of the Voice: A Theological Reading of 1 Corinthians 11:2–15." *NTS* 46 (2000) 520–36.

Welch, John W. "Chiasmus in Greek and Latin." In *Chiasmus in Antiquity: Structures, Analyses, Exegesis*, edited by J. Welch, 113–43. Provo, UT: Research, 2006.

———. "Chiasmus in the New Testament." In *Chiasmus in Antiquity: Structures, Analyses, Exegesis*, edited by J. Welch, 211–50. Provo, UT: Research, 2006.

Williams, David. *Paul's Metaphors: Their Context and Character*. Peabody, MA: Hendrickson, 1999.

Winter, Bruce. "Civil Litigation in Secular Corinth and the Church." *NTS* 37 (1991) 559–72.

Wire, Antoinette Clark. *The Corinthian Women Prophets: A Reconstruction through Paul's Rhetoric*. Minneapolis: Fortress, 1990.

Witherington, Ben. *Conflict and Community in Corinth: A Socio-Rhetorical Commentary on 1 and 2 Corinthians*. Grand Rapids: Eerdmans, 1995.

Wright, N. T. *The Resurrection of the Son of God*. Minneapolis: Fortress, 2003.

Wuellner, Wilhelm. "Arrangement." In *Handbook of Classical Rhetoric in the Hellenistic Period: 330 BC to AD 400*, edited by Stanley E. Porter, 56–82. Leiden: Brill, 1997.

Yarbrough, O. Larry. *Not Like the Gentiles: Marriage Rules in Paul's Letters*. SBLDiss 80. Atlanta: SBL, 1985.

Zamfir, Korinna, and Joseph Verheyden. "Text-Critical and Intertextual Remarks on 1 Tim 2:8–10." *NovT* 50 (2008) 376–406.